Thomas Mackay

Methods of Social Reform

Essays critical and constructive

Thomas Mackay

Methods of Social Reform
Essays critical and constructive

ISBN/EAN: 9783337295493

Printed in Europe, USA, Canada, Australia, Japan

Cover: Foto ©Suzi / pixelio.de

More available books at **www.hansebooks.com**

METHODS

OF

SOCIAL REFORM

ESSAYS CRITICAL AND CONSTRUCTIVE

By THOMAS MACKAY

AUTHOR OF " THE ENGLISH POOR "
EDITOR OF " A PLEA FOR LIBERTY," ETC.

LONDON
JOHN MURRAY, ALBEMARLE STREET
1896

PREFACE.

THE author desires to thank the proprietors of the various Reviews who have kindly given their consent to the republication of several of the articles reprinted in the following collection. He also wishes to express his gratitude to the numerous friends who, from time to time, have supplied him with information with regard to the local administration of the Poor Law.

TABLE OF CONTENTS.

METHODS OF
SOCIAL REFORM.

ESSAYS CRITICAL AND CONSTRUCTIVE.

———•◦•———

INTRODUCTION.

THE "State of the Poor" has now established itself as a permanent controversy, and, before long, it may be thrust into the fore-front of practical politics. This consideration will, it is hoped, warrant the author in his desire to reissue, at the present time, and in book form, a selection from the contributions which he has made, during the last few years, to this vexed and important inquiry. Some of the papers contained in this volume were originally delivered as addresses at Poor Law Conferences, or at gatherings of a kindred nature. Others have been reprinted from the reviews in which they originally appeared. The paper on *Poor Law Reform* and that on *Free versus Collective Bargaining* are now printed for the first time.

The choice of articles for inclusion in the

B

present volume, has been made with a view of illustrating two aspects of the problem which appear to the author to be of super-eminent importance. On the one hand, the absolute harmfulness of the collectivist principle, which lies at the root of our English poor law system, is strongly maintained. It is argued that the countenance given, by persons in exalted station, to proposals for its wider application, is seriously and mischievously diverting the attention of the poorer classes of the country from truer methods of progress. These proposals, which it is not here necessary to specify more particularly, amount in the aggregate to a policy of using taxation not as a means of providing for the public services, but as an instrument for redistributing property. On the other hand, it is the purpose of these pages to express a belief in the existence and possibility of those truer methods of progress, which consist in developing, on voluntary lines, the natural constructive forces of a free society. Briefly, the first portion of the volume is critical and destructive ; the second endeavours to indicate and explain, by means of concrete illustration, the nature of the true constructive elements of civilised society.

The paper on *Poor Law Reform* deals in a practical spirit with the present administration of the law. Though firmly convinced of the futility of any compromise of principle, the author is prepared to admit that the drastic remedies, which in his judgment are necessary if we hope for any large reformation, must be applied gradually, and in such manner as to carry with it the approval of public opinion. The only contribution which the author can make to this desirable end is to put on record his experience and conclusions without any attempt at compromise. For, whatever may be the case with regard to the application of sound principles, with regard to their enunciation, there is no room for compromise. The articles which follow on *The Poor Law as an obstacle to Thrift, The Interest of the Working Classes in the Poor Law, Old Age Pensions and the State*, contain, for the most part, negative criticism. The article on *The Abuse of Statistics* deals with certain statistical fallacies by which the view here maintained has been assailed ; while that on *The Co-operation of Charitable Agencies with the Poor Law* develops at somewhat greater length one of the methods of administrative reform which has been found most efficacious in bringing about a reduction of pauperism.

The articles on *People's Banks* and on *Free versus Collective Bargaining* lead the reader into a more hopeful atmosphere. The first directs attention to a most successful experiment in promoting a wider distribution of private property by the methods of acquisition and tenure recognised as legal by the consent of civilised society. This is contrasted with attempts to transfer property from one class to another by legislation and taxation, the pastime which occupies so much of the energies of political adventurers of all parties. It is argued that until our national enthusiasm can be diverted from the superstitious reverence with which their proceedings are followed, and our interest roused in favour of voluntary and constructive methods, our efforts after social reform must be cursed with sterility; indeed, such progress as the country is permitted to make will be made in spite of the empirical strivings of delegates representing greedy and aggressive majorities, animated by all the anti-social and retrograde instincts by which humanity is still influenced.

The ·last paper in the volume is designed to show that freedom of exchange, and not coercive combination, is the best and most beneficent guarantee for the continuous advance of labour in the social scale. A denial of this proposition seems to involve a fallacy which, in the author's judgment, is most unwarranted as well as most mischievous. Interference with freedom of exchange in the sphere of labour, whether brought about by legal, or extra-legal, but still coercive regulation, ignores an elementary truth in economics;

viz. that voluntary exchange brings a profit to both parties. *Ex hypothesi*, at the point of time when the bargain is effected, both parties are agreed that an exchange shall take place, and in the case of adult citizens, it is difficult to understand why they should be deprived of their liberty to act on what they conceive to be their own interest.

It is not denied that classes, at different times in the world's history, have been so depressed that the momentary advantage, derived from a free exchange, still leaves them in a miserable and unsatisfactory condition. Nay, further, it may be conceded that there are occasions when the poverty and degradation of a section of the community may warrant the confiscation and redistribution of property, in other words, a revolution ; but, even in this case, the subsequent redistribution has to be effected by means of the recognised tenures. The property which belonged to A may be taken from him and given to B, C, and D, but when this necessary or inevitable injustice is done, the right to hold or to sell emerges again as the only possible tenure by which men can satisfy their wish to profit by that sub-division of industrial energy which is the distinguishing feature of modern civilisation.

Most reasonable men will agree that in a normal state of society there is enough of equity and of happiness to warrant a resistance to revolution.

It then remains that, in a society which would avail itself of the advantages arising from a subdivision of labour, exchange is the only orderly process by which profit and wealth can be created and distributed. The reason that a man—or a class—can only secure what appears a poor rate of exchange for his services and property is, that he has nothing, in the opinion of his fellow men, of much value to offer. His services, such as they are, can only be converted to more valuable purpose, by allowing him to pursue freely the exchanges that are open to him. The mutual principle of exchange will lead him, in pursuit of his own interest, to seek better remunerated work. This, together with the willingness and ability of his neighbours to reward one industry better than another, provides a guarantee that, in the long run, and in proportion as the impediments to this distributing influence are removed, each unit of labour will be carried to the point or market where it can be employed most profitably to itself, and to the community at large. This automatic, natural, or voluntary principle of adjustment is no quick working panacea ; we may deplore the tarrying of the millennium, but we can find no surer or better guide ; all we can do is to clear away the impediments which stand in its path, and to preserve an unfaltering faith in the true beneficence of the reign of freedom.

The country has lately gone through the throes of a general election, and a party has been returned to power pledged to devote itself to what it vaguely terms social reform. This verdict of the constituencies has been interpreted as marking the intensity of the national wish to legislate about our social arrangements. Elsewhere, and probably more truly, the result of the late election has been imputed to popular disgust with a government whose social legislation, dictated by the noisiest, most mischievous, and at the same time least influential of its supporters has harassed and alarmed every respectable section of the community. There is some truth in both representations. The victory of the Conservative party has been gained, on the one hand, by promises of a wild and impracticable policy of state socialism, and, on the other hand, by the vote of those who support a party which, as they think, cannot, fortunately for the welfare of the country, do much to redeem these pledges.

It is not an altogether satisfactory situation. The desire for social improvement is very intense and very sincere, but it is quite another thing to admit that social reform, in any real sense of the term, can be promoted by legislative action. To take property from A and give it to B, C, and D, in order that they may buy old age pensions, or freehold houses, is a revolutionary proceeding, and no permanent and satisfactory superstructure can be built on such a foundation. Speaking at Doncaster on the 20th of July, 1895, Mr. Balfour very justly remarked (*Standard,* July 22, 1895) :—

"It was as impossible for us to live upon perpetual political revolutions as it was for an individual to obtain a wholesome diet upon pills. The Gladstonian Party seemed to think that a passionate love of Constitutional change was the great characteristic of Democracies. Nothing of the kind. All history was against that view, and probably the most vehemently Conservative population in the whole universe was the American Republic, where change was not desired, and where, if it was desired, it would be almost impossible under the multitudinous safeguards which their Constitution provided. The Anglo-Saxon race did not differ in that respect on the two sides of the Atlantic. As a Conservative people we must ever in the end oppose senseless and stupid revolutionary projects, forced forward by no national necessity, required by no social growth, and not called for by any real pressing need of the time. Such revolutionary proposals would from time to time be the expedient of the demagogue."

The English constitution is very well in its way, but there are elementary social truths of more transcendent importance. A social difficulty is not overcome, when it is solved by some coercive act of the legislature. If by an act of the constitution, poverty is given the right to endow itself at the expense of property, a revolutionary attack is aimed at an order of things far more fundamental and far more important than any political constitution.

The problems which these revolutionary proposals are intended to solve, will not be abandoned as insoluble, except by those who are inappreciative of the history of the past, and unduly sceptical of the possibilities of human progress in the future. The ever-recurring conflicts of interest—such as that which arises between the rich and the poor—can be solved by action which is at once mutual and voluntary. In the sphere of economics the most salient manifestation of this co-ordinating spirit of conciliation is to be found in the principle of exchange. In every exchange both parties profit. The law of the market, which is for ever driving commodities to a lower range of prices, is at the same time distributing and directing labour to more useful and, therefore, to it, better remunerated purposes. This is a fact attested by history and theory alike. Of the spontaneity of this natural order of progress, freedom is the guardian.

The moral of this would seem to be obvious. Social reform is the ardent aspiration of all men. Yet, alas! the highest intellect of the land, the most vehement enthusiasm of all but a small minority, a vast amount of time and of treasure are expended in hunting solutions that are no

solutions, but rather aggravations of our difficulties. A tenth part of a tithe of this spirit of
devotion directed to voluntary methods of reform,
accompanied by a recognition that this was the
true path of progress, would do more to bring
about the object of our desire than the legislation
of centuries.

No one, who has not learnt it by personal experience and observation, can form any conception
of the harm that is done to the best interests of
the poor by the illusory electioneering promises
which are thrown out so profusely by ambitious
political adventurers. The dead weight of
dependent inertia is thereby rendered heavier and
more impervious to the inspiriting and quickening
influence of the arts of independence and progress.

There are sections of our poorer classes, where
the feeling of personal responsibility has been
legislated and "electioneered" out of existence.
This spirit of dependence has to be exorcised,
possibly by the repeal of some legislation, but
mainly by the successful development of the
salutary instincts inherent in every free society.

Those who claim to lead and teach the people
must endeavour to divert men's minds from seeking
profit in the coercive or legislative spoliation
of their neighbours, and persuade them rather
to improve the value of their own services, and
the services of their children, by following and

interpreting the market; to retain and invest some portion of their earnings, to make use, in other words, of the necessary institution of private property as a protection against sickness, old age, and all the other economic ills to which flesh is heir. At every step in this process, voluntary effort is urgently required, not only from the poor themselves, but from the well-to-do who sympathise with them in their sufferings. The better administration of the poor law is largely dependent on the right development of voluntary charity. The better organisation of opportunities and inducements to save and invest, is an enterprise most urgently demanding the assistance of volunteers. The absolute failure of the Post-Office as an insurance agency, its comparative success, in spite of the unpopularity of aggravating official regulations, as a savings bank, performing moreover only a portion of the beneficent functions of a banker, suggest that there are vast fields of usefulness open to voluntary effort in connection with the thrift institutions of the labouring class.

The man who devotes himself to a political life derives, it may be hoped, some entertainment from his calling; if he is successful in obstructing or repealing legislation he may haply do some good, but the politician with his programme of constructive legislation is a pure source of calamity to the nation at large. This is a proposition which probably no one, unless himself actually engaged in politics, will seriously deny; our superstitious belief in the efficacy of politics is not due to conviction, but arises from pure idleness and disregard of the vast promise of reform which lies ready to be gathered by voluntary action. There are signs now that the nation is getting tired of the spectacle of political adventurers climbing to notoriety by playing experiments with the foundations of society. Lord Melbourne was probably right when he summed up his experience in the remark that mankind was not corrupt, but "damnably vain." These schemes of social reform by means of legislation are well meant, but to the increasing circle of those who take a scientific view of the fact that society grows naturally and is not made by spasmodic efforts of legislation, it is clear that their projectors are imagining a vain thing.

One last prefatory explanation seems desirable. There are those who, with some justice, are disposed to regard philanthropy as to some extent an unwholesome virtue. It is undoubtedly a dangerous calling for any man to take up, and in many cases it has a most mischievous effect upon the subjects of his experiments. In philanthropy, as in other virtues and vices, there are degrees of depravity. The man who "does his diligence," at his own charges, even if his action does not always show much respect for the higher possibilities of human nature, compels our respect. The vicarious philanthropist who, in a reckless race after a cheap popularity, uses the rate extorted from his neighbours to multiply the occasions of stumbling set before the helpless, miserable crowd who are only too ready to fall into dependence, is surely a very despicable creature.

This truth, and, in large measure, it is a truth, has never for long been absent from the mind of the author of these pages. The reader, it is requested, will observe that the methods of reform here advocated will reduce the necessity of philanthropic patronage to a minimum. Reform consists in a re-creation and development of the arts of independence. The plea, in fine, is not for more philanthropy, but rather for more respect for the dignity of human life, and more faith in its ability to work out its own salvation.

Lest the phrase, "the arts of independence," appear vague to the reader, it may not be unfitting in the close of this introductory chapter to explain more fully the meaning which the author attaches to it, and the place which it fills in his theory of society. The social creed, which underlies the view upheld in this volume, may be summed up in the proposition that human happiness and the right ordering of society have depended and still depend, in the main, on a recognition and acceptance of the doctrine of personal responsibility. All the constructive forces, which build up and then hold together the framework of society, take their rise and afterwards draw their life from this source. The personal motive, the executive element, if the phrase may be allowed, of a personally responsible unit, is, in this theory of life, sufficient to account for the purely automatic act of self-preservation, and also, and with equal naturalness, for the superior cogency of the social law which urges men to acts of self-abnegation and heroism. In other words, the personally responsible human being, left face to face with the experience of life, is prompted to action by motives of self-preservation, but, over and above this, the mutuality of the social life, in which he has of necessity become a part, suggests to him naturally, and with an insistence not to be denied, that course of social action which men call moral.

In the economic sphere of man's action, this truth, as to the mutuality of social life, is brought prominently forward in the theory which represents every economic action as a form of exchange. In this connection, speaking as an amateur, whose interests only fringe on the science of political economy, the author desires to express his great indebtedness to the writings of Mr. H. Dunning

MacLeod. By insisting that the phenomena of exchange are the sole subject matter of the science of economics, and that as a preliminary to their discussion, our so-called economic actions must be analysed and shown to be modes or forms of exchange, Mr. MacLeod has, in the opinion of the writer, introduced scientific order into a subject which otherwise is apt to degenerate into misty disquisitions on the nature of things in general.

Exchange is merely one manifestation of man's natural capacity for apprehending and shaping his conduct in accordance with the necessary mutuality of his environment. Its action has raised about us the material fabric of industrial society. Darwin has told us how it was the speculations of Malthus on the subject of population that supplied him with the first hint of his own famous hypothesis. In this instance the debt of the naturalist to the economist has been duly acknowledged. In a similar way, from a survey of the mere material growth of industrial society and from observation of the organising influence of exchange, we may derive an item of contributory proof for the hypothesis of a natural origin of ethics and for the opinion that ethical sentiment is a natural growth ; further, the same line of argument will suggest that it is unnecessary and unphilosophical to invent the hypothesis of a dual origin, in one part rational, in another ultra-rational. This reasoning does not depend on any particular theory of knowledge, nor does it preclude that effort of faith which derives the observed order of the evolution of nature from an initial act of miraculous creation. It assumes, what cannot be denied, the mere fact of personal consciousness. That granted, it is alleged that there is no break either historically or theoretically in the evolution of human activities from the automatic movement of self-preservation to the most carefully calculated action which we describe as moral or immoral. Social or moral sentiment has been dictated to us by the experience of the individuals who compose the race. Personal experience, issuing in personal action, has rejected the impossible creed that the units of society are warring atoms,[1] and has bound men together in the bonds of a recognised brotherhood.

In other words, personal responsibility is the automatic principle which has brought society thus far upon its journey, and there is no reason why we should seek to make it abdicate its

---

[1] This view, as far as the author can discover, is a figment imagined for rhetorical purposes by socialist writers, and imputed by them to their opponents, whom they have most inappropriately nicknamed individualists. Thus Dr. Westcott, Bishop of Durham, in a paper read at the Church Congress in Hull in 1890, says: "Individualism regards humanity as made up of disconnected or warring atoms," an absurd opinion held, as far as the author is aware, by no sane person, and of course easily susceptible of rhetorical condemnation.

authority for such voyage as lies before us in the future.

As necessary corollaries from this truth, several important and constructive principles seem at once to emerge. Personal responsibility necessitates personal action. The mutuality of life insists that our actions, in so far as they affect others, shall be by way of exchange ; the principle which should govern the limitation of personal freedom is thus at once suggested. The necessity to act or to live, limited as above stated, involves the necessity of exchanging services, and the earnings or wages of services. The necessity of exchanging services involves the principle of personal freedom. The exchange of the earnings of services necessitates the institution of private property. The term " necessity " is here advisedly substituted for the term " right." It is more accurate both histori-cally and philosophically. Thus the institution of private property does not rest on any metaphysical or empirical basis of " right," but on the fact that the experience of civilised society has every-where recognised it as the sole or necessary alter-native to an insupportable system of universal scramble. Communism, involving a community of property, is a mere postponement of the period of appropriation, a mere variation of the principle of division. Products, whether they be food, clothing, or shelter, must ultimately be personally appropriated. Every man has private property in his own dinner and his own coat. Under the present rule of private property, these things come to a man as the result of exchange—for the right of gift and bequest is involved in the larger right of exchange—conducted according to the recognised jurisprudence of the land. Under communism they would come to him, because they were awarded to him by the bureaucracy, and under anarchy, if such a thing were conceivable,[1] they would come to him as the spoil of a struggle like that of " the mammoths in their prime."

Private property is sometimes described as an evil ; it would be more correct to say that the limitation of supply, which renders it necessary, is an evil. Private property is a remedial measure forced upon mankind by the niggardliness of nature, which has limited supply. The problem is : How is this evil of limitation to be mitigated ? If not by means of a course of action in which the institution of private property is the first step, by what other means ?

Again, let us appeal to the verdict of the civilised world. The answer up to a certain point is clear. We cannot scramble for the good things of this

---

[1] The qualification in the text is inserted, because, it is submitted, a state of anarchy, in which voluntary observance of rule has ceased to exist, is inconceivable. Some new term is required for the philosopher's ideal of an anarchy distinguished by a rigid but *voluntary* observance of the dictates of morality and justice.

life ; we must recognise the necessity of orderly
appropriation. When we pass beyond this ax-
iomatic truth, opinion and practice become less
uniform. The bureaucratic theory of life still
holds, in an undefined or uncertain form. The
right of taxation is tacitly assumed to reside in
the sovereign power, and there are sections of the
community who desire to use taxation not as a
means of raising money for various necessary
public services, but as a method of distributing
property and the advantages of property on what
seems to the governing class a more equitable
principle. In view of the theory maintained in
these pages, such a method runs altogether counter
to the natural constructive forces of our social life.
Devices (such as a poor law, especially a poor law
which goes beyond providing relief of destitution),
designed to render personal appropriation unnecessary, are destructive of the organic principle
of progress. As above stated, orderly personal
appropriation is the first remedial step. It is a
retrograde step to reverse this process and to make
personal property a matter depending on the
caprice of the legislature. If, as seems unfortunately too probable, a tyrannical public
authority is to claim a right of ownership over the
private property of the individual, and to use its
power not for maintaining the public services, but
for redistributing wealth, a serious blow is aimed

at a fundamental principle of civilisation. Hitherto governments, monarchical and oligarchical, and therefore weak, have, because of their weakness, used their power of taxation sparingly. Their malversations amounted to jobbery, but not to revolution. A strong democratic government, animated by the prevalent spirit of philanthropic rapine, and officered, as seems inevitable, by wild-cat politicians of all parties, is a more serious danger. The necessity of curbing the power of the State over the purses of its subjects is a problem to which the nation before long will have to give serious attention.

State-socialism, it is affirmed, is a retrograde step. What, then, is the legitimate course of development? Property is in its essence monopoly, and as such is only a first step towards a remedy. Each monopoly or ownership of exchangeable property is of course limited to that property ; but the wants of the monopolist are by no means satisfied. He is impelled to increase the numbers of objects over which he can exercise monopoly, not for his own consumption, but for purposes of exchange. Monopoly is thus rendered innocuous, because it is tempered by the necessity of the monopolist to exchange. There lies, then, on every man a natural necessity to own his own person, to appropriate his own earnings, and to exchange his own services and commodities ; and the evil of primitive poverty will by this process be mitigated through the multiplication of property or monopoly in many hands, and through the principle of free exchange. By this means, and by this means only, can we reach the true socialisation of wealth.

Such, then, according to the theory here presented, are the constructive elements to which mankind must look for a better organisation of society, and it will follow that no system of public relief, however well ordered, has been, or ever can be, a healthy constructive force.

As an apology for this dogmatic presentment of his own view as to the origin of ethics and of society, the author may be permitted to remark that it is intruded here for the purpose of showing that the opinions set forth in the following pages are, as he believes, part of a reasoned theory of society, and, further, that he does not shrink from the logical conclusions which seem to follow from the premisses, but that, on the contrary, finding these larger conclusions reasonable and natural, he is the more firmly convinced of the justice of the view gathered in the narrower field of observation, in which he has been especially interested.

I.

POOR LAW REFORM.

THE PROBLEM DEFINED.

POOR Law Reform is an ambiguous phrase, and may be interpreted to cover a great number of contradictory opinions. At the outset, it may be stated that in the following pages the phrase must be taken to mean such an alteration in the poor law as will secure adequate relief for the destitute, and, at the same time, foster independence and reduce pauperism.

It is not necessary to discuss proposals for using the poor law as a means of bringing about equality of fortune and condition among all classes of the community. For though it is part of the Socialist programme to use taxation as a means of abolishing "Capitalism," and for handing over the wealth of the country to some form of collective tenure, it is not proposed, as I understand it, to use the poor law for this purpose. In a Fabian tract on the Reform of the Poor Law, it is admitted that "no instructed person would for a moment venture to run any risk of restoring the evil days of the old poor law." Again, "Socialists who object to an industrial system, which condemns to pauperism one-tenth of the population, believe that the greater part of the need for poor relief would cease if the owners of land and capital were compelled to restore to the workers collectively the tribute of rent and interest which is now exacted from them individually. Nevertheless, in a land of accident and sickness, poverty cannot be wholly extinguished until a complete Communism is reached. Some system of relief for the destitute must therefore continue to exist for a long time to come." It is a fair interpretation to put on this passage that a complete Communism is to be aimed at, not by the endowment of poverty through the poor law, but by expedients of taxation and "restoration" which do not here concern us. The quarrel of the Socialist is not specially with the poor law, but with the present mechanism of society, which, in his opinion, makes a poor law necessary. This argument against the endowment of poverty by the poor law is illustrated by the following criticism—reported to have been made on our English poor law system by a well-known continental Socialist. It is said that when Madame Louise Michel was in England, she was taken over some of our poor law establishments. She remarked that she now understood why England had had no revolution.   There is a certain amount of truth in the suggestion.   The more intelligent Socialists seem at times to appreciate the argument.   If the poor become satisfied with the provisions of the poor law, agitation becomes more difficult, and the Socialist's opportunity is gone : the necessary revolution becomes impossible.

The same view is taken for different reasons, by those who, like the present writer, believe in the possibility of independence for the poor. We argue in favour of a cautious and continuous restriction of the facilities for obtaining poor law relief, because we believe that this course will force the poor not into revolution, but into the orderly acquisition of property by means of the tenures already recognised by civilised society. We believe that the poor law has acted as a narcotic on the natural thrift and acquisitive instincts of the poor, and that at present it is one, at all events, of the chief impediments that stand in the way of working-class progress.

In passing, it may be remarked that, to an uninitiated bystander trying to appreciate and understand the Socialist position in this matter, it is difficult to reconcile this fear of returning to the old poor law and the indiscriminate relief of the able-bodied which was its characteristic feature, with the enthusiastic advocacy of State Pensions for the Aged, Collective Provision for the Sick,

Public Burial of the Dead, which are some of the items of reform recommended in the Fabian tract just quoted. If dependence on public relief is undesirable for the labourer during his working life, why should it be so desirable for him during his sickness and old age? Why should personal responsibility be the rule in the one case and not in the other? Is it not a singular comment on his philosophy, that the "instructed" Socialist recoils, as well he may, from condemning the labourer to have his maintenance measured out to him by a poor law bureaucracy, but is quite content to hand him over, body and soul, and the rest of the country with him, to the tender mercy of some glorified assembly of the "complete communism." With this inconsistency we have here nothing to do; the matter is mentioned only to justify the course followed in this essay, which is to treat the poor law not as an instrument for assimilating the fortune of the rich and the poor, but as a means of relieving destitution without at the same time becoming a discouragement to the desire to maintain independence at all periods of life.

Summed up, the position of the Socialist seems to be that though it is impossible to advance that "complete communism," which is the goal of Socialism, by an endowment of poverty *quâ* poverty, it is still desirable to endow sickness, old age, childhood, etc., etc., and to begin here that transference of responsibility from the individual to the state which one day will become complete communism. The theoretical Socialists are a small body, and this belief in the possibility and expediency of relieving men of their responsibilities for their children, their widows, their sickness, their old age, and the expenses of their burial is not shared by that large class of persons who like to describe themselves as practical men.

It is characteristic of the practical man that he abhors a logical conclusion as he would the plague. While he is certainly not of the opinion of the Socialist, he will not be at the trouble to draw the conclusion that if the Poor Law Amendment Act of 1834 proclaimed, and has since succeeded in establishing, the independence of the able-bodied, there is no ground for despairing of the independence of the poor in their childhood and widowhood, in their sickness and in their old age. The Socialist does not appreciate independence, or rather interprets it to mean dependence on the bureaucracy of a complete communism ; the practical man does value independence, but seeing the difficulty by which the subject is beset and having many other things to do, he is content to despair of the independence of the poor, nay, perhaps he will go further, and deem it a virtue to think merely of the adequacy of relief, and denounce those who still hold sacred the independence of the poor, as cruel and churlish doctrinaires.

The purpose of these articles is, if possible, to get a hearing for the views of those who do not despair of the independence of the poor, and who regard it as at least of equal value to any stall-fed content that can be bred of lavish public relief. The subject in these days is one of pressing import-ance. The practical man is assailed by rhetoric, by demography, by threats, by innumerable well-meant panaceas. His poor bewildered brain sees that if the state feeds a man, he ceases to be hungry ; if it gives him a pension in old age, he ceases to be destitute ; if it finds him work, he can no longer call himself unemployed.

This solution seems so simple, that the ordinary voter is ready to listen to the obvious remedies proposed by empirics ; he is unwilling to admit that pauperism, a disease of the body politic, requires the treatment of the specialist, and is as little a matter to be decided by voting as the practice of medicine. Over and above this danger, there is the now imminent risk of allowing this question to become a mere secondary issue in the game of politics. Optimists may argue, with some plausibility, that the verdict of the con-stituencies on a subject which has been presented to them fairly and squarely, is not likely to err. This may be so, but the misfortune is that this question has not been so presented. Issues, that appeared to them of graver import, have occupied exclusively the attention of leading politicians. None of them have been bold enough to face this question and attempt to educate public opinion. Agitation is not a weapon which those who take a scientific view of the pathology of pauperism find easy to wield. On the other hand, the condition of the poor is a theme on which it is easy to tear a passion to tatters. The ear of the politicians therefore has been secured by the more sentimental section of the philanthropic public. No prominent statesman has grappled with the real difficulties of the subject, and under pressure of the above-mentioned influences, the less responsible politician has been lavish of promises, some of which, there is reason to fear, he may be obliged to fulfil.

The danger is grave and imminent, and I do not think that the next section of this article can be devoted to a better purpose than to a recital of the precedent for making this a national rather than a party question, one to be treated by scientific rather than by electioneering methods of reform.

THE PRECEDENT OF 1834.

THE Poor Law Amendment Act of 1834 in more than one respect is an admirable precedent in poor law legislation. The bill was introduced by a Liberal Government in the first reformed House of Commons, and was supported by the Tory party, then led by Sir R. Peel and the Duke of Wellington, and passed through both houses by overwhelming majorities.

The difference of principle which then divided the two great parties in the state was intelligible enough. The country had just gone through the heated agitations attendant on the passing of the great Reform Bill. While the Whigs professed to trust in the popular aspiration as expressed by the new constituencies, the Tories put their faith in the constitution. To-day both parties are purely democratic, and the precedent followed by the democratic party of 1834 would seem to be equally binding on both parties at the present time. The Whig Government had a large majority, and if they had thought that the reform of the poor law was a matter on which popular suffrage was in a position to adjudicate in detail, they might have legislated at once. They felt, however, that this was not a matter which could be trusted to the chances of a faction fight on the floor of the House of Commons. They resolved, therefore, to await the report of the Royal Commission of Inquiry, which they had appointed in 1832.

This Commission, as is well known, examined the whole question of the administration of the poor law in the most exhaustive and thorough manner, and collected evidence which was absolutely conclusive in favour of the recommendations of its report. It is not too much to say that the debates which followed the introduction of the bill by Lord Althorp were dominated by the irresistible force of the testimony and reasoning contained in this historical report. The criticisms which were directed against the bill were for the most part aimed at the principle of central control. It has generally been assumed, and probably with justice, that under the circumstances a central control was an absolute necessity; and it was avowedly on the ground of expediency that Lord Althorp defended this device, which was without doubt the integral feature of the bill. The Government, in effect, did not feel itself strong enough to amend the law, being, as it were, mere delegates of a popular suffrage, which, though much more restricted then than now, easily becomes inflamed over a question of sentiment. They therefore appointed a permanent and non-elective body to carry out the necessary reform.

The Poor Law Amendment Act, 4 & 5 William IV. cap. 76, is in this respect a most remarkable piece of legislation. Direct legislation on the subject of poor law relief is in this Act conspicuous by its absence. The Act, it is true, made provision for the establishment of unions, and certain alterations in the law of settlement and bastardy, but these are minor matters. The principal operative part of the Act was the appointment of three Commissioners, to be styled the Poor Law Commissioners for England and Wales.

Section 15—to use the words of the summary given by Sir G. Nicholls (p. 290, vol. ii.)—"directs that 'the administration of relief to the poor throughout England and Wales, according to the existing laws, or such laws as shall be in force at the time being, shall be subject to the direction and control of the Commissioners,' who are authorised and required to make and issue all such rules, orders, and regulations for the management of the poor, for the government of workhouses, and the education of children therein, and for the apprenticing of poor children, and for the guidance and control of all guardians, vestries, and parish officers, so far as relates to the management of the poor, and the keeping, examining, auditing, and allowing or disallowing of accounts, and making and entering into contracts, or any expenditure for the relief of the poor, and for carrying this Act into execution in all other respects, as they shall think proper, and may suspend, alter, or rescind the same, 'provided always that nothing in this Act contained, shall be construed as enabling the said Commissioners or any of them to interfere in any individual case, for the purpose of ordering relief.' "

Again, in section 52, the Act, "after reciting that relief to the able-bodied is in many places so administered as to be productive of evil, and 'as difficulties may arise in case any immediate and universal remedy is attempted to be applied,' empowers the Commissioners by such rules, orders, and regulations as they may think fit, to regulate the same ; and all relief administered contrary to such regulations, unless in cases of emergency, is declared to be unlawful, and is to be disallowed."

The subsequent history of the question shows how right Parliament was in doubting its own power. The tremendous outcry which followed, and the virulence of the attacks directed against the new Commissioners, would probably have been sufficient to destroy or terrify into submission any government. The Commissioners were permanent officials, who happily had the courage of their opinions ; they did their duty, and withstood the wave of pauperism which was overwhelming the country.

At the same time, it is impossible to deny that there was a substratum of truth in the objection to a centralised control, and we are beginning to find some of the inconveniences now. If local bodies are set to run in leading-strings, they will not learn responsibility; some of them are sure to think that they could do their work better, if they were not so confined. The Commissioners and their successors, the Poor Law Board and the Local Government Board, have succeeded in abolishing some of the more glaring abuses of the old poor law, and, in spite of occasional clamour, they have refused to retreat from the position they have taken up. They have succeeded, from a legislative point of view, in rendering illegal all that was *explicitly* condemned in the Royal Commissioners' Report. At the same time, both individuals and associations gather wisdom from liberty of experiment; in the matter of poor law administration, liberty of experiment has not been allowed. No very flagrant maladministration has been possible, no parishes have, as under the old poor law, been brought to insolvency, and, as a consequence, public attention has not been concentrated on the subject. This comparative immunity from grave abuse is, of course, something gained, but

D

against this gain we must set the fact that the mass of voters, and of administrators also, have had no opportunity to learn by experience the wholesome nature of the regulations laid down by the Local Government Board ; and, on the contrary, there is a great disposition to kick over Local Government Board control altogether. Further, it is notorious that strong recommendations have been made for years from the Local Government Board to the local unions, to induce them to restrict out-door relief, also that these recommendations have been largely neglected. *Implicitly*, these recommendations were contained in the Royal Commissioners' Report, but neither the legislative nor the administrative powers entrusted to it have enabled the Local Government Board to have this advice carried out by the unions.

If we had had no central control, we should have had extraordinary and mischievous eccentricity of administration, but in all probability by this time we should have arrived at one of two conclusions : (1) Either that the powers entrusted to local administrators of the poor law were far too extensive, and that it was necessary to curtail them (just as the powers which were abused under the old poor law were curtailed), if the country was to escape the demoralisation and bankruptcy of pauperism. This curtailment might have taken place by direct legislation, or, as before, by appointing a commission with explicit instructions to legislate. (2) Or we should have come to the conclusion that poor law administration, being in its nature judicial, was not a matter to be entrusted to an elective body.

These remarks are not made with any desire to ignore the admirable work done by the Local Government Board. The country advisedly adopted a certain policy of reform ; probably at the time it was the only possible scheme. All that the Commissioners and their successors, the Poor Law and Local Government Boards, were explicitly told to do, they have done, and they have made a gallant effort to impose on the local unions recommendations implicitly contained in their original instructions. Here the policy of central control has to some extent failed, and there are signs of considerable reaction even against those salutary rules which seemed most firmly established.

As already remarked, we have for all these years enjoyed a certain immunity from graver forms of maladministration, but we have prevented the local voter and the local administrator *from finding out by experience* the disastrous consequences of many of the experiments which they are now clamouring to try.

If the poor law guardian is to be a purely

elective officer it is plain he can only be controlled by an enlightened popular voter. Now a popular voter is, as a rule, a very ill-informed person on this question, and often an interested party. Most of us who have followed this question have had occasion to meet suggestions made by eager but inexperienced voters and administrators by reference, perhaps, to the parish workshops of 1848, or to the parish farm and the other abominations of the old poor law ; these instances, which are so convincing to the serious student of the question, are like water on a duck's back to these enthusiastic philanthropists. "Those were not fair trials," they exclaim ; "let us try it again and see what we can do." And unless this difficult matter is handled with patriotism and courage by our party leaders, these experiments will be tried again, and a course adopted which may go far to condemn our working class to another century of dependence.

The precedent of the conduct of parties at the time of the Poor Law Amendment Act is, I submit, one worthy of imitation. Responsible politicians on all sides should enter into a self-denying ordinance that they will not make capital with the groundling vote by misrepresentations on this difficult and dangerous subject.

1834 AND 1895.

THESE considerations appear to me to warrant
the expression of a hope that this difficult problem
may be kept out of party politics. If the parliament of 1834 felt itself unable to legislate, much
more would it be dangerous, at the present day,
to allow political parties to enter into a reckless
competition to gain the popular vote. The faith
of Lord Althorp and his colleagues in popular
government had just been tried by a fiery ordeal,
and they might well have been justified if they
had insisted in committing poor law administration
entirely to the arbitrament of the newly created
constituencies. They recognised, however (and the
truth is just as obvious to-day as it was then), that
the duty of the poor law guardian is in part that
of the physician and in part that of the judge.
Pauperism is a disease requiring scientific treatment. Further, the taking of relief from one class
and giving it to another is a judicial function,
which ought not to be performed solely at the
dictate of the persons who are to receive. Now
obviously scientific laws of health are not to be

determined by popular suffrage, nor ought judges to be chosen, because of the subserviency of their views, by the majority of litigants in a pending suit. This were to poison the administration of justice at its source.

Here, perhaps, is the place to enter a protest against the assumption that in this or any other country the poor have an inalienable right divine to have a compulsory levy made on society in their behalf. By custom and by legislation the absolutely destitute have been given a guarantee of maintenance, but society has a right to prescribe the manner in which this maintenance shall be given. As experience has amply proved, this legal endowment of destitution introduces a most dangerous and at times demoralising influence into our social arrangements. A heavy onus of proof therefore lies with those who wish to extend the provision for the poor beyond the relief of destitution. If an effective test of destitution can be devised and applied, no serious disintegration of society need result, but those who contend that the legal endowment of poverty can never be made a salutary constructive influence in the life of the poor, must continue to insist that even the guarantee of maintenance, held out to destitution, is an unnatural and disturbing element introduced into the living organism of society. Its real necessity is by no means proven. Its apparent necessity arises mainly from the fact that the system has created its own dependent population. The power, which a local majority already possesses, is an infringement, perhaps an unnecessary infringement, of our liberties, and it is in accordance with all the best precedents of our constitutional history that its exercise shall be jealously watched and carefully circumscribed.

Now as well as in 1834 there are two logical and extreme courses open. (1) It may be argued, This is a scientific and judicial question. We will appoint functionaries, a new branch of the civil service, to administer a definite law without fear and without favour. Our present law is very imperfect and very indefinite, we will amend it, and put in the hands of our new functionaries a precise and well-understood instrument. (2) Or it may be said, This is a matter which cannot be withdrawn from popular management. We are now definitely committed to a trust in the people. True, in a sense, this is a judicial and scientific problem, but the people are quite competent to determine its merits. We will, therefore, confide the matter quite frankly to a popular constituency. We must, however, be careful to see that the constituency is really autonomous, that it has a real opportunity of learning by experiment what is right and what is wrong in dealing with this subject. The law obviously can only enforce on such popular bodies the minimum amount of control in the right direction, but there is a danger (and this is now more apparent than in 1834) that popular bodies may be elected utterly unconvinced of the wisdom of the control put on them, and they will find very little difficulty in evading this control. If we want *a really autonomous* body to go right, we must give it power to go wrong. It is a bold measure, but as we are allowing the people to be its own physician and its own judge, let us do what we can to give it opportunity of deciding between right and wrong. With this end in view let us, if possible, narrow by definite enactment the powers which guardians may exercise, and within these limits leave them free to use their discretion. We will not disfranchise those who by themselves and by their friends may be interested as possible recipients of relief, nor, on the other hand, will we obscure the merits of this complicated question by absolving them from payment of rates, and setting them to vote what apparently is a levy on other people for their own benefit. We shall insist upon direct payment of rates by all voters, and though the smaller ratepayer may still persuade himself that he will profit as a recipient of a lavishly distributed bounty rather than suffer as a payer of a mischievously wasted and therefore tyrannical impost, still that is an

anomaly in popular representative government,
which cannot be altered, and the dangers of which ·
cannot in this case be wholly avoided. These
were the extreme alternatives before the Government in 1834, these are the alternatives before
the country to-day.

In 1834 the Government avoided both, and took
a middle course, adopting a compromise which,
as already hinted, contained both the advantages
and disadvantages inseparable from such · expedients. Can the same course be followed
to-day, or, if not, to which of the two obvious
alternatives above described shall we incline?

The reason why we have again to face this
problem, after an interval of sixty years, is that
the disadvantages of the compromise seem now
to be greater than its advantages, or at least to
be asserting themselves somewhat strongly.
Briefly stated, it is this. We have still an
electorate, and, in many cases, a local administration absolutely indifferent to the scientific aspect
of the question, and often, with the mandate of a
corruptly influenced election before their eyes,
incapable of performing judicial functions. Mean-
while, the democratic power has grown, and the
influence and control of the central authority
is perfectly unable to cope with it. Thus, although
the crisis is by no means so severe, we have
practically come back to the old order of things.

Again, the case of the able-bodied unemployed has taken its place in the forefront of the agitation against the poor law. A few years ago the duty of the public authority towards the unemployed seemed to be a matter settled for ever in the spirit dictated by the Poor Law Commissioners' Report, but the controversy has again been opened.

The causes of this seem to me to be very similar now to what they were in the period preceding 1834.

A protective tariff, restricting that expansion of industry and production which is indispensable in countries where population is increasing, finds its counterpart to-day in the restrictive regulations of trade unionism, and in the penalising legislation directed against private enterprise. These restraints upon the natural expansion of industry, which otherwise had proved commensurate with the increased ambitions and increased numbers of our population, caused then and cause now a certain difficulty in finding employment for the less competent workmen in all trades, and for the natural growth of population. The remedy applied in those old days was the parish farm, the roundsman system, and the general degradation of the labourer by the poor law. To-day we have the restrictive policy of trade unionism, reckless and wasteful public expenditure which together constitute a burthen and a menace to the development of industry. On the other hand, our casual wards, and an enormous multiplication of voluntary shelters, have already consolidated a large dependent population. We have circulars issued from the Local Government Board, suggesting the creation of public relief work. Such at least is the interpretation which nine men out of ten will put on the cautiously worded electioneering circular which various presidents of the Local Government Board have thought it consistent with their duty to issue. Some of the London Vestries bluntly replied that they were not relief authorities, and that they would have nothing to do with the matter. Others, putting the only practical interpretation on it which seems possible, have for the last two or three years spent unnecessarily large sums in street cleaning and other similar work. The expectation excited has grown in volume, and every winter the clamour of persons who want work to be found for them is louder. One vestry, which has made itself prominent by giving up contract work and by the disuse of street cleaning machinery in order to give hand-broom employment to the unemployed, found the pressure on it growing greater, and summoned a meeting of other vestries to discuss proposals for starting public works on a gigantic scale, the creation of light railways for removing the refuse of London, and the reclamation of waste

land by the sea shore. It is the old experience
over again. Restrict the legitimate expansion
of trade in one direction, and open a door leading
into a *cul de sac* of rate-supported industry in
another direction, and the old problem of 1832
is brought back again in all its essential features.

It is a splendid material for political intrigue.
A promise of legislation on the subject may be
made to serve as the decisive trump card in
the great Irish tragi-comedy. Politicians protest
that their intentions are honourable, and in
private life their assurances would be readily
accepted, but in practical politics circumstances
are too strong for them. Many avowedly believe
in the inspiration of the majority, and accept the
doctrine of delegacy. Yet, if the history of the
subject teaches us anything at all, it is that true
methods of poor law administration are not likely
to be learnt by listening to the advice of an
uninstructed public opinion.

It is submitted that the first step to be taken
now is that which was taken sixty years ago, viz.
*Inquiry by an authority altogether independent of
politics.* The Royal Commission of 1832 was
composed of men entirely independent of party
politics. Not a single member of the House
of Commons was nominated to serve on this
important inquiry. The mere fact that a man
was a politician seems to have been enough to

disqualify him for the onerous duty of serving. They were men of high character and position, and they had no object in view but to bring out the truth. This plan seems to me to be more likely to prove productive of useful result than that now in use, which is to embark the leading agitators of irreconcilable schools of opinion on what ought to be a judicial inquiry, and trust a tribunal of hostile witnesses to worry through without coming to blows.

LORD ALTHORP'S statement on February 1, 1832, with regard to the necessity of the appointment of the Commission, was as follows :—

"That the general question of the poor laws was a subject of great magnitude, and involved such a variety of important considerations, that any member of the Government, or of that House, would not be justified in bringing forward a measure, that would apply generally to the whole collective system of the poor laws of this country. . . . He must observe that all the evidence which had been taken before the different committees on this subject had been derived from gentlemen who came before those committees with preconceived opinions on the subject, and who seemed to want a knowledge of the working of the different systems that prevailed in different parts of the country."

Such a knowledge, he said, was absolutely necessary ; the Government therefore was of opinion that the best course to pursue was, by means of investigation and inquiry on the spot, to find out the effects of the different systems as they existed in the different parishes throughout the country.

Ministers therefore would await the report of the Commission.

At the present day this plea for inaction on the ground of the ignorance and inability of ministers and government might not be true to the same extent. It would, however, be less than the truth as to the absolute ignorance and prejudice of the constituencies on the subject; and to-day the opinion and knowledge of the constituencies is much more important than it was in those earlier days when the doctrine of delegacy was unknown.

There is, therefore, the same necessity for inquiry, but rather for the sake of the constituencies than for the sake of the Government.

For it is one of the singular features of this controversy that there is a practical unanimity of opinion among all who have had any experience of the subject. A short tenure of office at the Local Government Board is sufficient to make even the keenest politicians aware of the devastating influence of a lax administration of the poor law.

The voice and recommendations of the permanent officials of the Local Government Board are also unanimous. Students of poor law literature will find it difficult to recall the name of any writer of repute who has not urged the necessity of a restrictive policy. Among what is called the instructed public there is only one opinion on the subject. The difficulty is to bring the force of this experience to bear on the popular imagination.

Nothing, in my judgment, would be so conducive to this end as an exhaustive inquiry by some authority of a judicial character and independent of all political party. Such commissioners, of course, would not discover anything that is not very familiar to those who have paid attention to the question of poor law administration. Still, they would collect much material together, and they would restate the issues of the problems, and pass judgment with an authority that could not be gainsaid.

Would the effect of this report enable the legislature to proceed in the right direction?

I propose in subsequent sections to set out the nature of some of the evidence which lies ready for the consideration of any commission of inquiry which may be appointed. When he has considered this, the reader will be in a position to form his own judgment on the proper course to be followed by the legislature in the present crisis.

Throughout the hearing of the evidence, it may be well to bear in mind the three courses which are open to the legislature. (1) They may determine that poor law administration, like the judicial functions of the bench, is not to be entrusted to popularly elected authorities. We must appoint poor law administrators, as we appoint judges, with some sort of regard to their qualifications for the office. (2) They may decide that the matter must, for good or for evil, be given over to a popular electorate (as is already done by Sir H. Fowler's bill). All we can do in this case is to take guarantees for reasonable administration, (*a*) by insisting on direct payment of rates, and on the disfranchisement of those who pay no rates; or (*b*) by restricting the at present very wide power of guardians, on the ground that the existing license is a source of very great mischief where guardians administer laxly. (3) Or they may decline both of these courses and, following the example of 1834, may decide to strengthen the hands of the Local Government Board and give it explicit instructions to bring to an end certain forms of maladministration, and leave it to the Local Government Board to choose the time and the manner in which it thinks best to enforce its advice. In other words, Parliament and the Government may say, as in 1834, Poor Law Reform is not a matter which can be carried out in detail by an elective assembly. We will appoint a judicial body, and, laying down for its guidance certain principles of action, leave to it the onus of legislation.

There is much to be said both for and against all these alternatives. The only utterly indefensible course is that followed by the legislature

E

with regard to the Local Government Act,
1894.

Lord Rosebery's Government was avowedly trying to provoke the House of Lords to a trial of
strength. The handing over of local administration
to an electorate, the majority of which pays no
rates direct, seemed a point on which the House of
Lords would have been justified in acting ; but
the tactics of the game, in the judgment of the
Duke of Devonshire, made this intervention undesirable. The Opposition in the House of
Commons had felt obliged to imitate the Government in avoiding any cause of offence to that
irresponsible section of parliamentary voters whose
good will is commonly supposed to be fickle and
venal. No one had been found bold enough "to
bell the cat." The Opposition, therefore, must
share with the late Government the responsibility
for the result, which is that an important measure,
one which purports to be the foundation of our
system of local government, has ostentatiously
set aside the time-honoured constitutional maxim
that representation and taxation must go together.

The utterly contradictory arguments used by
ministers in support of this portion of their measure
bring into relief the true nature of the situation.
Sir H. Fowler's uneasy shifting from one argument
to another wholly contradictory of it, and the
remarkable collapse of the Opposition, suggest

that, in this instance at all events, our system of party government has failed to protect society from a gross injustice, which is bound in the future to give rise to trouble and disaster. Sir H. Fowler, as minister in charge of the bill, represented it to be a measure based on trust in the people ; the people paid no direct rates, but they smoked and drank beer and spirits, and grants were made from the Imperial treasury in aid of local burdens ; economical administration would, therefore, be to the interest of those who paid duty on tobacco and beer. By the time the bill got into committee, Sir H. Fowler seems to have grown ashamed of this utterly inadequate argument, and to the complaint of those who said that trust in the people did not carry with it the corollary that we must trust in the wisdom of one section of the people when engaged in spending the money of another section, he replied that sufficient check against abuse was to be found in the control of the Local Government Board. A more futile and insupportable argument could not easily have been found. It is notorious that, without infringing the rules laid down by the Local Government Board, a perverse local body can easily multiply its pauperism to an almost indefinite extent, and exercise unchecked their power in a manner destructive to the character of the poor and ruinous to the interests of the rate-payers. And, secondly, it is equally notorious that evasion of the law as laid down by the Local Government Board is extremely easy, and of daily occurrence.

No impartial person, who will candidly examine the course of this bill through the Houses of Parliament, can fail to be convinced of the utter unfitness of such assemblies (in their present temper, at all events) to arrive at any reasonable conclusion on this delicate question. The difficulty of a body like the House of Commons in dealing with a subject like bimetallism is obvious enough. Poor law reform is not perhaps so complicated or so abstruse, but it has the additional disadvantage that it cannot be discussed in the dry light of logic and common sense alone. Every disputant has his eye on the electorate, or rather on a section of the electorate, whose misfortunes indeed entitle it to every consideration, but from which it is idle and dishonest to pretend that we shall derive a true diagnosis of the disease with which it is afflicted.

THE NATURE OF THE EVIDENCE.

WHILE it is not possible for a single writer to gather evidence from so wide a field of observation as a commission of inquiry, there is yet a great deal of information ready to hand in blue books and pamphlets, and in the reports of the proceedings of the poor law conferences. The more formal treatises on the subject, though perfectly sound as to the doctrine they lay down, have been published some years, and as a consequence are rather belated in the accounts they give of more recent and successful experiments in poor law administration.

With a view of bringing my narrative within reasonable limits, and not from any lack of material, I propose in the next section to give an account of what I believe to be sound administration in a town, and in a rural, union, mentioning by way of illustration similar but not identical experiments tried elsewhere, and contrasting it with examples of what I believe to be bad administration.

First, however, a word of caution should be said

as to the value of such comparisons, in so far as they are based on statistics alone, for in my judgment nothing is more calculated to mislead than indiscriminate comparisons and indiscriminate use of poor law statistics.

The truth is that poor law administration is not a matter on which a comparison of statistics can throw very much light. It is much more a question of common sense. The problem, from a statistical point of view, may be thus stated : How many persons have been obliged, in any given union, to abandon their independence and accept, either an addition to their income or a complete maintenance, from the rates? Obviously any numerical answer to this question must be largely affected by two considerations. (1) The nature of the relief offered and the ease with which it can be obtained. (2) The character and circumstances of the population of the union.

In very many statistical inquiries—even those conducted by demographists as reputable as Mr. Booth—these two considerations are often entirely overlooked. It is the most usual thing in the world to compare the percentage of pauperism per head of population, as shown in several different unions. It is then triumphantly pointed out that there is a low rate of pauperism in Wharfdale and in Penzance, as well as in Bradfield,

Brixworth, and Atcham. Again, there is a fairly high rate of pauperism in the London Union of St. George-in-the-East and in Manchester, as well as in Barnstaple and Honiton. The administration in these Unions differs largely. In Bradfield, Brixworth, and Atcham, in St. George-in-the-East, and in Manchester, the proportion of out-door relief to total relief is very small, while exactly the opposite conditions prevail in Wharfedale, Penzance, Barnstaple, and Honiton. It is argued, therefore, by Mr. Booth, that administration has very little to do with the rate of pauperism. A moment's consideration shows the absurdity of such an argument. The conditions of land tenure and industry may in many unions be such as to make a high rate of pauperism impossible. Such, one might guess, was the case in Wharfedale, a Yorkshire valley where the holdings are small, and where the work of the farm is done by the members of the farmer's family, or by hired and unmarried labourers living on the farm. A lax system of poor law relief need not have more effect on such a population than it would have on the inhabitants of Belgrave Square. The only way of arriving at the result of different systems of administration is by watching the effect of a change of policy in one and the same union.

Naturally, that is, apart from the influence of

administration, the tendency towards pauperism varies largely in different unions. Racial and economical considerations are involved, too numerous and complicated to be here fully discussed. One or two points may be mentioned. There is the drift of the vagrant population at certain seasons to the towns, attracted by fortuitous charity, and still more by the improved accommodation given by the infirmaries and workhouses. These persons, if the tabulation admitted of it, should be deducted from the list of the settled poor, as is generally done with vagrants and lunatics. The very serious nature of this drift of unsettled pauperism can be best gathered from the fact that out of 9584 admissions to the Whitechapel workhouse and infirmary during the year ended Lady-day, 1895, only 871, *i.e.* 9·1 per cent., came from their own or friends' houses. The other 90 per cent. were practically homeless.[1]

In computing numerically, therefore, the pauperism of large towns, the fact must be remembered, that we are dealing also with a portion of the unsettled pauperism of the whole country. The official statistics give us no assistance in estimating the amount of this population.[2] There is evidence,

[1] Report of Guardians of Whitechapel Union for year ended Lady-day, 1895.
[2] For a fuller discussion of the ebb and flow of this unsettled population, and its disturbing influence on the statistics of the subject, see pp. 244, 250.

however, to show that it has a tendency to con-
centrate itself in some unions rather than others ;
in unions, for instance, where there are philanthropic shelters and common lodging-house accommodation, and also in unions where the
infirmary and workhouse are, by reason of their
superior comfort, want of discipline, or some other
reason, popular with this class. Increased comfort
and cleanliness, it should be observed, are generally
to be found in unions where the guardians are
restricting out-door relief, and concurrently paying
more attention to the proper management of
their in-door establishments. It is fair, however,
to add, that, in one instance at least, a union workhouse appears to be very popular with this class,
not on account of the liberal scale of its in-door
management, but rather by reason of the free and
easy nature of its regulations.

The most valuable comparison, then, will be
between different methods of administration in
the same union.

Even in this case, however, changes of condition
will go a long way to invalidate conclusions drawn
merely from statistics. Thus, in comparing the
pauperism of to-day with that of fifteen or twenty
years ago, it must never be forgotten that, as
already stated, a very great change has come over
the administration of our in-door pauper establishments. Previous to 1867, sick, lunatic, and imbecile

paupers were for the most part retained in the same
buildings as other paupers. In 1866, there were in
all the London workhouses only 111 nurses, and
only 3 trained night nurses ; the rest of the service
was performed by the able-bodied paupers. As a
consequence of the passing of Hardy's Act, there
were at the date of the House of Lords' Inquiry
of 1888 at least 11,000 beds in separate infirmaries—many of them in every respect equal to
hospitals—and over 1000 trained nurses. Similar
improvement has taken place in the provision
made for pauper children. Separate schools,
cottage home schools, and systems of boarding
out, have been adopted with a view of making
the education of pauper children more efficient.
The general management of the workhouse has
in many respects been largely improved. The
term workhouse is now an entire misnomer. For
the aged and infirm the workhouse is an almshouse
and not a task house. In many places kindly
visitors vie with one another in doing all they can
to relieve the monotony of the inmates' lives. The
fare, though simple, is adequate, and a principal
grievance of the inhabitants is that the airiness and
cleanliness of the dormitories is more agreeable to
the dictates of sanitary science than to the comfort
of persons accustomed to small, close, and sometimes crowded rooms. Further, Parliament has,
in its wisdom, decreed that persons, who are

chargeable for medical attendance only, shall not
be, like other paupers, deprived of their parliamentary franchise.

All these considerations must be taken into
account when we compare the pauperism of the
present time with that of twenty or twenty-five
years ago. But for the greater comfort and
advantages, deliberately introduced into our poor
law establishments, there can be no doubt that
in-door pauperism would be much less than
it is.

To a certain extent, it will be urged, the improved
conditions of existence in a poor law institution
are counteracted by the higher standard of living
among the poorer classes which has happily
become possible of late years. Unfortunately,
however, much turns on the word "possible."
There is a class, which seems to lack motive to
avail itself of its possibilities. An increase of
income does not suggest to it saving, thrifty effort,
or even the purchase of articles which give employment to labour. Too often it only means a somewhat more lavish scale of living while the income
lasts, or a cessation of work on a variety of
pretences, a disagreement with an employer, or a
desire for leisure, which less euphemistically might
be termed a love of idleness. With this class, the
increased possibilities of life have not raised them
above the hand to mouth existence, and their

attitude is the cause of all the difficulty of poor law administration. Our present inquiry may perhaps lead us to think that this love of a purely proletariate life is fostered by the remedies applied; in other words, by the fact that the ordinary administration of the law guarantees an eligible maintenance from the rates to sickness, old age, widowhood, and orphanhood. These contingencies are the natural competitors of claims of mere self-indulgence. They supply the motives which urge men to the first steps to rise above the merely proletariate life. If the so-called remedies for pauperism take the form of making these first steps unnecessary, it is obvious that the remedy may very easily become a cause of disease.

One other *caveat* as to the danger of reckless comparisons must be mentioned. The point is very obvious, and has already been indicated, but it is so important that it deserves to be explicitly stated. In dealing with poor law statistics, it is idle to attach the same weight to out-door pauperism as to in-door pauperism. The amount of out-door pauperism is a matter turning entirely on the caprice of the various boards of guardians; it will be found, singularly enough, that proportionately it is smallest in the poorest unions of the metropolis, mainly because a resolute resistance to the encroachment of its demands has been found to be the only alternative to bankruptcy. In-door relief, on the other hand, is guarded by an automatic test of a constant nature.

People do not become in-door paupers till they have determined that it is best for them to give up such livelihood as they have outside, in exchange for a maintenance in some poor law establishment. The question is affected, as already indicated, by the varying value of the maintenance offered in the workhouse, but subject to this qualification the numbers of in-door pauperism are the only poor law figures of any value as an index to poverty. On the other hand, the amount of out-door relief is governed by totally different factors ; the applicant gives up nothing, but is actuated by the universal desire of all mankind, viz. to add to his resources. Against this universal pressure there is no barrier except the caprice of guardians and the easily evaded rules of the Local Government Board.

The giving of out-door relief has a further disturbing influence on the statistical aspect of the question. In the majority of cases, notwithstanding the increased comfort of the in-door establishments, a diminution of out-door relief brings also a diminution of in-door relief, and for a reason that is obvious enough. When a population is trained up to expect relief at their own homes in every crisis of life, naturally a greater dependence is placed on this source of income than in places where such relief is not obtainable. The dependent feeling originated and fostered by out-relief increases as life goes on, and children and friends more readily absolve themselves from the duty of supporting the aged ; and, notwithstanding the decrease of old age pauperism as a whole, in places the tendency of old and infirm people to gravitate to the workhouse is strengthened and confirmed.

If we wish, therefore, to arrive at any statistical estimate of the amount of necessary destitution, represented by the poor law returns, we should consider only the in-door pauperism ; and, from the in-door pauperism in unions where out-door relief is freely given, we should deduct a certain percentage, if we wish to make due allowance for the artificial manufactory of pauperism above referred to.

THE ADMINISTRATION IN WHITECHAPEL.

LET us first consider the case of a town union.

The following account of the administration of the law in Whitechapel is taken, slightly condensed, but almost verbatim, from a pamphlet written by Mr. Vallance, the clerk of the union, and used by him as a basis for his evidence given before the Lords' Committee of 1888.

Up to 1870 the system followed for the relief of apparent distress was the granting of small doles of out-door relief; the in-door establishments—at that time consisting of a mixed workhouse for the adult sick and healthy poor, and a separate school at Forest Gate—being reserved for the destitute poor who voluntarily sought refuge in them. Out-door relief in money and kind was given to the able-bodied unemployed in return for work done under the rules laid down by the Out-door Relief Regulation Order. Under this system the administration was periodically subjected to great pressure; the aid of the police had frequently to be obtained for the protection of the guardians, the officers, and the property of the union. The matter came to a climax in the winter of 1869-70; and the guardians determined to reform a system which was felt to be fostering pauperism and encouraging idleness, improvidence, and imposture, whilst the relief in no sense helped the poor, being, as a rule, utterly inadequate. Voluntary charity merely consisted in indiscriminate almsgiving ; no intelligible distinction was observed between the functions of charitable and poor law relief, and much additional distress was the result of this thoughtless and indiscriminate benevolence. It was an object with the guardians to lay down a distinction between legal and voluntary relief, to interpret the former as relief in the workhouse or some other poor law institution, the latter as personal sympathy and helpful charity. They began, therefore, by restricting out-door relief in "out-of-work" cases, and they practically suspended the Out-door Relief Regulation Order, and applied strictly the principle of the Prohibitory Order. The first of these orders permits out-door relief to be given to able-bodied men and their families, in return for work done in a Labour Yard. Such relief may not take the form of wages, but must be proportionate to the requirements of the man and his family. Relief in large towns is, as a rule, administered under this order. The Prohibitory Order, as its name implies, forbids all out-door relief to the able-bodied, except in cases of sudden and urgent necessity.

The labour yard was closed in Whitechapel in 1870, and has never since been re-opened. During this process of restriction about one in ten of those offered in-door in place of out-door relief accepted the offer, and these gradually withdrew, and the in-door pauperism resumed its normal condition.

The out-door relief of all kinds was next carefully reviewed. Pains were taken to make it adequate, temporary, and usually conditional on some promise of effort to avoid application to the rates in future—for instance, a man would be relieved temporarily on condition of his promise to join a benefit club. Widows with dependent children were in some cases given temporary relief, pending inquiries as to their friends and efforts to place them in a position of independence. Employment as " scrubber " at the Infirmary was obtained in some cases, and, failing other arrangements, the guardians offered to receive some of the children into their district school, and the mother was left free to provide for herself and one or two children, a responsibility which, in the experience of the guardians, a widow might fairly be called on to discharge.

Out-relief was given to the aged and infirm only in those cases where there was evidence of thrift, and when the guardians were satisfied that there were no children or relatives whose duty it was to support the applicant. The class

F

was not found to be numerous, and, with the better organisation of charitable funds which resulted from the adoption of a definite policy by the guardians, it was, later on, dealt with entirely by the Tower Hamlet Pension Committee and other voluntary relief agencies.

The system of out-door relief thus gradually came to an end, and no new cases—other than those of sudden and urgent necessity relieved by the relieving officer in kind—have now for about twenty-five years been added to the out-door relief list.

Contemporaneously with this discontinuance of out-door relief, a great improvement took place in the in-door establishments. The time of the guardians was not consumed in the vain task of trying to adjudicate impartially on the claims of the many applicants for out-door relief, and they were therefore able to devote more attention to the in-door arrangements.

The change in the character of the Whitechapel workhouse and its allied establishments is due partly to this cause, and partly also to the fact that the guardians there have availed themselves very freely of the powers given them by the Metropolitan Poor Act 1868. It was charged by the anonymous author of a pamphlet entitled "Plain Words on Out-Relief," that the abolition of out-relief in Whitechapel had brought about

a great increase of expenditure. The answer, of
course, is that the expenditure in question followed
naturally on the passing of the Metropolitan Poor
Act, and was quite independent of the action of the
guardians with regard to out-door relief. The rise
in expenditure has been just as great in other
unions, where there has been no corresponding
decrease in the expenditure on out-door relief.
The great change cannot be brought out more
clearly than by quoting from a letter written by
Mr. Vallance to the Local Government *Chronicle*,
and reprinted in the Report of the Whitechapel
Guardians for the year ended Lady-day, 1894. The
great increase in salaries and also the general cost
of in-maintenance has been caused "by reason of
the operation of the Metropolitan Poor Act, 1868,
which had not appreciably affected expenditure
in 1870, but which later brought into force the
separate infirmary system, with its abolition of
all pauper service, and the elaborate net-work
of small pox and fever hospitals, etc., under the
control of the Metropolitan Asylums Board.
In 1870 the separate infirmary, with all its
attractiveness to the sick poor, was not in
existence; the official staff attached to the
infirmary department of the workhouse being
then represented by two visiting medical officers
and four nurses, whilst in 1892, there was a
separate infirmary certified for 590 sick poor, with

three resident medical officers, hospital-trained
matron and assistant, a staff of forty-two highly
trained nurses, paid servants, washers, scrubbers,
house-labourers, and the various other workers
necessary in an institution exclusively devoted
to the sick, and from which all pauper labour
is excluded. The cost of the staff of the infirmary
alone in 1892 was £6103; additional to which
£1263 was charged to Whitechapel in respect
of the official staff of the Metropolitan Asylums
Board."

These improvements, all pointing to a more
considerate and efficient treatment of the sick
poor, have been willingly undertaken by the
Whitechapel Board and are the result of the Act
of 1868.

THE STATISTICAL RESULT.

THE statistical result of the Whitechapel method of administration can be most conveniently given by a somewhat lengthy quotation from the Report of the Guardians for the year ended Lady-day, 1894.

" The retrospect of twenty-five years' administration, which was contained in the last year's Report, was a personal one,[1] but inasmuch as the early winter of 1869–70 was the real turning point in the history of the modern poor law in Whitechapel, and as the present year (1894) marks the close of a quarter of a century of uniform adherence to principles then laid down, it may be fitting —at the risk of some repetition—to append the following statistical table, exemplifying the gradual nature of the restriction of out-door relief and its contemporaneous effect, if any, upon the in-door pauperism. It will be seen that the sixth week of the quarter ended Lady-day, 1870, has been taken as a starting point, that being the week in which

[1] This refers to Mr. Vallance's personal connection with the Board which dates from 1868.

the highest pauperism was reached; the table being so arranged as to show the number of paupers relieved, the ratio per cent. of in-door and out-door paupers, and the amount expended in out-door relief in that and the corresponding weeks of the intervening years up to 1894, viz. :—

	In-door Paupers relieved.	Out-door Paupers relieved.	Total No. of Paupers relieved exclusive of Lunatics in Asylums.	Ratio per cent.		Cost of Out-door Relief (*i.e.* in money and kind).	
				In-door.	Out-door.	During the 6th week of the Lady-day Qtr.	During year ended Lady-day.
	(1)	(2)	(3)	(4)	(5)	(6)	(7)
						£ s. d.	£
1870	1419	5339	6758(*a*)	21·0	79·0	168 17 4	6,685
1871	1219	2568	3787	32·2	67·8	120 14 3	6,073
1872	1000	1568	2568	38·9	61·1	75 18 7	4,730
1873	1163	845	2008	57·9	42·1	50 4 5	2,654
1874	1154	609	1763	65·5	34·5	36 11 1	2,114
1875	1170	346	1516	77·2	22·8	22 9 0	1,406
1876	1268	186	1454	87·2	12·8	16 19 7	916
1877	1203	122	1325	90·8	9·2	12 2 9	873
1878	1221	141 (*b*)	1362	89·6	10·4	11 0 6	731
1879	1431	143 (*b*)	1574	90·9	9·1	9 15 3	592
1880	1464	128 (*b*)	1592	92·0	8·0	9 7 7	546
1881	1582	121 (*b*)	1703	92·9	7·1	8 17 4	528
1882	1478	105 (*b*)	1583	93·4	6·6	7 6 11	584
1883	1482	91 (*b*)	1573	94·2	5·8	4 8 10	521
1884	1418	77 (*b*)	1495	94·8	5·2	4 2 9	463
1885	1370	74 (*b*)	1444	94·9	5·1	4 8 1	309
1886	1305	70 (*b*)	1375	94·9	5·1	3 3 5	167
1887	1247	61 (*b*)	1308	95·3	4·7	2 7 11	131
1888	1356	63 (*b*)	1419	95·5	4·5	2 10 11	117
1889	1308	46 (*b*)	1354	96·6	3·4	1 15 7	86
1890	1258	52 (*b*)	1310	96·0	4·0	1 16 3	84
1891	1345	71 (*b*)	1416	95·0	5·0	3 5 4	77
1892	1342	56 (*b*)	1398	96·0	4·0	2 14 10	67
1893	1518	47 (*b*)	1565	97·0	3·0	1 19 2	72
1894	1623	30 (*b*)	1653	98·2	1·8	0 6 6	45

It is to be observed that in 1870 the imbecile paupers were maintained in the Workhouse and are accordingly enumerated in col. 1.

In 1871 those paupers had been transferred to Imbecile Asylums, and had ceased to be so enumerated until 1879, when they were required to be again included in the return of in-door paupers. This will explain the sudden diminution in the in-door paupers in 1871, and the sudden rise in 1879.

(*a*) The figures for 1870 may be regarded as exceptional to the extent of about 2000 paupers, there being at that period a severe temporary pressure upon the administration; but it is nevertheless interesting to note that the experience of the winter of 1869–70 induced the Guardians to voluntarily suspend the Out-door Relief Regulation Order early in the following year, and to apply strictly the principle of the Out-door Relief Prohibitory Order.

(*b*) These figures include 30 boarded-out children in 1878, 36 in 1879, 42 in 1880, 52 in 1881, 55 in 1882, 60 in 1883, 49 in 1884, 49 in 1885, 54 in 1886, 48 in 1887, 41 in 1838, 38 in 1889, 42 in 1890, 37 in 1891, 34 in 1892, 30 in 1893, and 26 in 1894.

"Adopting, moreover, the forms of comparison of last year and bringing the figures down to the latest possible date, we find that the mean numbers of *in-door paupers* (inclusive of vagrants) relieved in the year 1870 and 1893 respectively were as follows:

	1870.	1893.
England and Wales...	156,800	192,512
Metropolis	36,441	59,901
Whitechapel	1,311	1,374

thus showing an increase in England and Wales of 22·9 per cent.; the Metropolis of 64·3 per cent.; and Whitechapel of 4·8 per cent.

"Taking next the *out-door paupers*, the mean numbers relieved in the above-mentioned years were—in

	1870.	1893.
England and Wales... ...	876,000	566,264
Metropolis	114,386	47,472
Whitechapel	3,554	312

thus showing a decrease in England and Wales of

35·3 per cent. ; the Metropolis of 58·5 per cent. ; and Whitechapel of 91·2 per cent.

" Or, taking both the *in-door and out-door paupers,* the mean numbers relieved were—in

	1870.	1893.
England and Wales... ... 1,032,800		758,776
Metropolis 150,827		107,373
Whitechapel 4,865		1,686

thus showing a decrease in England and Wales of 26·5 per cent. ; in the Metropolis of 28·8 per cent. ; and in Whitechapel of 65·3 per cent.

" The *expenditure upon in-door relief* in 1870 and 1892 (being the latest return appended to the Report of the Local Government Board, 1892–3) was in

	1870.	1892.
England and Wales ... £1,502,807		£2,044,062
Metropolis 420,006		757,361
Whitechapel 13,076		15,932

thus showing an increase of expenditure in in-door relief in England and Wales of 36·0 per cent. ; in the Metropolis of 80·3 per cent. ; and in White-chapel of 21·8 per cent.

" The *expenditure upon out-door relief* in 1870 and 1892 was—in

	1870.	1892.
England and Wales ... £3,633,051		£2,374,380
Metropolis 412,817		181,406
Whitechapel 6,685		799

thus showing a decrease of expenditure in out-door relief in England and Wales of 34·6 per cent. ; the

Metropolis of 56·0 per cent. ; and Whitechapel of 88·0 per cent. ; or, excluding the cost of 'boarded-out children' (£485), the decrease of expenditure in out-door relief in Whitechapel will be found to be no less than 95·3 per cent.

"Taking also the quinquennial periods from 1870, the ratio of each form of pauperism to population in England and Wales, the Metropolis, and White-chapel, respectively, stood as follows, viz. :—

YEARS.	England and Wales.			The Metropolis.			Whitechapel Union.		
	In-door.	Out-door.	Total.	In-door.	Out-door.	Total.	In-door.	Out-door.	Total.
1870	7·1	39·4	46·5	11·5	36·0	47·5	16·6	45·0	61·6
1875	6·2	27·6	33·8	11·6	20·3	31·9	17·0	9·2	26·2
1880	7·1	24·7	31·8	13·0	13·7	26·7	17·6	5·5	23·1
1885	6·8	21·8	28·6	13·8	11·6	25·4	18·9	4·5	23·4
1890	6·6	20·7	27·3	14·1	11·8	25·9	17·7	4·3	22·0
1893	6·5	19·3	25·8	14·1	11·1	25·2	18·4	4·1	22·5

"These figures need no justification. They are absolute in themselves, and are free from the objection that they involve fallacious deductions. Of late, more than one attempt has been made to reach logical conclusions as to the results of a given policy of administration, by a comparison of pauperism and expenditure in or between individual unions, or by a calculation of the ratio of pauperism to population in certain unions. It is, however, entirely misleading to compare White-chapel—with its migratory population, represented by the 8000 beds, or thereabouts, in common lodging-houses, shelters, refuges, &c., and from which the pauperism is largely, if not mainly, recruited — with another union, even of the poorest character, but with probably a more settled population ; whilst it would be equally inconclusive to compare pauperism, or expenditure, in different unions, with population, without due regard to the character of such population."

The report hardly makes enough of the exceptional difficulties of the situation in Whitechapel ; but even in face of these it is satisfactory to note the great reduction of pauperism which has been achieved by a courageous application of sound principles of administration. To see the full extent of the vast improvement that may be effected, it is necessary to turn to a rural union, such as Bradfield, to be presently noted, which lies remote from the demoralising influences of the poorest and roughest quarter of the largest metropolis in the world.

What is less satisfactory, but equally plain from a consideration of these figures, is the unnecessarily high average of pauperism maintained throughout England by reason of the fact that many boards of guardians still obstinately adhere to every form of abuse which the law unfortunately enables them to exercise.

BETHNAL GREEN.

BETHNAL GREEN is a union contiguous to White-chapel, where unfortunately the guardians have taken a different view of their duty. Practically the Bethnal Green Board gives out-door relief to all applicants. During a great part of the year their relieving officers are besieged by importunate crowds ; interim relief, under the plea of sudden and urgent necessity, is given by the Relieving Officers to able-bodied men in a way that is probably illegal. The most inadequate sums are given, and it is not too much to say that the out-relief system followed in Bethnal Green is simply a centre not for the distribution of adequate relief, but for the dissemination of the virus of pauperism. If we turn to the in-door system what do we find ? First, that for the last twenty years the Bethnal Green Board has lived in a perpetual state of warfare with the Local Government Board, because of the disgraceful condition of its workhouse and the absence of all proper accommodation for the treatment of the sick. The case of Bethnal Green is a very remarkable one and deserves more attention than it has hitherto attracted. It has all along been a union where the old plural vote had little effect. During the debates on Sir H. Fowler's bill, its mismanagement was quoted, as an instance of the level to which the "one man one vote" principle, irrespective of ratepaying, could reduce a constituency. The unsatisfactory administration of the law in Bethnal Green attracted the attention of Sir Walter Foster, Under-Secretary of the Local Government Board, and on receiving a deputation from Bethnal Green on the subject of an infirmary site, he is reported to have spoken his mind very freely as to the disgraceful condition of the workhouse. Some reforming members of the board who were present urged that Sir Walter should print and publish his remarks. At the moment, in view of the fact that Sir H. Fowler's bill was assimilating the franchise of the whole country to that which already obtained in Bethnal Green, the exigency of party politics or some other cause prevented this, but in the interest of the poor of Bethnal Green it is desirable that some publicity should be given to the facts, of which the following are cited as a sample.

In January, 1894, it was reported at a meeting of the Board that the guardians had been served with a summons by the Sanitary Authorities for not carrying out their orders with respect to the drains and insanitary and dirty condition of the house. The medical officer of the Union, Dr. Knox, appearing as witness before the Select Committee of the House of Lords, admitted that the Bethnal Green Workhouse was the worst institution of the kind in London; that it was so bad that it could not be amended, but must be pulled down. Further, it is stated that Bethnal Green is the only Union in London which engages pauper nurses in the sick wards, and that the accommodation is so grossly inadequate that the workhouse is always over-crowded.

Yet with all these inconveniences the Bethnal Green Workhouse is not unpopular. Dr. Hunter was able to say, in his article in the *Contemporary Review*, March, 1894, that Bethnal Green was among the In-door Relief · Unions, that is, the unions which gave more than the average amount of their relief inside the house. As already stated, there is no disposition to refuse out-door relief, and the paupers who enter the house do so from choice, or because they belong to the vagrant class and have no homes.[1] Here is a description given by one of the inmates in a letter addressed to the Board and to the Local Government Board. After drawing attention to the opinions expressed by certain members of the Board in their addresses before the election in regard to the classification

[1] For proof of this see p. 241.

of inmates according to character and disposition, the letter went on to say, " The unfortunate inmates were herded together like cattle. On Sunday the place was a regular pandemonium· Casuals came in and stayed till Monday, and the language used by some of them was disgusting, while the time was passed in playing cards and dominoes, in whistling, howling, singing of obscene songs, and dancing." It would not be fair as a rule to. quote the criticisms of a pauper inmate as conclusive evidence, but in this case the substantial accuracy oɪ the description is not seriously denied. Some time ago, a new master was appointed, and a complaint was brought before the board by some of the inmates that the door between the apartments of the male and the female inmates of the house was locked at night. It appeared that for many years this had never been closed. These things seem hardly credible, but they are vouched for to me by unimpeachable evidence.

What must be the class of people who flock into this rate-supported common-lodging house? What a terrible injustice this laxity of discipline inflicts on the more respectable inmates! Contrast this pandemonium with the clean and orderly workhouse and infirmary at Whitechapel, with its medical officers and trained nurses.

CLASSIFICATION.

TAKE, again, the question of classification. Every agitator on the poor law declares himself to be in favour of better classification, but few of them have any conception of the difficulties which beset the question. Mr. Vallance, whose competence and ability will be readily acknowledged even by those who differ from his view on poor law relief, has always declared that for himself he would be very unwilling to have the responsibility for classification according to character and merit thrust on poor law officials. It would, in his opinion, be an exercise of arbitrary power which could not, without much risk of abuse, be entrusted to poor law officials. The cry for classification in the mouth of the agitators is somewhat inconsistent. In one breath they are complaining of the harshness and cruelty of the poor law official, and yet they clamour to clothe him with new and arbitrary powers. They are backed up in this demand, not by conscientious officials like Mr. Vallance, but by the electioneering promises of the representatives of Bethnal Green. Classification admittedly is desirable ; but, as Mr. Vallance has shown, the only practicable classification must be a voluntary one. If the buildings are adequate, there need be no over-crowding, and inmates will classify themselves.

The Local Government Board, very properly, insists on a threefold classification, the able-bodied, the sick and infirm, and the young, and these are divided again according to sex. The able-bodied in the workhouse are very few in number, and the plan pursued at Whitechapel is to isolate them from one another, as far as possible, and to keep them all employed in some useful work. There is no oakum picking, but the inmates are employed in painting and carpentry according to their ability. They are not, of course, paid wages for this, and they are made to understand that if they wish to become independent they must go out and seek work in the ordinary channels of trade. The isolation is agreeable to the more respectable, and is distasteful to the idle, gossiping loafer. With regard to the women—more especially women coming into the infirmary to be confined of illegitimate children—it has been urged, and with some degree of plausibility, that classification according to degree of respectability should be attempted. A closer consideration of the question, however, confirmed by the experience recorded by Mr. Vallance, will, I think, bring most reasonable persons to a different conclusion. The disabilities and sufferings of women in this unfortunate class are more than sufficient, and it is difficult to imagine a crueller suggestion than that they should be herded together and marked out as a class with which no one is to associate.

Mr. Vallance has recorded an instance of a provincial union where this classification took place. Unfortunate young women, who, to the eye of some functionary, appeared more depraved than others, were collected together apart from the other inmates, with the result to be expected. The insult and the degradation called into activity all their worst instincts, and Mr. Vallance has described to me his last sight of the whole party being dragged off to the police-court charged with riotous and obscene conduct. The plan pursued in Whitechapel is quite different. There are, of course, a considerable number of women in this condition passing through the infirmary. It is the business of the matron to see them, and it is not difficult for a woman of sympathy and common sense to learn something of the character of each. When the women are able to go about, the matron makes it her business to send them to work in different parts of the establishment. One goes perhaps to the kitchen, another to the

G

laundry, or to the scrubbers. If they are anxious to make a new start in life, some lady is induced to interest herself in the matter, and employment outside is obtained, and, during the year to which my information relates, I am told that fifty-one women were helped in this way and given a chance, at all events, to live a respectable life. If unfortunately, as may occasionally happen, paupers of this class show themselves perverse and unmanageable, it is perfectly easy for a judicious official to isolate such persons by finding them employment in remoter parts of the establishment. These arrangements are made not by way of punishment, but merely in the ordinary routine of the domestic work of the institution.

The treatment of the sick is entirely a doctor's question. It is the duty of the guardians to secure the services of a competent medical man, of a duly qualified staff of nurses, and to see that sufficient and suitable accommodation is provided. The fever hospitals under the metropolitan asylums boards are open for infectious cases, and such further classification as is necessary must of necessity be left in large measure to the doctor.

The classification of the aged and infirm, again, is a question much debated. Mr. Vallance's advice may be quoted again. It is that ample accommodation be provided, that the wards should be divided up as far as possible; some small tables and movable chairs, with a few screens, the last given perhaps by some charitable person, will enable the inmates to arrange themselves in groups. The kindly association presided over by the Countess of Meath, known still as the Brabazon scheme, has been extremely useful in finding simple employments to beguile the idle hours of the aged and infirm. A friend, who has devoted the best years of his life to the onerous duties of a London poor law guardian, told me how he once sought counsel on this point from an old man who had for years been an inmate of a certain London workhouse. The old fellow unexpectedly came into some money and left the house. Some months after, my friend met him in the street, and in the course of conversation asked him his candid opinion on the management of the workhouse, and the question of classification in particular. The old man said, " Don't you bother yourself about that ; we classify ourselves ; if you were to classify us you would classify us all wrong. You should give us a better pudding on Friday, but otherwise I have no complaint to make."

This, I think, is the common sense of the matter. For the able-bodied, discipline and task-work is necessary, but the aged and infirm are not required to work. They should be kept employed to save them from utter weariness, but for them the workhouse is an almshouse, and the most considerate treatment is to leave them, as far as possible, free to choose their own friends and associates. After all, it must be remembered, the most respectable are not of necessity the best company. A great deal of this talk about classification is merely bred of presumption and ignorance.

With regard to the children, there is little difference of opinion. Separate schools are indispensable. Admittedly some of the London schools have grown too large. Others, again, leave little to be desired. The plan of having cottage homes is also recommended, but it is extremely costly. Boarding out is, in a limited number of cases, a successful method of bringing up pauper children. Obviously, however, this method is only available for deserted or orphan children, and if carelessly supervised it is liable to terrible abuses. Miss Mason, the Local Government Board inspector of boarded-out children, has more than once dwelt on the fact that it is at times very difficult to find a sufficient supply of suitable foster-mothers. The great majority of pauper children must continue to be brought up in the schools, and if some of the many futile hours devoted by guardians to "discriminating" on the merits of applicants for out-door relief could be given to the schools, these important institutions might be greatly improved.

Here our brief account of the reformation at Whitechapel must end.

STEPNEY AND ST. GEORGE-IN-THE-EAST.

A SIMILAR reform was, about the same time, begun and carried out in the contiguous union of Stepney, and in 1875 the example was followed by St. George-in-the-East.

In Stepney the account given by Mr. Jones, for many years relieving officer in that union, dwells specially on the policy of insisting that out-relief, when given at all, shall be adequate. In Stepney he represents that it had the following effect. The out-relief list, when the reform began, was very extensive, and the relief given grossly inadequate. To make it really adequate, the guardians must have faced a very large extra expenditure. In justice to the ratepayers, this was a matter requiring careful consideration. The claims of each applicant for out-relief were therefore carefully scrutinised, with the final result, that a disuse of the method of out-door relief quite as complete as in Whitechapel became the rule at Stepney.

The remarkable feature in the case of St.

George-in-the-East was that the change was made suddenly.

"On Jan. 1, 1875, the number of paupers in St. George-in-the-East (population about 47,000, and the district as poor as any in London) was 3047; of these 1248 were in receipt of in-door relief, and 1799 of out-door relief. The guardians *suddenly* set to work to revise their out-relief list, with the result that on Jan. 1, 1876, the numbers were: indoor, 1258; outdoor, 548; total 1806." (*The Administration of the Poor Law*, a pamphlet by A. G. Crowder, Guardian of St. George-in-the-East, 1888.)

If, as is now generally admitted among those who have paid any impartial attention to the matter, a restriction of out-door relief is a good thing, it becomes a very interesting and important matter to decide by what method a transition is to be made.

It is, I think, possible that in practice there was not so much difference in the method followed as would at first sight appear. In none of the unions, as I believe, were any *new* cases of out-relief put on the books after the decision of the guardians to reform their administration. The St. George's Board, it is possible, acted more boldly, because the policy of the Whitechapel and Stepney Boards had already proved the advantage and possibility of a change; its action in dealing with the cases already on the out-relief list seems to have been more drastic, but the policy of all the unions had this most important and vital feature in common, that tacitly it was agreed that no new cases should be put on the list. This, I expect, is the secret of the continuity of policy in these three unions—a continuity in the case of Whitechapel and Stepney of a quarter of a century. Considering what human nature is, considering the class of men who are responsible for local administration, more especially in the poorer parts of London, I do not believe that they could have resisted the temptation to use the patronage at their disposal, unless a custom equivalent to an absolute rule of the board had stood in the way. As is well known, the tendency to restrict out-relief has been general throughout the country, but its restriction has been very gradual, and unions are liable to a reversal of policy. The continuity of policy in these unions has been due partly to the presence on the board of one or two men, who had thought the matter out and were trusted by their colleagues, but even more to the fact that practically no applications for out-door relief are now considered.

BIRMINGHAM AND MANCHESTER.

A DIFFERENT practice has been adopted for bringing about a reduction of out-door relief in other urban unions. In Birmingham, in Manchester, and in Paddington, the process has been more laborious. There, the general understanding that no more cases shall be put on the out-relief list has not been reached. Rules have been laid down for the administration of out-relief, and a somewhat laborious system of inquiry and cross visiting has been instituted. Each case is considered on its merits, but the result has been a very large reduction of out-door relief.

In Birmingham a Special Committee of the Board was appointed on Oct. 4, 1882,

"to examine into the whole question of out-door relief, as administered in this parish, with power to inquire into the system adopted in other large towns, and to report any suggestions or alterations they might consider it desirable to make."

The Committee recommended the appointment of a superintendent of the Relief Department, whose duties should be to attend all relief committees, to see that the orders of the committees were carried out, that the regulations of the guardians were adhered to, and to exercise a general supervision over the officers and arrangements of the Relief Department.

They also recommended the appointment of a *cross visitor*, as assistant to the superintendent. His duties were to conduct, "independently of the Relieving Officers, inquiries with regard to such applicants for or recipients of relief, as may be referred to him by the superintendent, and to report to him." Next, recommendations were made with a view to re-arranging the staff of the Relieving Officers. The question as to the number of cases which each officer can supervise was left open till the results of the appointment of the superintendent and cross visitor could be ascertained.

It was further urged that steps should be taken to secure uniformity of action in the different relief committees of the Board ; that, for this purpose, the following rules should be adopted.

"That out relief be refused to the following classes of applicants for relief, except in special cases—
  (1) "Single able-bodied men.
  (2) "Single able-bodied women.
  (3) "Able-bodied widows without children.
  (4) "Married women (with or without families) whose

husbands, having been convicted of crime, are under-going a second or subsequent term of imprisonment.

(5) "Married women deserted by their husbands, whether with or without families.

(6) "Persons residing with relatives where the united income of the family is sufficient for the support of all its members, whether such relatives are liable by law to support the applicant or not.

(7) "Widows with children, during the first six months of their widowhood, if on the death of their husband, they receive money from a club, which, in the opinion of the committee, was lavishly spent in mourning or funeral expenses.

(8) "Any person who fails to satisfy the committee that their destitution has not been caused by improvidence and intemperance."

The report further recommends that a Central Out-door Relief Committee should revise the decisions of the Sectional Relief Committees in doubtful cases.

Relief, further, should only be given for a short period ; and attention is also called to the practice of the Whitechapel Committee in relieving the children of widows in the district schools without requiring the parent to come into the house.

These relief regulations were put into force on January 1, 1884. The Central Relief Committee was duly appointed. In 1884 they were called on to revise fifty-two decisions of the sectional com-mittees. This necessity for revision steadily decreased till, in 1889, there were no revisions at all; in 1890 there was one. In 1891 there were two. A very similar result attended the work of the cross visitor. In 1884, forty-nine cases were struck off the list by the Board on the report of the cross visitor, while in 1890 and 1891 only one and three cases were reported and dealt with as un-satisfactory. The reduction of out-door relief made it possible to reduce the number of Relieving Officers in 1891 from six to five.

Relief committees issue orders for admission to the workhouse from time to time to persons who are recipients of out-door relief, either as a test of destitution, when the case seems undeserving of out-relief, or when the home conditions are unsatis-factory. In 1884 one hundred and seventy such orders were made. In 1889, twenty-one; in 1890, twenty-eight; in 1891, twenty-two. In 1889 and 1890 none of these orders were accepted, and in 1891 only three of them were used.

In 1883, prior to the New Regulations, there were 1138 orders for the workhouse given; of these 344 were used. This number has gone on steadily decreasing till, in 1891, only forty-five orders were given; of these only twenty-one were applied for, and only fourteen of these were used; "therefore," says Mr. Fothergill, the Superintendent of out-relief, in his report to the Board in 1892, "it may be presumed that there was no real necessity for the applications in these cases where the orders were not used."

Of the general result of this system the following figures will speak :—

PAUPERS RELIEVED ON JAN. 1, EXCLUSIVE OF LUNATICS.

Years.	Out-door.	In-door.	Total.	Proportion of paupers to population, one in
1883	4905	2550	7455	33
1884	4496	2643	7139	34
1885	3810	3043	6853	35
1886	3514	3028	6542	37
1887	3108	3158	6266	39
1888	2388	3147	5535	44
1889	1851	3135	4986	49
1890	1263	3037	4300	57
1891	1183	3088	4271	57
1892	904	3003	3907	62

With regard to the increase in the workhouse, it is to be observed that there has been a continuous improvement in the infirmary treatment of the sick poor, and that to this cause much of the in-door pauperism is to be attributed. " The opening of the New Infirmary," says Mr. Fothergill, in his report for 1889, "has thrown a great responsibility on my department, for the cunning schemes that are planned to secure admission are many, and, when they are not successful, insults and abuse are heaped upon the relieving officers. The fame of the infirmary has spread far and wide, and large numbers come seeking the benefit of the improved provision made for the sick here." The report goes on to give instances of persons who had travelled long distances in order to avail themselves of the benefit of the infirmary.

The figures above quoted show that the number of admission orders given by the Board both in the case of first applications and to persons in receipt of out-door relief, has steadily diminished. The great majority of the inmates of the workhouse and infirmary were admitted on the authority of the master of the workhouse on their own application, and each year a considerable number of out-relief paupers voluntarily gave up their allowances and asked to be admitted to the workhouse. In 1884, the first year of the new regulations, as many as forty-nine took this step. These considerations account in a perfectly natural and not unsatisfactory manner for the slight increase in in-door pauperism.

The history of the Manchester and Paddington Boards is not dissimilar. An interesting account of the history of poor law administration in Manchester is given by Mr. Alexander McDougall, J.P., Vice-chairman of the Manchester Board of Guardians.[1]

---

[1] See p. 304 of a volume entitled, " The Organisation of Charities, a report of the sixth section of the International Congress of Charities at Chicago." Baltimore : the John Hopkins Press. London : The Scientific Press, Limited, 428, Strand. 1894.

About twenty years ago rules almost identical with those at Birmingham were adopted by the Board, with the following statistical result :—

OUT-DOOR RELIEF.

For the year ending March 29, 1873, average number of persons receiving relief on one day was . . . 3198
For the year ending March 25, 1893, average number of persons receiving relief on one day was . . . 594

Decrease . . 2604

IN-DOOR RELIEF.

For the year ending March 29, 1873, average number of persons receiving relief on one day was . . . 2298
For the year ending March 25, 1893, average number of persons receiving relief on one day was . . . 2718

Increase . . 420

Commenting on these figures, Mr. McDougall remarks :—

" This large reduction in the number of persons granted out-relief has not been at the cost of hardship and suffering. Careful inquiry has failed to discover any cases of necessity unrelieved because of strict adherence to the regulations. On the other hand, it has raised the respectability of out-relief, and made really worthy persons less disinclined to apply."

It may here be pointed out that the argument of those who advocate an absolute rule against out-relief is that with regard to "really worthy persons" it is the business of private charity to meet such cases, and that, according to their testimony, no insuperable difficulty has been found elsewhere in solving the problem in this way ; see Mr. Vallance's remarks *re* Tower Hamlet Pension Committee, p. 66. "The collateral results," Mr. McDougall continues, "have been most beneficial; the character of notoriously pauperised localities has been changed. Out-relief, readily granted, causes groups of improvident persons to localise. These nests of pauperism are soon broken up when out-relief becomes restricted to exceptional cases only." Mr. McDougall next dwells on the improvements made in the infirmary and in the workhouse generally. "There is but little unwillingness," he says, "on the part of the sick poor to go into the infirmary; it has become popular even to an extent not desired by the guardians, as it is a fact that sick persons from a distance are attracted." This fact is universal in most populous places. In response to a very proper feeling of humanity, great improvements have everywhere been made, and this fact must be held largely responsible for the increase in the numbers of in-door paupers.

Mr. McDougall then describes the assistance which has been given to the reform of public relief by the Manchester and Salford District Provident Society, an association which works very much on the lines of the Charity Organisation Society of London. With regard to the aged, an account is given of the efforts of one of the guardians (I believe that Mr. McDougall himself is the person in question), who has raised from voluntary sources a small pension fund, which he pays out to a number of destitute, respectable old people. "The number of such persons," he says, "even in a large population is not great, because the majority of aged persons have children able to contribute to their support;" a view of the situation which confirms the already expressed opinion that if charitable people will unite in taking a reasonable attitude on the subject, there is no reason why the guardians should not make their rule against out-relief well-nigh absolute, and leave the hard cases to be dealt with by private charity.

A RURAL UNION.

IT remains to add a brief narrative of the reform of administration carried out in a rural district. The Bradfield Union comprises 62,650 acres, situated ⅚ in Berkshire and ⅙ in Oxfordshire, to the west of Reading, having a total rateable value of £136,979. The population was 15,853 in 1871, and in 1891, 18,017, in spite of a transference of a populous part of the Union to Reading in 1889. It is, in the main, an agricultural union. An agricultural labourer earns a nominal 12s. to 15s. per week; but with extras and harvest money, etc., really makes about 17s. to 20s. per week. The average rent of a cottage and garden is 1s. 6d.

On January 1, 1871, there were in receipt of poor relief 999 out-door and 259 in-door paupers (exclusive of lunatics in asylums and vagrants), a total of 1258, or one in thirteen (7·7 per cent.) of the population. The total poor law expenditure for the year was £10,865, and the poor rate stood at 24½d. in the pound, entailing a cost of 13s. 8½d. per head of population.

On January 1, 1893, the corresponding figures were as follows: out-door paupers, 22; in-door, 99; total, 121, or 1 in 148 (0·67 per cent.). Expenditure during the preceding year, £1995; poor rate, 3½d. ; cost per head of population, 2s. 2½d.[1]

[1] The above facts are given on the authority of an interesting

At the annual meeting of the London Charity Organisation Society in 1891, the Chairman of the Bradfield Union, the late Mr. Bland-Garland, gave a most remarkable and impressive narrative of his experience.

" I am only a country guardian," he began ; " I have only the old story to tell you—nothing whatever new— the old story as told by the Poor Law Commissioners of 1834, which has been shamefully neglected by guardians ever since—neglect which has caused more misery, in my opinion, to the poor of this country than all other causes put together. How does the restriction of out-door. relief promote thrift and independence ? It is the chief cause of pauperism. I hope I shall persuade many of you before I have finished that four-fifths of the pauperism of this country is due to out-door relief, that drunkenness and crime contribute comparatively in only a very small measure to it. . . . It is a far-reaching evil, much more so than is generally supposed. Not only the recipients are pauperised by it, but the whole neighbourhood for a considerable area learn to depend upon it, when it is given freely. They are all looking forward to it when their time comes. The actual numbers in receipt of it are no criterion to the numbers that, though not in receipt of it, are being pauperised by the expectation of it. I can speak very strongly from my own personal observation of twenty years on this subject. I doubt not that, as we

paper, p. 350, contributed by Mr. Willink (who succeeded Mr. Bland-Garland as Chairman of the Board) to the International Congress of Charities at Chicago. The full title, etc., of the Report is given on p. 94.

have hundreds of thousands at the present day in England and Wales receiving out-door relief, and being, of course, paupers, we have millions who are prepared to be paupers, and who would, if it were not for the malign influence of out-door relief, be exerting themselves to provide for sickness and old age."

Mr. Bland-Garland's address, which has been reprinted by the Charity Organisation Society under the appropriate title "From Pauperism to Manliness," goes on to explain the result of the refusal of out-door relief. In the old days some seven hundred medical orders were given during the year. An old medical officer told Mr. Bland-Garland that in the village where he had lived for thirty years, every one (tradespeople as well as labourers) used to get medical attendance from him. This was made to cease, and all orders were given on loan, and, where practicable, repayment was enforced. In 1890, twenty-four orders only were given; "the people have got to be too independent now. They have learnt to stand on their own legs, and to go into the medical officer's clubs, and to be independent of the guardians."

From 1876 to 1890, 55 widows with 213 children had made application. Of these, only 1 widow and 11 children accepted the offer made by the Board to receive them into the workhouse.

" The remaining fifty-four widows and 202 children who declined to go into the workhouse are far better off than similar widows and children were when they got out-relief. As a matter of course the children of widows in receipt of out-relief are brought up as beggars and pauperised from their infancy, and the pauperism hangs to them. . . . You may consider that hereditary pauperism. . . . The widows, it is very easy to see, are improved. They are free from the incubus of pauperism. They can demand full remuneration for their labour. They could not do that when they were receiving the pauper dole. They only got a pittance then from their employers. Those that require assistance from their relations get it far more readily than they did when they received the pauper dole. I would say from my heart that one of the happiest circumstances of my life is that we refused to give any more out-door relief to widows, because I see plainly, all over the Union, that they are far better off, and far happier than ever they were before."

Then, after referring to the reduction of the rate, he goes on—

" It becomes comparatively easy now for me or any of my fellow guardians to say to the gentlemen who reside in the parishes where we occasionally find a poor person, or couple, whom we would rather not bring into the house, 'Well, now, this is a subject for private charity. We recommend you to get your neighbours to contribute to a small pension for life for these people.' We always say what the pension ought to be, in order that it may be sufficient, if possible. We are enabled to add, to give force to the recommendation, 'You know now that you only pay a $5\frac{1}{4}d$. rate, instead of a $24\frac{1}{2}d$.

Surely you can afford it.' And we find that very effective."

He then gives some account of the increase of thrift, due, as he argued, to the better administration of the law. Medical clubs showed an increased membership of 148 per cent. and Friendly Societies of 150 per cent.

"It is said that the restriction of out-door relief is a hardship to the poor, because it drives them into the workhouse. It does nothing of the kind, ladies and gentlemen. It drives them into thrift and independence. How can it drive them into the workhouse, when it has reduced the number of inmates of our workhouse to less than one-half, when we have done away with all out-door relief, you may say?"

The same kindly but clear-headed authority dwells in this same address on the pains taken by the guardians with the children who come under their care. They do not "board out," which he thinks more suitable for large unions. The children are kept in a part of the house separate from the adult paupers. They are sent to the village school and mix with the other children. They are taught to use their hands, and are brought up in a healthy way. Care is taken in the selection of masters and mistresses for them, when they are ready to go out into the world, so that they may not be taxed above their strength.

This careful and sensible policy is rewarded

with success, and it is satisfactory to learn that the children so brought up do not relapse into pauperism.

One last quotation from this interesting address enables the reader to appreciate the difficulty of providing for exceptions by rule.

"As to the exceptions in favour of out-door relief, you must lay down some rules, I suppose. Some unions that have been reformed have laid down a great many rules. But with too many rules I think you may get into great difficulties. Our exceptions have been simple ones. We simply make an exception in favour of giving a widow four weeks' out-door relief after the commencement of her widowhood, in order that she may have time to make her arrangements. Beyond that we only give out-door relief to temporarily urgent cases arising from sickness or accident. Well, we find these exceptions are so clearly defined that no one leans upon them. The evil of exceptions is that they tend to become the rule. When they go beyond what I have just stated they become dangerous. People then begin to lean upon them in the expectation of getting this poison— out-door relief."

A GENERAL CONCLUSION.

It is no part of the purpose of this article to insist on the superior merit of one method of reducing out-door relief as against another. Personal and local considerations must in most cases decide the precise policy to be followed by any reforming board of guardians. All that can be done at present is to direct public opinion to the necessity and practicability of administrative reform. The possibility of legislative reform is a matter on which it is more difficult to speak with confidence. The treatment of pauperism is a science, and locally elected, democratic science is a conception, not likely to be realised in our time. The other horn of the dilemma is, that no centralised authority might be sufficiently powerful to apply the requisite measures of social surgery. A legal provision for the poor is a dangerous principle, creating a large proportion of the pauperism which it relieves. It has, however, become an integral part of our social life, and if we cannot abolish it, we must control and limit it, as best we can. A formal inquiry conducted by some competent and impartial tribunal might, like the similar inquiry of 1832–34, create such a volume of opinion throughout the country, that the legislature might be able to take away from the local authorities some portion of the powers which at present are too often used to the detriment and demoralisation of the poor. Till that is done, all that the poor law reformer can do is to urge on the local authorities that they should voluntarily adopt the principles and practice of one or other of the models which have been briefly and imperfectly sketched on the foregoing pages.

II.

THE POOR LAW
AS AN OBSTACLE TO THRIFT.[1]

INFORMATION as to the relation of Friendly
Societies to methods of administering poor law
relief prior to the passing of the Poor Law Amendment Act of 1834 is of necessity very scanty. Our
principal source of knowledge is Sir F. Eden's
"State of the Poor," three vols. 4to, 1797. Of
course, many facts as to the poor law and as to
Friendly Societies are to be obtained from various
and separate other sources, but no one has so
clearly appreciated the close connection which
subsists between the two as Sir F. Eden. His
second and third volumes are devoted to a
statistical account of all matters relating to the
poor in "several agricultural, commercial, and
manufacturing districts." The facts set down by
the author are, for the most part, the result of
personal inquiry, and in his passage from town

---

[1] Republished with some additions from *Insurance and Saving.*
A report on the existing opportunities for Working Class Thrift.
Charity Organisation Society Series. Sonnenschein & Co., 1892, to
which volume the present essay formed an Introduction.

to town, this most painstaking investigator
enumerates, in almost every instance, the number
of Friendly Societies in each town or district, and
in many instances gives very elaborate details as
to their rules, membership, etc. Sir F. Eden was
a keen observer of human nature, and no dealer
in panaceas; he saw very clearly the close
connection between the alternatives of Friendly
Society insurance and the less honourable maintenance to be obtained from the rates. This
action in setting the two things in statistical
juxtaposition is the beginning of a long train of
circumstantial evidence, all tending to show that
the relation between the two is very close.
Unfortunately, it is not a subject on which Government has collected any statistics. It is obvious
that if various eligible forms of poor law relief are
curtailed, there must be more inducement to
provide for emergency by means of insurance and
saving. That this is, in fact, the case we hope to
be able to prove by an array of figures and instances
which, if not so full as could be wished, are yet
significant and convincing.

In the preface to his work, Sir F. Eden, speaking
of the characteristics of Friendly Society members,
remarks, "that rejecting, as it were, a provision
gratuitously held out to them by the public, and
which was to cost them nothing—(the poor law)—
they chose to be indebted for relief, if they should

want it, to their own industry and their own frugality. And I would fain hope that I do not deserve to be set down as wanting in respect for parliamentary wisdom, if, in a case like this, I should declare my preference of the wisdom of the people. I cannot recollect any act of the legislature for many years that has either produced such important national advantages, or been so popular, as the institution and extension of Friendly Societies."

Again : " I do not find," he says, "that any parish has been burthened with the maintenance of the member of any Friendly Society, nor are the instances numerous of the families of members being burthensome."

Again : " There are great objections to all compulsory schemes for erecting Friendly Societies ; whatever benefit is intended the poor, obliging them to subscribe is, in effect, taxing them. . . . Why use force, when mutual convenience will probably make that palatable which legislative direction may render nauseous? Few of us will be driven, but most of us may be led."

In another passage he remarks : "Any attempt to combine those voluntary associations with parochial taxes will, I am persuaded, do much harm, and lessen that sense of independence which a member of a benefit club totally unconnected with a poor rate now enjoys."

He estimates that the aggregate Societies in England and Wales amounted to something like 7200, with an average membership of 90, or, in all, 648,000. These clubs spend each about £62 per annum, or, in all, £421,000, and the subscriptions amount to something like £500,000 per annum.

Later on he sums up the situation with his usual impartiality and caution (vol. i. p. 615) : "Whether Friendly Societies will or will not eventually contribute to reduce the poor's rate, the limited extent of my inquiries does not allow me peremptorily to decide. That, however, these institutions increase the comforts of the labouring classes who belong to them will be evident from comparing the condition of those who are members of them, and of those who in the same village are contented to rely on the parish for relief. The former are generally comparatively cleanly, orderly, and sober, and consequently happy and good members of society, whilst the latter are living in filth and wretchedness, and are often, from the pressure of a casual sickness or accident, which incapacitates them from working, tempted to the commission of improper acts (not to say crimes), against which the sure resource of a benefit club would have been the best preservative. . . . Although, however, I cannot speak confidently on the probability of a great reduction of the poor's rate being the consequence of an extension of Friendly Societies *whilst that national tax has no bounds assigned to it but what depend on the caprice, humanity, or discrimination, of overseers and justices of the peace,* I flatter myself the reader will in the course of the following pages meet with some not unimportant information relative to the state and progress of these useful institutions."

The words in italics give the key to the situation, for in the existing state of the law it was useless to think of any extension of business-like Friendly Society insurance.

The close connection between the extension of Friendly Societies and a decrease in pauperism is here fully recognised, and the fact is further recorded in the preamble of the 59 Geo. III. c. 129, which sets out : " Whereas the habitual reliance of poor people upon parochial relief, rather than upon their own industry, tends to the moral deterioration of the people, and to the accumulation of heavy burthens upon parishes ; and it is desirable that encouragement should be afforded to persons desirous of making provision for themselves and their families," etc.

It is, perhaps, worthy of note that in 1802 (according to the " Insurance Cyclopædia," *sub voce* " Friendly Society") there were more Friendly Societies in Scotland, in relation to population, than in England. In 1824 the Highland Society of Scotland published a valuable " Report on Friendly or Benefit Societies, to which are appended tables showing the rates of contribution necessary," etc.

The leading part which Scotland took in this matter of Friendly Societies is capable, perhaps, of explanation. In Scotland, down to the time of Dr. Chalmers, there was no universal compulsory assessment for the poor—and so it happened that a very poor and sparsely populated country took the lead in this matter before its richer and more populous neighbour. The proverbial thriftiness of the Scots is due, in part at all events, to their exemption from this demoralising law, and a common saying in the north, " Thrift went out with the new poor law," bears witness to the far-seeing wisdom of Dr. Chalmers and those of his compatriots who opposed the introduction of the English system into Scotland.

Mr. Sturges Bourne's Select Committee on the Poor Laws, 1817, remark in condemnation of the system then existing in England—

" The system . . . is peculiar to Great Britain; and even in Scotland, where a law similar in principle was about the same period enacted, the intelligent persons to whom the administration of it has been entrusted, appear by a valuable report—for which your Committee are lately indebted to the prompt exertions of the General Assembly of the Church of Scotland—to have had so much foresight and judgment as to its effects, that they have very generally and successfully endeavoured to avoid having recourse to its provisions for a compulsory enactment."

There is a grim pleasantry in a parliamentary committee dwelling with approval on the foresight and judgment of intelligent persons who thus generally and successfully evaded the provisions of an act of the Legislature.

Mr. Sturges Bourne's Committee on the Poor Laws, which sat in 1817, paid considerable attention to the Friendly Society question. The Committee were of opinion, "that it will be expedient to enable parishes to establish Parochial Benefit Societies, under the joint management of the contributors and the nominees of the parish." The insuperable objection to subjecting Friendly Societies to parochial assistance and parochial supervision does not appear to have been urged on the Committee's attention. In the apology for a subsidised Friendly Society which follows this suggestion, the Committee urge that persons joining a society drawing subsidy from public funds, should be subjected to a poor law rather less favourable than that applied to the general community. Similarly Mr. Charles Booth, the most logical, but the most impracticable of State pension projectors, has at the present time suggested that when the universal endowment of old age has been enacted, the system of out-door relief shall be brought to an end. This suggestion to barter one form of legal relief, which has proved mischievous, for another form which in the opinion of its projectors would be attended with beneficial results, is one to be received with grave suspicion by all those who would deal with facts and not with names. The incident is recorded, because it marks a growing appreciation of the rivalry and antagonism which must exist between Friendly Societies and every system of legal relief. The evidence tendered to the Committee on this head is of very considerable interest. Mr. William Hale, treasurer of the parish of Spitalfields, spoke to the great increase of pauperism and to the breakdown of the national independence and character of the people owing to the operation of the poor laws. He qualifies this statement by the remark—

" I speak of that class of the poor who have been in the habit of taking regular parochial relief, for there are many who can still say, ' Thank God, I never have been a pauper;' many of them belong to benefit clubs; it is rarely we have an application from any person who belongs to a benefit club, and very rarely that I observe any individuals apply for relief who have been in the habit of saving any money; if it is only thirty or forty shillings, a man possessed of that will preserve it and aim to increase it; but it is the individuals who have never saved anything, let their earnings be what they will;

they know they can take parochial relief, and with them present enjoyment is better than future comfort."

The Rev. Richard Vivian, Rector of Bushey, tells of a reduction of pauperism in his parish, an event which at this date was extremely rare. He attributes the decrease to better management of the poor law, mainly in the direction of resisting the allowance system, *i.e.* out-door relief to the able-bodied, and secondly to two benefit clubs, which numbered 360 members, men and women, out of a population of 1060.

Mr. George Moncrief, merchant, of Edinburgh, spoke of the large number of Friendly Societies in Edinburgh, and stated that pauperism was practically unknown among members of Friendly Societies. The Committee also took evidence from Mr. Morgan, a distinguished actuary of the day, who had devoted attention to Friendly Society insurance.

After the passing of the Poor Law Amendment Act, 1834, a very rapid increase took place in the deposits at savings banks, and in the membership of Friendly and Provident Societies.

The vast change introduced into the administration of the law is strikingly shown by the following "Summary of what Sussex Pauperism was under the old system, and what it is after a little more than one year's experiment under the new." ("Encyclop. Brit.," 7th edition—Poor Law.)

Population	205,936
Able-bodied paupers at the time of forming the Unions (*i.e.* previous to the passing of the Act of 1834)	6,160
Number of able-bodied paupers, March, 1836 .	554
„ „ „ June „	125
Reduction in rate	45 per cent.

The above may be taken as a specimen of the result of the new law in a southern agricultural county. The change, in fact, involved the abolition and disendowment of the able-bodied pauper.

The able-bodied population, whose subsistence on the rates was withdrawn by the provisions of the new law, not only maintained itself, but proceeded to extend and consolidate the system of saving, self-help, and insurance, which has since grown to such remarkable proportions. That this is so the following facts afford proof.

In the Appendix to the Fourth Annual Report of the Poor Law Commissioners (pp. 220–222), Mr. Tufnell, after citing many indications of improvement in the condition of the labouring class, gives it as his opinion, "that their welfare seems to have been on the whole in a state of steady advancement since the enforcement of the regulations of the new poor law. As one proof of this I beg to refer to the following table, which shows *the deposit during the last seven years in the savings banks in the two counties of Kent and Sussex from Friendly Societies, and from depositors of sums under £20.* I have selected these two classes of depositors, as amongst them, more than in any other class, the labouring population are chiefly to be found " :—

Date.	Kent Savings Banks.	Sussex Savings Banks.	Observations.
	£	£	
Nov. 20, 1831	93,694	41,164	Years previous to the passing of the Poor Law Amendment Act.
,, 1832	87,592	39,889	
,, 1833	91,317	41,686	
,, 1834	94,918	43,466	Poor Law Amendment Act discussed & passed.
,, 1835	97,613	45,897	Poor Law Amendment Act brought into *partial* operation.
,, 1836	106,156	50,148	Poor Law Amendment Act brought into universal operation.
,, 1837	110,156	51,409	

The three years previous to the passing of the Poor Law Amendment Act were by no means unprosperous, yet it will be perceived how slowly deposits increased, and that in 1832 there was a large diminution.

In the same report is to be found the following

table, showing the increase of the various classes of depositors in the Tunbridge Wells savings banks between 1831 and 1837 :—

	1831.	1837.	Increase per cent.
Servants . . .	361	483	34
Agricultural Labourers .	46	137	200
Children . . .	357	388	9
Journeymen and Apprentices	39	57	46
Charitable Societies. .	14	26	86
Benefit Societies . .	4	5	25
Small Shopkeepers . .	8	16	100
Small Farmers and others .	54	68	26
Total . .	883	1180	34°/o

Of the Friendly Societies the same authority remarks that "they are now more generally established on principles calculated to secure a certain provision in sickness and old age, instead of those injurious institutions hitherto so prevalent which seem intended only to minister to the profit of publicans, and which are usually founded on principles that must inevitably cause their dissolution when old age overtakes the members." He goes on to cite, by way of specimen, the numbers that have annually belonged to three Benefit Societies —the first a Friendly Society in Sussex, the second and third Kentish Societies :

Years.	SUSSEX.	KENT.	
	Numbers.	Numbers.	Numbers.
1831 . . .	84	—	461
1832 . . .	64	37	477
1833 . . .	56	363	519
1834 . . .	48	356	533
1835 . . .	49	353	609
1836 . . .	64	420	611
1837 . . .	98	478	770

These figures all point to an acceleration of steady growth after the passing of the new law.

"These contrasts," says Mr. Tufnell, "are, however, far less favourable to the present system than they would appear, had not the failure of the crops and the hardness of the seasons during the last year and a half pressed with peculiar severity on the labouring classes of this district."

As to the effect over the whole country, the following facts are given on the authority of Mr. Tidd Pratt, for many years Chief Registrar of Friendly Societies (*see* Fourth Annual Report of Commissioners, p. 84): "The Benefit Society Act passed in 1829, and the number enrolled from July, 1829, to August, 1830, in the first year was 510, and in the second 560, in the third year 1180. (This last number was abnormal, the witness goes on to explain, owing to a change in the law.) In 1833, 470; in 1834, 350. Since that, under the

Poor Law Amendment Act, the next year was 700, the next 670, the next 739." The witness was further asked :

Q. 1671. Have you any reason to know that the increase in the number of depositors (*see* table below) is at all attributable to the Poor Law Amendment Act?—A. From conversations which I have had with parties who have spoken to me respecting Friendly Societies, I should say decidedly it has.

Q. 1672. Will you state the nature of these communications?—A. The communications have been these : Upon parties forming Benefit Societies they have stated to me that heretofore it was no use belonging to a Benefit Society, because if a man belonged to a Benefit Society, whatever allowance he was entitled to was deducted, the overseer made no allowance, and therefore that it was no use to belong to a Benefit Society, for if he did he would get less than if he belonged to no Benefit Society ; the consequence was that it was better for him to save his money in any way, than contribute to a Benefit Society ; in addition to which it has been stated to me in letters that now is the time that parties must look to themselves, as they *could not receive out-door relief under the new law.*[1]

---

[1] It should be remembered that our present out-door relief system is due to the fact that the Poor Law Board and Local

Q. 1673. From those different communications have you reason to suppose that the Poor Law Amendment Act has led to this great increase of deposits?—A. I have no doubt that it has, particularly with regard to Benefit Societies.

Q. 1674. Do you know whether within the last year the increase of deposits has been in the larger or smaller sums?—A. Decidedly in the smaller.

Q. 1675. May not the reason of that be from the change in the Act of Parliament?—A. No; when I say smaller sums, I mean sums of £5, £10. The Act of Parliament applies to £20.

The following table is drawn from official returns. [Slightly abridged from the return published (p. 87) of the Fourth Annual Report of the Poor Law Commissioners.]

Government Board have never used the discretion vested in them to carry out, to its logical conclusion, the maxim of the Poor Law Commissioners' Repert, *viz.* "That the fundamental principle with respect to legal relief is that the condition of the pauper ought to be, on the whole, less eligible than that of the independent labourer;" and secondly, that all distribution of relief in money or goods to be spent or consumed in the pauper's own house is inconsistent with the principle in question. The Prohibitory Orders of the Board have never prohibited out-relief to the aged. A large number of exceptions to the General Prohibitory Order have been allowed in other cases, with the result that many of the evils of the old poor law are still with us. This view attributed to the "parties" conferring with Mr. Tidd Pratt was strictly logical.

"AN ACCOUNT OF THE NUMBER OF DEPOSITORS AND OF THE SUMS DEPOSITED IN SAVINGS BANKS AT THE CLOSE OF THE LAST QUARTER OF EACH OF THE YEARS FROM 1830-1837, BOTH INCLUSIVE."

Years.	INDIVIDUAL DEPOSITORS.					FRIENDLY SOCIETIES.					
	No. of Depositors.	Increase.	Amount.	Increase.	Decrease.	No. of Depositors.	Increase.	Decrease.	Amount.	Increase.	Decrease.
			£	£	£				£	£	£
Nov. 20, 1830	421,129	—	13,729,089	—	—	4,533	—	—	714,112	—	—
,, 1831	430,166	9,037	13,739,907	10,818	—	4,655	101	—	678,334	—	35,778
,, 1832	433,277	3,111	13,581,760	—	158,147	4,154	—	501	571,428	—	106,906
,, 1833	467,357	34,080	14,486,548	904,788	—	4,319	165	—	603,756	32,328	—
,, 1834	501,199	33,842	15,433,788	947,240	—	4,575	256	—	619,097	15,341	—
,, 1835	537,731	36,532	16,461,846	1,028,058	—	4,975	400	—	666,074	46,977	—
,, 1836	587,488	49,757	17,705,228	1,243,382	—	5,394	419	—	726,142	60,068	—
,, 1837 Including returns to July 18, 1838	624,560	37,072	18,498,044	792,816	—	5,791	397	—	785,109	58,967	—

The above figures show conclusively that, as might have been expected, a restriction of the maintenance provided by the rates at once increased the useful activity of savings banks and Friendly Societies.

It can further be shown that it is only within the last fifty years that the Friendly Society movement has put off its convivial and less serious aspects, and assumed the character of a business-like system of insurance.

The figures as to membership in Friendly Societies in these earlier days are somewhat obscured by the frequent secessions which took place. The Manchester Unity of Oddfellows, now the wealthiest and one of the best managed of the affiliated societies, was definitely constituted as an affiliated order in 1822. In 1834 it numbered about 60,000 members. In 1846 the number had risen to 251,727, notwithstanding the fact that there had been in 1844 a secession of 21,461 members (Baernreither, *English Associations of Working Men*, p. 256). The Foresters were re-organised in 1834 under their present title of Ancient Order of Foresters, and from that period their growth has been continuous. The Hearts of Oak, the largest of the centralised societies, dates from 1842. It is not possible to enumerate all the provident institutions which took their rise on the decade following on the reform of the poor law ;

a long list of the Friendly Societies originating about this time will be found in the article, "Friendly Society," in the "Insurance Cyclopædia."

It may seem invidious to dwell on the fact that the vast improvement in the aims and management of Friendly Societies, which has taken place within the last fifty years, would have been impossible but for the determined courage of the first reformed Parliament, which, despite much sentimental opposition, took the first step in restricting the degrading but yet enticing alternative of the maintenance provided by the old poor law.

It remains for this present generation to complete the work of reform which was commenced in 1834. It is significant; but, if our argument is correct, it is also very intelligible that arrangements for making provision for old age are still very far from complete. On the upper stratum of the working-class the poor law has long ceased to exercise any dangerous fascination, and it is in the great Trade Unions belonging to this section of the labouring class that the largest and most successful effort has been made to provide for old age. Thus the largest item of expenditure in the Amalgamated Engineers is for superannuation pay.[1] But in the

---

[1] See Appendices, Howell, "Conflicts of Capital and Labour." From this it appears that in 1889 this society expended £40,170 on superannuation, out of a total expenditure of £132,560. In 1876 the superannuation expenditure was only £12,538.

classes which are more or less "submerged," to use a phrase which is now classical, it is to be feared that men still look on old age as a time for which the rates, and not they themselves, must provide. Guardians, too, often from ignorance or a mistaken tender-heartedness, lend themselves to this view and give old age pensions out of the rates, thereby setting up a disastrous competition with the more honourable methods now under consideration.

Those reformers who at the present day demand a further restriction of the maintenance provided by the poor law, rely on these figures as evidence of the beneficial result likely to follow administration based on the same principle. They rely, moreover, on the assumption that human nature is not very different now from what it was in 1834, and they proceed to substantiate their position, first by the evidence of experienced witnesses conversant with the present administration of the law and of Friendly Societies; and secondly, by quoting a few concrete instances in which the truth of the foregoing views have been locally demonstrated.

First, to quote the opinion of the experts. Chapter vi. of the Fourth Report of the Friendly Societies' Commission (1874) is entitled, "On the Connection between the Poor Law and

Friendly Societies," and is full of information of the most important character.

The Commission had evidence put before it to show that in some districts "the labourer calls in the parish doctor on the slightest account whatever, and always looks to the poor law for relief in old age ; and, under these circumstances, it was hardly surprising to hear from many experienced witnesses that the poor law acts as a direct discouragement to providence, either preventing labourers from joining clubs at all, lest they should waste money by doing for themselves what they have learnt to expect others to do for them ; or leading them to join such clubs as will not interfere with their receipt of what they have begun to consider as their own property, as a sort of rent-charge on the land for their benefit, and as part of the wages they are entitled to for their labour." One witness tersely expressed the feeling among the poor of the south of England to be, "that the poor law is the best benefit club, because everything is taken out and nothing paid in."[1] To this may be traced the popularity of

[1] Poor law reformers often meet with the argument that the poor ratepayer does put something into the poor law club, and that for this reason he is entitled to draw out for his necessities on his own terms. A moment's reflection will show the fallacy of this argument. The poor law rate is not an insurance premium, but is a compulsory levy for the relief of those who are destitute. It is obvious that if ratepayers pay a *premium*, all are equally entitled to relief, and all poor ratepayers at any rate will apply

the "sharing-out clubs," which may be said to be framed in such a manner as to secure for themselves a release from the burthen of aged and infirm members, whose maintenance is forthwith suffered to fall upon the rates, which become, in fact, the virtual superannuation pay of this kind of Friendly Society.

The allusion of the Commissioner, whose words are here summarised, is to the practice of "sharing-out clubs" to dissolve at the end of each year, and to begin again with the New Year. Owing to this system, old men and men in chronic ill-health are allowed or even forced to drop out of these associations just at the time when there is most need for assistance.

The foregoing statement is, we conceive, of the very greatest importance. The extreme laxity of

---

for it, and the rate must be multiplied to an enormous extent. If men are to pay an adequate premium for the benefit which they expect to receive (the only terms on which the benefit can he honourably accepted), they will obtain their requirements much more cheaply from a Friendly Society or other insurance agency than from the State. Unfortunately, some colour is given to the statement that the poor man puts nothing into the poor rates, by the provisions of the Small Tenements Act and the Poor Rate Assessment Act of 1869, by which owners of houses below a certain value are in certain circumstances rated instead of the occupiers. This custom obtains very largely in London. Of course the occupier does not escape taxation, for the owner takes care to recoup his expenditure in rates by obtaining a higher rent, or by giving a worse house for the same money, while the real incidence of the poor rate, which in the end falls heavily on the poor man's dwelling, is concealed from his view.

guardians in granting out-door relief to the aged explains, to a very considerable extent, the slow progress which has been made in the task of providing for old age. Even in the best clubs, subscription for superannuation in old age is not popular, and it is probably altogether a mistake to suppose that a lifelong subscription for a deferred annuity is ever likely to be a popular or wise form of investment. The man who is saving and frugal is more likely to be actuated by a wish to provide for his wife and family, and for his own sickness and want of work. If he succeeds in putting by something for these objects, the money will come in useful if he survives to old age. It is not possible for men of small means to earmark each portion of their savings exclusively for one particular purpose. Dr. Baernreither (p. 393) discusses the reasons which have prevented the superannuation scheme of the Foresters and Manchester Unity of Oddfellows from becoming a success. Many members have made other arrangements for their old age, some by saving, and some by subscription to the superannuation fund of their Trade Union ; but while, no doubt, the more provident and enterprising of the class have taken these steps, a portion of the lower grades of labour continues to look forward with apathetic indifference to the disablement of old age. We should like here to disavow any intention of imputing this fact as a reproach to the working-class. We are fully aware of the almost heroic self-denial which is required to enable a working man with a family to make provision for his old age. But it is well to remember that exactly the same remark was often made during the early stages of the controversy on poor law reform. Is it reasonable, it was asked on the eve of the great reform of 1834, to tell a poor man to provide for a numerous family and for his period of want of employment? Yet the first reformed Parliament passed the stringent provisions of the new poor law, which prohibit out-door relief to the able-bodied, and no sane person at the present day wishes to lead the country back to the old state of things. The increased stringency of administration is sought, not on account of the saving to the rates, not on behalf of the intelligent artisan population on whose motives and conduct the poor law has no influence, but for the protection of the lower grade of labour against its own weakness. There never was a time when all classes of society were more anxious to remove the reproach of pauperism from our midst. Little progress, however, can be made while a lax administration of the law continues to decoy the less fortunate among the labouring class away from the ladder of self-respect and voluntary effort, by which the more successful of their class have already climbed to a measure of independence and security. No amount of "jerrymandering" can ever make maintenance on the rates an honourable solution. We appeal to members of Friendly Societies to urge the Legislature to withdraw from guardians of the poor their present power of competing with Friendly Societies by the giving of out-door relief, to the detriment not only of the ratepayer, but of the character of the poorest class. There is a natural but as yet unrecognised alliance between those who would restrict the attractions of the poor law and those who have done and are doing so much for the independence of the poor by the work of Friendly Societies and savings banks. It is to be hoped that the identity of their aims will bring about a better understanding between the two.

At Boards of Guardians, where out-door relief is given, a very great difficulty has arisen with regard to allowances to be made to members of Friendly Societies in receipt of sick or old age allowances in cases where such allowances are insufficient for the maintenance of the man and his family. It has been argued that it would be an encouragement to thrift if poor law relief was given as a reward to members of Friendly Societies, and without fully taking into account the allowance given by the club.

There is, however, a poor law minute issued on this subject by the Poor Law Board in 1870, which seems unanswerable. The Board points out "the great difficulty in drawing distinctions between annuities from Benefit Societies and other kinds of property. If, instead of subscribing to a Benefit Society, a man had invested in a savings bank, he would have shown himself equally prudent, and his widow might equally claim to have the property thus bequeathed to her left out of account if she asked for parish relief. Property left to a widow in cottages, or derived from a policy of insurance on the husband's life, might be held to establish a similar claim. The result accordingly would be that a vast number of persons not destitute would be encouraged to become paupers. The principle of leaving property bequeathed to widows out of account in granting relief would establish the principle that the rates were not the very last resource of the poorest class, but a collateral insurance fund, to which not destitution alone, but the receipt of annuities from other sources would establish a claim."

With regard to suggestions[1] made by other witnesses as to the wisdom of Poor Law Guardians discriminating in favour of members of Friendly

---

[1] The most reasonable of these was that of the Rev. C. P. Tidd Pratt, who suggested that when necessary, out-door relief should be given to a member of a Friendly Society, but that only in-door relief should be given to other persons.

K

Societies, the report sums up, "it would be impossible to lay down any rule in the matter which should not conflict with the principle of the poor law, viz. that every person has a legal right to have his necessities relieved without regard to his deserts. . . . It should be remembered that guardians have to deal simply with destitution and not to expend a charitable fund, and the tendency of holding out such favours to members of Friendly Societies is to encourage men to insure for less than their real need with a Friendly Society, and to count on poor law relief to make up the sum required for their support. It cannot but be a mistake to deceive people into supposing that they are not receiving relief when they are in point of fact receiving it, and to hold out as an inducement to them to join clubs, a promise that they may thus become paupers on more favourable terms. . . . We may remark that the best managed Friendly Societies object most strongly to any connection with poor law administration." The truth of this sentence will not be disputed by those who are acquainted with the literature of the Friendly Society movement. If proof were wanting, it is to be found in the strenuous opposition that is being offered by the great Friendly Societies to the modern proposal to put out-door relief on a better footing by re-introducing it under the title of State pensions.

The leaders of these societies are well aware, though politicians ignore the fact, that a man, who by fault or misfortune comes to be dependent for the necessaries of life upon rates or taxes taken from his neighbours, is a pauper. Their aim is to achieve lifelong independence for their class, and they see very clearly that to sit down content either with out-door relief or old age pensions from the rates is by no means the goal which they have in view. To do this, argues one of the Friendly Society journals, " is to admit that the income of the workers of Britain is insufficient, and that it is necessary to pauperise them." The proper remedy, it insists, is to struggle for better wages if that be necessary, and by no means to sit down content in perpetual pauperism under the title of State pensioners. There is no analogy, in the minds of the Friendly Society leaders, between the policy of free education and free or assisted pensions. It may be sound policy in the interest of the future generation to absolve men from the responsibility of educating their children, but it is clearly, in their opinion, contrary to public policy to absolve a large class of the community from the task of supplying themselves with the first necessaries of life during a portion of their lives. What society requires for its reformation is not that each man when he comes to the age of sixty shall find that his fairy godmother, the State, has put a balance at his bankers, but rather that, during his life, he shall have followed the prudent course of so limiting his responsibilities to his income, that at sixty he finds himself in possession, by his own exertion, of adequate provision for his old age. The valuable thing is not £ *s. d.,* but the character and the capacity for further progress which is created by this wholesome discipline. To remove the necessity of providing for old age would be to remove one of the most potent influences of civilisation.

We can see nothing in these proposals for State-aided pensions which differentiates such relief in any way from our present system of out-door relief, and in our opinion it would have exactly the same demoralising effect on the thrifty instincts of the people. In proportion as the conditions attached to it tend to make it in any real sense an education in personal thrift by requiring a serious effort from the insurers, in exactly that proportion does it tend to become inoperative as regards the lowest class whom it is specially designed to affect.

Let us look at one or two of the alternative proposals more closely. Sometimes it is proposed that the whole population on reaching a given age shall be entitled to a pension, and it is argued that as every one will accept the State pension dole, no one need feel pauperised; but the "submerged," for whose benefit all this agitation arises, cannot be taxed ; to them the pension will be more or less pure gain, and it is surely absurd to persuade them that they are not accepting poor law relief, and that they are therefore justified in declining effort and resting content with their position. Or, again, if the rate is based on actuarial calculation, and if no one may participate who has not contributed in full, in what way will this benefit the submerged, who, of course, would not contribute ? Even those persons who, in such a scheme of compulsory thrift, have money taken from them which they would otherwise have wasted, are not really bettered by the transaction. Repugnance is by such methods bred against the whole idea of insurance, and the voluntary exercise of thrifty instincts is neglected, and it is these last alone which have social value.

At other times it is argued that the pensions are only to be given to poor people who require them, and who have lived thrifty and respectable lives. Now, it may be true that any man may go without question into a free library without being pauperised, but if at the age of sixty he has to render account of all his life, and to be cross-examined thereon by some parochial board, it is obvious that he is put in a very humiliating position, and is precisely in the same position as those who, at present, come before Boards of Guardians to claim out-door rather than in-door relief. And will not the parochial board re-introduce into the system of pensions all the abuses of the present out-relief systems? The pension board will do as present Boards of Guardians do, and will give pensions to their own tenants, poor relations, and dependants. Nor will it be possible to avoid a discouragement to efforts made by the poor to provide for themselves. It will be their interest not to do so; and if they do provide for themselves, they will be aggrieved when they see neighbours, who have wasted their means, living on a fund contributed by their industry.

Before concluding this brief review of the opinion of experts, it is desirable to add a few extracts from the Local Government Board reports. The great experience of the officials of the Board, more especially of the poor law inspectors, gives a weight to their opinion which will be universally recognised. In the circular addressed by the Board to the inspectors in 1871 it is remarked:—

"A certainty of obtaining out-door relief in his own home whenever he may ask for it, extinguishes in the mind of the labourer all motive for husbanding his resources, and induces him to rely exclusively upon the rates instead of on his own savings for such relief as he may require. It removes every incentive to self-reliance and prudent forethought on his part, and induces him, moreover, to apply for relief on occasions when the circumstances are not such as to render him absolutely in need of it."

In the same sense Mr. Baldwyn Fleming, in the 21st Local Government Board Report, writes :—

" Upon one of the questions of the hour, namely, thrift by means of Friendly Societies, the unnecessary grant of out-door relief has a distinctly hostile influence. A working man might truly say that he saw little good in joining a Friendly Society, because the amount he received from it would be deducted on estimating any claim for relief from the rates. If he did not belong to a benefit society he would at once get a proportionately larger amount of relief, and, therefore, it is a pure waste of money in him to pay into a club. This may be answered by saying that the guardians need not take club payments into account, but if they did not, they would compel the ratepayers to give the man more than his necessity required, which would be indefensible.[1] Hence the grant of out-door relief militates against Friendly Societies in two ways :—

" (1) It is a positive inducement not to enter, because the provision it affords is better than is given by Friendly Societies, inasmuch as medical attendance and what are

---

[1] The course which Mr. Fleming rightly calls indefensible has, since he wrote, been expressly countenanced by Parliament. All persons interested in the great cause of the independence of the poor must reprobate that ill-considered electioneering measure known as the Out-door Relief (Friendly Societies) Act, 1894.

known as medical extras (stimulants, meat, expensive medicines, etc.) are supplied free of cost.

" (2) The members are actually placed in a worse position than those who are not members, if the necessity for relief should arise. They have spent money upon club payments, and have to keep on so spending money, while they get less relief than men who are not in a club. Thus, out-relief must compete, and compete very mischievously, with provident societies. On the other hand, in-door relief does not, and cannot, compete with them."

Mr. (now Sir H.) Longley, in his exhaustive report on out-door relief, published in the 3rd Local Government Board Report, p. 185, writes as follows :—

"The suggestion that a man in receipt of regular weekly wages may be fairly called upon to secure his widow (if able to work for her living) against dependence on poor law relief, is not so impracticable as it may at first sight appear. . . . The cost of making provision for this special contingency need not, it would seem, press unduly upon the husband, while the general adoption of the more stringent rule of relief to widows would, it is to be hoped, encourage him to make the necessary sacrifice. But even a less substantial provision than this would, I believe, in many instances rescue a widow from pauperism. It is frequently found that a widow, willing and able to work, requires some help to make a start, or to 'take advantage of some' special opportunity of obtaining employment. A lump sum of no large amount, secured to be paid to her at her husband's death, would in these cases be of the utmost service. Assistance of this kind is supplied to widows more frequently than is generally known, by subscriptions raised among the fellow-workmen of the husband, or among the poorer neighbours. Indeed, I have been led, in the course of these inquiries, to believe that what amounts almost to an interchange of charitable assistance among the poor of London is not uncommon, and that they assist each other in distress to an extent which is little understood, and for which they receive but little credit. It is scarcely possible to conceive a form of charity which combines so completely its highest reciprocal benefits, with the absence of the mischief so frequently incident to almsgiving."

The same authority, a few pages earlier in his report, remarks on the same subject—

"Believing as I do that the present system of relief to widows of this class has largely contributed to deter them from making the special exertions to maintain themselves and their families, which their unfortunate condition calls for, I must protest against the doctrine that their position is to be treated by the dispensers of poor law relief as anomalous, even in theory; and this, because the condition of a widow with a large family, however deplorable it undoubtedly is, is one of the ordinary contingencies of human circumstances, which may, in some degree or other, be provided against, equally with sickness, or accident, or other bereavement. The difference between these contingencies seems to be one of degree rather than of kind, and though no doubt the widow's condition is specially hopeless and forlorn, yet, from one point of view, that of the wife of a working man disabled by lingering sickness, and who is prevented by the need of her constant attendance upon him from exerting herself to support their family, is still more helpless than that of a widow."

To this testimony must be added the weighty words of Mr. J. J. Stockall, the Friendly Society representative on the Royal Commission on the Aged Poor. The memorandum which he appends to the majority report of the Commission, is so short, pithy, and characteristic of that honourable love of independence, which inspires the whole body of the Friendly Society membership, that I venture to reproduce it verbatim.

"Having signed the report, with which, on the whole, I cordially agree, I think it well to express my opinion that danger may arise to a portion of the class who now make provision in some measure for old age for themselves in the various friendly and other thrift societies, should they be induced to depend upon relief from the rates, or a pension from the State, as a part of their subsistence in old age, and to look for it as a right, rather than depend upon a provision made entirely by themselves. Such provision, as the evidence brought before us clearly proves, is increasingly being made by the labouring classes. I fear and believe it possible a worse evil may be created than any now supposed to be existing under the administration of the present poor law, if rate or State aid should come to be received with complacency by any material proportion of those who now provide for themselves. In my opinion, the granting of such aid would lead to entire dependence upon the State of a great number of those who now, without the hope of such assistance, are nerved to make provision for themselves, by which process self-respect is gained and character given to the nation.

" I entirely concur in all our recommendations which favour a different treatment to persons of good character, as distinguished from that apportioned to the wastrel and drunkard. While holding that the former class are entitled to such consideration as would make their lives as happy as possible, I am not prepared to endorse the view that these deserving poor should be encouraged to look upon parochial or State provision with satisfaction, or as a desirable source of provision for their old age."

The relation of voluntary charity to provident associations does not strictly fall within the limits of our subject, the briefest reference therefore must suffice. If charity is distributed by great official institutions without due precaution, if it is given indiscriminately and inadequately, it can be just as disastrous in its effects as the poor law. This is not the place to combat the evils of great institutional systems of charitable relief, or to repeat again the danger of indiscriminate and inadequate methods ; it will be sufficient to remind those who administer such funds of their great responsibility in this matter.

Miss Octavia Hill told the Lords' Committee that in London it was well-nigh impossible to make provident dispensaries compete with the gratuitous medical relief given in hospitals, but that in some of the suburbs of London, where hospitals were less plentiful, no such difficulty arose. The hospital system, as at present organised, is largely antagonistic to a due development of the thrifty instincts of the poor, and reform is urgently needed to make these great institutions auxiliaries and not competitors of provident institutions.

To those who distribute charitable relief in money or kind, the necessity of circumspection is urged, lest they discourage thrift by habitually putting the unthrifty in the same position as the thrifty. The argument which condemns any attempt to give easier terms of becoming a pauper to the Friendly Society or provident man, does not apply with the same force to charitable funds. It is rather distinctly the duty of the administrators of these funds to supplement with considerate courtesy and kindness the efforts of those who have tried to help themselves. It is not too much to say that some proportion of the charitable funds which are every year distributed throughout the country is from neglect of due caution directly inimical to the development of methods of self-help. We venture to quote a paragraph from the report of one of the District Committees of the Charity Organisation Society.

" The uniform action of the associated charities of this district as represented by this Committee has, it is to be hoped, done something to influence public opinion among the poor. Great stress, for instance, is always laid on the rule that to qualify themselves for charitable, rather than poor law relief, the applicants should have made some reasonable attempts to provide for their own wants. For many years applicants have been daily asked in this office : Do you belong to a Friendly Society ? Have you ever put by anything for a rainy day ?—and when it is found that relief is readily given to those who can make a satisfactory answer to the questions, and that a majority of those who have neglected these precautions altogether are referred to the less agreeable machinery of the poor law (in this Union only in-door relief is given by the guardians), the Committee hopes that this perpetual iteration of sound advice has produced some effect."

It is urged that the precaution here described is a wise one. One of the objects which all co-operation of poor law and charitable agencies must have in view, is that the whole machinery of relief shall cease to compete with the noble institution of self-help which the working-classes of England have made for themselves, without any assistance from Government or from the rich.

It remains now to bring forward a few specific instances of the disastrous way in which poor law relief laxly administered competes with the honourable but arduous independence attainable by means of subscription to a Friendly Society, or some other method of thrift.

The following story is told by Mr. Vallance, clerk of the Whitechapel Board of Guardians, in a paper read at a poor law conference some years ago :—

"I well recollect, some years since, the case of a man, with a wife and several children dependent upon him, who, on account of his own sickness, was relieved by the guardians in money and kind. By a singular coincidence, his next-door neighbour—a man employed in the same department of the same factory, earning no more than the other was capable of earning, and having the same number of children dependent upon him—was also at home suffering from sickness. This man, however, had been thrifty and industrious, and was, at the time, in receipt from a sick club of about the same amount as his neighbour's pauper relief: and, in his enforced confinement to his home, became an observant student of the operation of the poor law as exemplified next door. He saw the relieving officer periodically visiting his neighbour's house ; he saw the wife as she started upon her weekly errand to the relief office, and he saw her and her children returning home laden with parish bread ; and reflection taught him that he, a provident man, was being taxed for the maintenance, in equal comfort with himself, of his neighbour, an improvident man. Under a sense of injury, this man came to me shortly afterwards and complained, in unmeasured terms, of a system of relief which recognised the claims of bare walls and floors without regard to the habits of life which occasioned them, whilst the cleanliness and comfort of his own cottage, and his efforts to maintain his independence, not only debarred him from participation in 'parish relief,' but imposed upon him a portion of the burden of his neighbour's maintenance."

The next quotation is from Mr. Fawcett's book on " Pauperism," p. 40 :—

" An event which lately happened in a western county will serve as a striking illustration of the extent to which prudential habits are discouraged by the distribution of large parochial funds among those whose improvidence is their sole title for public support. Not many months since a report appeared of a large meeting which had been held of Somersetshire colliers. The meeting appears to have been suggested, and everything connected with it arranged, by the workmen themselves. The object of the gathering was to promote the formation of a Friendly Society. There was at first an unanimous feeling in favour of the proposal ; presently it was mentioned by one of the speakers that those who became members of the Friendly Society would lose all chance of obtaining parochial relief. The whole tone of the meeting changed ; the hint having once been given, it was quickly seen that the amount which they might subscribe to the Friendly Society would simply reduce the rates. A resolution was ultimately passed that the society should not be established as long as a claim to a share of the rates was forfeited by belonging to it. It is difficult to over-estimate the mischief which such an occurrence must produce. Colliers are proverbially an improvident class, and a movement which must have promoted the development of prudential habits amongst them was prematurely nipped in the bud by an extraneous circumstance, which legislation has created and has power to control."

The remarkable dispauperisation of the Union of Bradfield has been quoted (p. 98).

The Chairman of this Union, Mr. Bland-Garland, read a paper at a poor law conference on December 12, 1888, on "State Relief and other Obstacles to Thrift." After commenting on the improved condition of the labouring class in his Union, he says : "To give you direct proofs of increased thrift is a more difficult task. I cannot, of course, have access to the books of the savings banks or those of the great collecting insurance companies, but I have obtained returns of nearly all the Friendly Societies that are established or have branches within the Union, including even the public-house clubs (the members of which have much decreased in number), and also of the medical clubs, and they show that the member-ship of the Friendly Societies has increased 148 per cent. since 1871, and that of the doctors' clubs 152 per cent.; this is satisfactory as far as it goes." It is worth emphasising the fact that these figures come out even though there had been a great reduction in the membership of the old rotten public clubs, which are happily now becoming a thing of the past. The difficulty of giving direct proof is very great, as Mr. Bland-Garland justly remarks, but it is really not a point on which the public is entitled to ask for proof. In the seventeen years under review, 1871–1888, 1116 paupers became merged in the independent population. It is not reasonable to ask that Mr. Bland-Garland should be ready with detailed information as to the sources of income which, under their present happier circumstances, have enabled these persons to remain independent ; he has said enough to show that increased membership in Friendly and Provident Societies has had something to do with it.

Very similar has been the experience in Brixworth in Northamptonshire, where the same sound policy has been followed. On January 1st, 1870, there were in the Union 1101 out-door and 104 in-door paupers, in all 1205, or one in every 11 of the population. The out-door list has gradually been diminished, till on January 1st, 1890, there were 39 out-door and 92 in-door paupers, or one in every 101 of the population.

The Chairman of this Union, the Rev. W. Bury, writes, "The history of Friendly Societies in our Union during the last twenty years might be summed up in few words. The disappearance of utterly rotten ones ; the honest endeavour on the part of a large number of local clubs to strengthen their position, stimulated thereto by the restriction of out-door relief ; their failure to do so ; and the very large and increasing accession of strength

L

to the affiliated orders, such as the Oddfellows. Medical clubs during the same period have completely covered the Union." In his evidence before the Royal Commission on the Aged Poor Mr. Bury gave some interesting particulars as to the popularity of investment in co-operative trading in his neighbourhood, all tending to show increased activity of thrifty instincts ; a result which it is impossible not to connect with the fact that the imagination of the poor is no longer attracted to an expectation of maintenance on the rates.

In an elaborate statistical paper by Dr. J. Milsom Rhodes, read before the Manchester Statistical Society, and now published by Knight & Co., Fleet Street, great pains have been taken to show by a series of maps the relation of poor law relief to the growth of thrift of various forms. Information is defective, as it is difficult to localise accurately the results of different systems; but one or two points are worth mentioning. Staffordshire is a county of importance both as regards population and manufactures, and in this respect it contains some of the essential conditions for an extension of co-operative enterprise. The out-door pauperism in this county is 26·4 per thousand of population as against 5·5 in-door paupers. Is this the reason that Dr. Rhodes is able to comment on the "extraordinary sudden drop in the number of co-operators in Staffordshire as compared with the surrounding counties"? "It is a remarkable fact," says the same authority, "that nearly all the counties on the north of the line that represents the 1*s.* poor rate are believers in co-operation to a much greater extent than those south of it." The parts lying south of this line have the larger amount of out-door pauperism. Again, he asks, "In looking at the map, the question suggests itself—Why is the number of depositors so high in Berkshire and Shropshire? No doubt the existence of manufacturing industries to some extent accounts for it, *aided probably by the restriction of out-door relief to very exceptional cases, thereby encouraging habits of thrift.*"

In Berkshire in-door pauperism is 8·9 as against 19·6 of out-door pauperism per thousand. In Shropshire the figures are 7·0 in-door as against 14·1 out-door. We have already alluded to the probable connection of an increase of thrift with the strict administration of the law pursued in Bradfield, a large Union in the former county. In Bradfield 6·8 per 1000 are in-door paupers, and 2·1 out-door paupers.

We conclude with an apposite quotation from Dr. Rhodes's paper. "Let us endeavour," he says, "to impress by every means in our power upon the new democracy the great facts that the last thing in the world that a working man should desire for himself is the 'Statute of the Forty-Third of Elizabeth.' Let him quit the Forty-Third of Elizabeth altogether, and, as Carlyle said, 'rejoice that the Poor Law Amendment Act has, even by harsh methods and against his own free will, forced him away from it. That was a broken reed to lean on if there ever was one, and did but run into his lamed right hand. Let him cast it far from him, that broken reed, and look to quite the opposite point of the heavens for help. His unlamed right hand, with the cunning industry that he has in it, is not this defined to be the "sceptre of our planet"? He that can work is a born king of something. Let a man honour his craftsman-ship, his *can do*, and know that his rights of man have no concern at all with the Forty-Third of Elizabeth.'"

III.

THE WORKING CLASSES AND THE POOR LAW.[1]

THE subject proposed for our consideration in this article is the INTEREST OF THE WORKING CLASS IN THE POOR LAW, in the administration of the law as it at present is, and in proposed reforms of the law as from time to time they are brought forward.

The working class is now master, and I for one do not believe that they will be less just or less wise than those who in times past have possessed themselves of political power in this country. At the same time I do not believe they will be either more just or more wise. The history of our poor law is a long record of error, and it is impossible to assume that the advent of the working class to power will prevent error in the future. The new poor law of 1834 put us on the way to reform, but we must all confess that our progress has been very partial. The new poor law was

[1] A paper read at the South Eastern Poor Law Conference, November 2, 1891.

one of the first acts of the first reformed Parliament, and at the present moment there is a new democracy engaged in taking possession of the reins of government, and it lies in its power to make or to mar our poor law system for another generation.

It is therefore extremely desirable that those of us who have distinct views on the question should arrange our ideas, both for our own enlightenment and in order that we may discuss intelligently with the working class members of the constituencies what their true interest in this matter is.

Now the workman has an interest in the poor law: (I.) as a payer of rates; (II.) as an earner of wages, profiting by the spending and investing of the savings of his neighbours; and (III.) as a possible recipient of relief.

I. *As a payer of rates.*—Those of us who have been in the habit of speaking and writing in support of a strict administration have generally been somewhat apologetic in referring to the saving in the rates, as though the rates were the interest of the well-to-do only.

It has been proved over and over again that a strict administration will reduce the rate. In Bradfield, as we know, it has in 17 years reduced it from over 2*s.* to less than 6*d.* in the pound. Or take the Union of Stepney—I quote from a

table drawn up by Mr. Jones, late Relieving
Officer in Stepney—and compare the expenditure
in 1869 under the old lax system, and in 1887
under strict administration ; it shows a saving
of £6891 for the half year, or at the rate of nearly
£14,000 per annum. This £14,000 a-year is left
to fructify in the pockets of ratepayers mainly
composed of the working class.

I have been at some pains to find out in one
or two instances the amount of the burden laid
on the poorer class of property in a certain East
End Union. On a house rated at £54 the taxes
are £21 6s., of which £8 2s. is poor rate, *i.e.*
rather more than one-seventh is to be added for
poor rate. A house assessed at £19 pays £7 in
taxes; the taxes are paid by the landlord, who
lets the house for 12s. a-week. A very simple sum
will show that more than 2s. 7d. of this 12s. is to
recoup himself for taxes paid, and, of this 2s. 7d.,
1s. 1d. is for poor rate. A third house, assessed
at £12, should pay £4 10s. taxes, but as it is a
compound house, let under 8s. 6d. per week, the
landlord, on paying the taxes, receives a commission of 14s., and the taxes actually paid are
£3 16s. The house is let at 8s. a-week (and
probably sublet in single rooms), so that about
1s. 6d. a-week out of 8s. is for taxes, and of this
1s. 6d. about 7d. is for poor rate.

I need hardly point out that the fact of the

landlord paying the taxes is no relief to the tenant, for when the landlord fixes the rent he takes the taxes into account, and I have no doubt that fractions of 6*d.* are settled in round figures in his own favour.[1] The system of allowing the landlord to compound for taxes is, I venture to think, a bad one, as it is much better that those who really pay should know exactly how the

---

[1] I have left the text as originally written, for, to the best of my belief, it represents substantially the facts of the case. To my own knowledge, some landlords in the poorer parts of London did raise their rents on the passing of the Free Education Act. The power of the landlord to shift some of the burden of new taxation to the shoulders of the occupier, seems to be a question distinct from the economic problem as to the ultimate incidence of rates. There can, I think, be very little doubt that Mr. Goschen's Select Committee on Local Taxation were entirely right when they reported "that the evidence taken before your committee shows that in many cases the burden of the rates, which are paid by the occupier, falls ultimately, either in part or wholly, upon the owner. . . ." Obviously, a tax put on a certain class of property is a deduction, to that extent, from the profitableness of that property, and ultimately must fall upon the owner. An owner, in such circumstances, will higgle with more determination, and in many cases will succeed in obtaining a better rent. If he fails, he will be less ready to repair his houses, or when he builds a new house, he will build a worse house, or he will build no more houses at all. There is only one market for capital, and if the enterprise of housebuilding is to continue, it must give the normal return to the capital engaged in it. It may effect this, by charging more for the same house, or by limiting supply till increased demand raises the rate of rent; or it may, by restricting repairs or building a cheaper house, obtain the same rent for a worse article; in every case, ultimately the consumer or occupier is injured as well as the owner, and, in all probability, of the two he can the least afford it. It is a neglect of these considerations which is mainly responsible for the unsatisfactory housing of the poorer classes.

matter stands. That the poor feel and resent the burdensome growth of the rates there can be no doubt, but they regard the matter as inevitable.

Some years ago I was sent by Mr. Barnett, of St. Jude's, to canvass some of the poor ratepayers of Whitechapel, to induce them to vote for taxing themselves for a free library. I have often since thought over my reception. The notion of a library was received politely, if not with enthusiasm, and the word "free" was very grateful; but when they understood that it meant even a trifling addition to the rates, I generally found that my embassy was in vain, for all of them asserted that they had other and better uses for their money. I have still a lively recollection how one old fellow drove me from his presence with many opprobrious words. This was many years ago, and the Act has since been adopted in Whitechapel, but I very much doubt if a majority of the poorer ratepayers were wittingly parties to the arrangement.

To speak seriously, the struggle to make ends meet is very desperate—a few pence a-week represent a man's subscription to his club and to his saving account. Yet, if we take the case of the man paying 8s. a-week rent, he is paying 7d. a-week for the support of those who have neglected to belong to a club or to save.

The poor are not indifferent to a reduction of the rates, but they argue: Do not let us be too hard on the poor creatures who have to come on the rates ; let us pay our money cheerfully and be done with it. If, however, we can show them, as I believe we can, that a lax administration is the very reverse of kindness to those who are ready to fall, I am sure that the argument from the rates will be and ought to be a very useful auxiliary in this important controversy.

It will be argued perhaps: Well, if the rate presses so heavily on the poor, let us have a graduated rate of Income Tax, and let us absolve the poor altogether from the payment of poor rate. This is not the place to discuss the general principles of taxation ; but, even if we admit that the principle of a graduated rate of taxation is admissible for the purpose of meeting some portion of our national expenditure, it is, I venture to say, utterly inapplicable for the purpose of poor law rating. If the poor are absolved from contributing according to their ability, they will cease to have any claim to administer, for it is inconceivable that in any civilised community a class shall administer, and administer with a preponderating influence, a fund from which they alone derive benefit, but which is drawn entirely from the pockets of another class of ratepayers.

II. *As to the interest of the workman as a wage*

earner.—Is it to his interest that heavy rates should be extracted from the ratepayers' pockets to be spent in the relief of the poor? Let us follow from an economical point of view the raising and spending of the rate.

It is taken from an unwilling ratepayer, who no doubt thinks he could find better use for it. There are the tax-collector, the assessment officers, the vestry, poor law, and audit officials, to say nothing of local government inspectors galore. They are all necessary and highly useful persons, but it is obvious that to filter a fund through their hands is an expensive way of dissipating the money of the community.

Finally, the relief, such as it is, reaches the pauper—and who is the pauper? Is he not in many cases the man who has gone through life with his mind's eye fixed on this poor law dole? He has through life qualified himself and his family to receive it; and how has he qualified himself? He has belonged to no Friendly Society, for he says, "The poor law is the best club—I put nothing into that." He puts no money in the savings bank for the same reason. It will not do to argue: Paying rates is paying a premium of insurance, and those who pay rates are entitled when their time comes to get relief on their own terms. The poor rate is a compulsory levy for the destitute, and is not an insurance premium.

If the payment of rates was designed to entitle us to the honourable benefit of an insurance policy, on each occasion when we wished to have an addition to our income the poor rate would have to be multiplied a thousand-fold. Further, the pauper and his thriftless ways are a cause of low wages, for he is always in more needy circumstances than his fellows, as it is part of his habit to keep himself qualified for relief by being destitute, and he is, therefore, the less able to stand out for a good wage. He brings up his children in the same spirit; he never seeks, by an insurance or otherwise, to make provision for his wife or for his children, for he sees that the law will provide; and in their turn, when he is old, the children whom he has neglected will neglect him, and leave him to be a permanent burden on the rates.

In a word, this fund, which we are at so great pains to collect, to administer and to audit, is a standing endowment for the encouragement of those who have a disposition to loaf through life. For I believe it is too often this fatal facility of obtaining relief that has hung like a nightmare over the man's better nature, and has prevented him from stirring himself and becoming a useful member of society.

Compare with this picture the fund which may be saved by a strict administration. In round

figures it is in Bradfield a reduction from 2*s.* to
6*d.* in the pound ; in London it is counted in
thousands of pounds. The money is either spent
or is invested. Now I defy any one to spend or
to invest money without giving employment to
labour. Even if we buy the stock of an established
railway, we set free the funds of the seller, who
perhaps is going to build a house or to embark
his money in some new and more adventurous
industry. ⬩ Nothing can deprive the working class
of its share of this saving, and it will come to
them with less deduction for the cost of management, and it will come to them in the honourable
form of wages for work done.

I do not of course argue that the unfortunate,
or even the vicious, pauper should not be maintained when he actually becomes destitute, but I
insist that in the interest of the wage earner it
is necessary to administer the law so as to deter
people, except in the last resort, from throwing
themselves on the poor rate.

Economy in the administration of the poor law
does not filch away from the poor a fund which
in any sense is a benefit to them, but, on the
contrary, it is the saving of a fund which must
be devoted to the encouragement of industry and
to the payment of honestly earned wages.

Before leaving this second branch of my subject,
I will touch on a fallacy which has an attraction

for many minds, more especially, I think, among the working class. It is that poor law relief could be made less degrading to the poor and less burdensome to the ratepayers, if fair wages were given to the labourer by the poor law authorities in return for remunerative labour. Sir G. Nicholls, the historian of the poor law, speaking of a proposal of this kind made by Sir M. Hale in the time of Charles II., remarks: "The assumption that this is possible is opposed to sound principle and at variance with all subsequent experience." Let me illustrate this by an example.

A while ago, when times were bad, we heard of agricultural land going out of cultivation because it could not be got to pay. This state of things inspired a good many dwellers in towns, most of them living within the sound of Bow Bells, with the notion that here was a fine opening for pauper labour. Some of you gentlemen live in the country and know what farming is, and I appeal to you if it is not an absurd and ridiculous reflection on your skill and your enterprise to suggest that London pauper labour, marshalled by the worthy tradesmen who act as London guardians, is likely to succeed where you have failed. I think you will agree with an agricultural friend of mine, who was asked what labourers in his part of the country would do if they were set down to get their living out of land which farmers had abandoned. " I do not know," he said, "but if they were wise they would run away."

From this example you can see why all attempts to make relief work remunerative to the community must fail. *Ex hypothesi*, relief work must be work which it will not pay experts to do in hope of profit ; it follows surely that it cannot be done by amateurs paying the market rate of wages, except at a loss so heavy and continuous that bankruptcy must arrive if such method of relief is made a normal part of our system. If, on the other hand, less than the market wage is paid, a good day's work for a good day's pay is not given, and cannot fairly be demanded ; and such a system, if adopted on any large scale, means the degradation of labour just as much as the present pauper allowance.

III. It remains for me now to discuss *the interest which the workman has in the poor law as a possible recipient of relief.*

I began my paper by suggesting that there is an analogy between the present time and the present temper of the public, and the time previous to the passing of the Poor Law Amendment Act.

I believe that there are exactly the same parties using exactly the same class of arguments, and it is for the general public, more particularly the working class (for with them the responsibility now rests), to say to which side they will cleave. This same principle of division will be apparent in every other crisis in our poor law history. Let me illustrate what I mean by two examples.

The two most beneficial reforms in our poor law system within the last century have been : (1) "the Act to prevent the removal of poor persons until they have become actually chargeable" (35 George III. cap. 101, passed in 1795) ; and (2) the Poor Law Amendment Act. It is almost incredible to us that the abominable tyranny of the old law of settlement should have had its supporters. That law, as you are aware, bound the labourer to the place of his birth. He was not allowed to leave his native place to search for work, as the authorities of the place to which he came could remove him, *not because he had become chargeable*, but lest in the future he might become chargeable.

Adam Smith remarked, " There is scarce a poor man in England who has not in some part of his life felt himself cruelly oppressed by this ill-contrived law of settlements." Yet the system had its supporters, and we should be wrong in thinking that they were more cruel and indifferent to the sufferings of the poor than the present generation. Each man has, they argued, his right of maintenance and asylum at the place of his birth. This is his birthright ; let him resist all temptation

to give it up. There he is a part of the constitutional economy of England. Let him rely on
this, and not on his own ability to go out and
do battle with the difficulties of life. He is far
too poor and too ignorant for independence. It
is far best for him, and we shall compel him to
preserve the certainty of maintenance in the place
of his settlement.

Again, my second example refers to the time
of the reform of the poor law forty years later,
when many estimable people, headed by the
Times, declared that it was the height of cruelty
to throw the able-bodied labourer on his own
resources, and to hold him responsible for his
wife and children. Under the old law relief was
regularly paid in aid of wages, and generally the
allowance was regulated according to the number
of his children. This last practice had been sanctioned by the applause of the great commoner,
Mr. Pitt. The poor law commissioners, whose
duty it was later on to expose and cause this
state of things to cease, were for a time the best
abused people in England. Sir G. Nicholls has
recorded somewhere in his book a list of all the
nasty adjectives which were applied to him and to
his colleagues.

Now I ask with confidence, Is any one prepared
to go back on the policy of these two reforms, a
policy which I would describe shortly as being

M

a vindication of the right of the working class to achieve its own independence. I do not for one moment believe it. The workman has set his back with determination to the miserable flesh-pots of settlement and poor law relief, and has passed on from one point of progress to another. He has competed with his employer and exacted a better wage ; he has organised his trade union, his friendly society, his co-operative store, his building society ; he supports savings banks and insurance offices ; and these things are all of them the work of the last fifty years, and have been rendered possible by the restriction of poor law relief, which has ever been a most fatal competitor with thrifty effort and self-help.

The workman has still, it is true, much to seek, and, as in the two former crises which I have mentioned, he has well-meaning but timorous, and I venture to add most dangerous, counsellors, who urge him to take what he yet requires from the rates. There are many such proposals in the air, and they are termed by their inventors, " Projects for Poor Law Reform." In the past the gift from the rates has been accursed ; its rejection has developed enterprise and self-help, the foundation not only of temporary and present success, but of continuous future progress. Is the operation of cause and effect different to-day ?

I will advert to two of these proposals, and I

will quote some genuine working-class criticism on each, with a view of showing how very hopeful we should be that wise counsels will prevail.

One enthusiastic reformer urges that we should have what he calls "Collective Provision for the Sick"; that is, that all sick persons should be tended in hospital at the public charge.

Hear, however, as a comment on this, the words of a writer in the *Co-operative News*, the organ of the workman's co-operative movement, and written for workmen by workmen. He is speaking of Dr. Rhodes's contention that medical relief is too often the germ of pauperism. He says: "Thus easily relieved, thoughtless people come to regard medical relief not as pauperism but as a right. . . . The connection with the relieving officer is established, and the facility of lifting a burden on to other shoulders once enjoyed is nearly certain to lead to further applications for aid, when work is scarce or money runs short. . . . We shall not occupy space in drawing obvious inferences, but satisfy ourselves by passing on a warning note which may cause co-operators to think out for themselves plans whereby, through the stores, they can encourage or supplement the work of friendly societies, the provident clubs and dispensaries, and the similar agencies, which both foster thrift and keep many off the slippery paths to pauperism." This, I venture to say, is the true note of the independent English working man. The proposal for placing all hospitals and medical treatment on the rates comes, not from a working man, but from a middle-class gentleman who, to do him justice, does not propose it in his own interest, but rather as a short cut by which his poorer neighbours, for whom he has a profound sympathy, may get all that they want.

Lastly, I would say a word or two on the subject of the proposed State Pensions. The workman has provided, and is providing, for his sickness, for his children, and for many other occasions for which poor law relief was formerly thought necessary; but it is alleged that he has not provided for his old age—therefore, says the tempter, let us put pensions, or a portion of the cost of pensions, on the rates.

Friendly Society papers and Friendly Society speakers have, as far as I know, rejected the proposal unanimously. Here is a passage from the *Oddfellows' Magazine*, commenting on the suggestion (and a very insidious suggestion it is) that the Friendly Societies should be used as intermediaries for receiving the Government grant in aid of pensions—

"No thought of Government or rate-provided subsidy must enter into the calculations of those who would lead the Order along the path which ends in superannuation. No sane person could imagine that assistance or subvention would be given unless accompanied by inspection and a proportionate measure of control. This would prove a deathblow to the principles on which the Unity has reared itself to its present proud position, viz. self-help and independence. When interference enters the door, independence will fly out of the window, and the decadence of the Manchester Unity will have commenced."

I next quote a sentence from the admirable presidential address of the High Chief Ranger of the Ancient Order of Foresters, delivered in August of this year (1891). A considerable portion of his speech is devoted to a criticism of this proposal for free or assisted pensions. I quote only one sentence. It goes to the root of the matter.

" If it be proposed to create a system of State subsidy open to all, then the plan is one for the replacement of individual effort by State aid, without any need for it in the great majority of cases. If, on the other hand, unsolicited assistance is to be given to certain classes of the community, a distinction will be made invidious to those included, and unjust to many of those excluded, which may go far to supersede the teachings of our societies as to the independence and equality of men. In any case it seems a peculiar method of promoting the depauperisation of the people to keep a certain—or rather uncertain—number of them off the rates for a few years by making a far larger proportion dependent on subsidies from the taxes for nearly the whole of their lives, and during the prime and vigour of manhood."

I commend to your notice the whole of Mr.

Radley's admirable speech ; it is reported in *Unity* of September, 1891.[1]

I see that Mr. Rankin, M.P.,[2] Chairman of the National Providence League, and a great promoter of national pension schemes, has admitted that if the proposal meets with the opposition of the friendly society world, it will be impossible to carry any legislation of this nature. Unless a complete change comes over the attitude of these societies, there can be no doubt that all such proposals will be vehemently opposed, and there perhaps we might leave this very impracticable suggestion.

But I think it is extremely important that those who are interested in the cause of poor law reform should take this opportunity of assuring the Friendly Societies of their sympathy and support in opposing this measure. And for this reason I cannot regret the controversy. Those who, in season and out of season, have urged the working class to cut themselves adrift from the assistance of the rates and from the poor law, have met with a good deal of abuse, and their motives have been misrepresented. There is a chance, I hope, that some of these misunderstandings may be explained away ; for there is a natural alliance between those who

[1] Price 1*d*. Office: 231, Pentonville Road.

[2] Speaking at Birmingham on November 18, 1891, Mr. Chamberlain made a similar admission.

seek to shut more and more closely the door which admits the poor to the degradation of pauperism, and those who are developing with such admirable success aids to thrift and independence. It is not too much to say that the dispauperisation of the country can be achieved only by an alliance of this kind, and I think it well that we should pay attention to this proposal, and seek to establish a closer understanding among those who in all classes hold a brief *for the independence of the poor.*

We can, moreover, I think, make some contribution to securing the rejection of this proposal by arguments drawn from the experience of wise poor law administration.

Advocates of State Pensions have appealed to poor law statistics and refer to Mr. Burt's Return, according to which there were on August 1, 1890, 245,687 paupers over sixty-five years of age. Now of these 190,935 were out-door paupers and only 54,752 in-door.

This simple analysis shows to persons who know anything of poor law work how worthless are arguments drawn from such figures, for obviously they merely indicate certain eccentricities of administration. Let me give a brief illustration of my meaning.

There were in 1871, in the Union of Bradfield, 1256 paupers — in the year 1888 there were only 142.

If a statistician had come to Bradfield in 1871 he might have argued that, as one in every thirteen of the population was a pauper, therefore exceptional legislation was necessary. Take him to Bradfield in 1888, and he finds that there is only one pauper to every 126 of the population, and that pauperism has steadily decreased, and is still decreasing, under a certain policy of administration, and he will admit that here, at all events, the curse of pauperism is being rooted out. And how has this come about? The story is familiar: it has been accomplished by a wise, firm, and humane administration.

Apply the same firm measure to this mass of pauperism which is presented to us by Mr. Burt's Return, and it will vanish as it is vanishing at Bradfield. The measure pursued at Bradfield has been the restriction, I suppose I might almost say the abolition, of out-door relief, with the happy result that while the out-door pauper has almost disappeared, the in-door pauperism has also diminished by more than a half.

I think that we shall be justified in drawing a very different inference from Mr. Burt's Return from that drawn by our State-pension friends, viz. that if the working class, to whom the responsibility has now passed, will but courageously withdraw the dole of out-door relief, our labouring population will be borne certainly and inevitably into a still larger measure of inde-pendence.[1]

But, it will be asked, where are the old age annuities which we might expect to find among the dispauperised inhabitants of Bradfield? For it does not, for some reason, satisfy our State-pension friends to see the labourer rescued from pauperism—they will not rest content unless they see him in the enjoyment of an annuity.

It is not possible to set out in statistical detail all the little economies of each individual in a rural union who does not become a pauper. This does not prove that these economies do not exist.

Mr. Garland, the Chairman of the Bradfield Board, has told us that in his Union the member-ship of local provident and medical clubs has increased 150 per cent. Obviously the books of savings banks and insurance agencies are not open to public inspection, but undoubtedly the poor of Bradfield have their share in the general increase of savings among the working class, of which I add a few items. Co-operative capital has increased from £4,000,000 in 1874 to £10,000,000 in 1888; the cash sales, on which a dividend of 1s. to 3s. in the pound is returned, have risen from £14,000,000 to £28,000,000.

[1] For more detailed comment on Mr. Burt's Return, see Mr. C. S. Loch's "Old Age Pensions and Pauperism." Sonnenschein & Co., 1892.

Building societies had capital of £12,000,000 in 1875 and £51,000,000 in 1888. Savings banks, Post-Office alone, have increased from £23,000,000 in 1875 to £58,000,000 in 1889. Fourteen insurance companies doing business with the poor had in 1879 £726,000 insurance funds, and in 1887 the amount had risen to £5,000,000; the total sum insured was the enormous one of £83,000,000, of which £71,000,000 was on adult life. This is what is called industrial insurance. As to the value of this, opinions may differ, but it discloses, at all events, a great potentiality for saving. Of the ordinary insurance effected by the working class, it is more difficult to speak in figures. One company alone is insuring £5,500,000 every year, principally among the working class, and the total insurances in force in this company cannot be less than £30,000,000. The Friendly Societies insure mainly against the risk of sickness, but superannuation allowance is in many societies payable to those who suffer from the infirmity of old age. By the trade unions very large sums are paid as superannuation to those incapacitated by old age. The curious will find some interesting account of this in the appendices to the new edition of Mr. Howell's " Conflicts of Capital and Labour " (Macmillan, 1890).

I might say a good deal of the costliness and general impracticability of the proposal and of its commonly admitted futility, unless it is accompanied by compulsion; but time is pressing, and I will confine myself to asking you a question, which I think will enable us to answer these eager searchers for annuitants.

Do any of my readers know among their own circle a single person who is providing for his old age by beginning at the age of twenty-five to purchase an annuity? I expect I could number our united experience of such persons—I had almost said of such foolish and eccentric persons—on the fingers of one hand.

Then why on earth should we try to tempt or to compel the working class to do a thing which is evidently so unusual among the general community?

The fact is that old age is not a risk which a prudent man, as a rule, will seek to cover by insurance. Insurance is obviously designed to cover an uncertain risk. Old age is certain, and it is also remote.

A prudent man insures against the risks which may come suddenly and early, like death, sickness, want of work; when he has done this, and while he is doing it, he collects a home about him, he starts his children in life, he increases his deposit at the bank. When old age comes he has children bound to him by gratitude for early care; he has his little capital at the bank, in furniture, and perhaps a little business ; his life is probably insured, and he is not the less an honoured guest in his children's home because he has some small savings to bequeath. This sort of thing is going on in many a working-class family, and I venture to think it would be the height of presumption for the rough hand of the law to interfere to coerce or cajole the workman into preferring the remote risk of his own old age, which he may never live to see, to the more obvious claims of sickness, wife and children, more especially as a patient frugal attention to these will not leave his old age unprovided for.

IV.

OLD AGE PENSIONS AND THE STATE.[1]

OUGHT old age to be a public or a private charge? That is the issue which the country is being asked to try.

The principle at stake is one of far-reaching importance. If it is desirable to relieve the inhabitants of this country of responsibility for providing the necessaries of life in their old age, it is obvious that the same principle may be extended to other risks of life. A certain section of the advocates of a State pension admit this, indeed base their advocacy on this very ground. They conscientiously believe in the possibility of Socialism. They desire to see the functions of the State gradually enlarged till at length they absorb all the activities of our social life. They look forward to what they term a complete "Socialisation" of all the instruments of production, and to a time when the whole population shall be first

[1] A paper read before the Society of Arts, February 22, 1893.

the salaried and then the pensioned servants of a vast bureaucracy. To make the State responsible for the maintenance of old age is to them, therefore, only one step in a much larger revolution. It is not my intention to dwell on this aspect of the question, though it seems to me to be the only logical position which can be taken up by those who desire to make a public provision for old age, otherwise than is already provided by our poor law. I content myself by remarking that, for the present, the difficulty of this view appears to me to be considerable, for though, up to a certain point, a well-organised government might discharge the responsibilities of mankind, as these are at present estimated, no government can remove from individual men their power of creating responsibility. By responsibility I mean, of course, such things as marriage, and the consequent demands of wife and family, the hunger arising from the consumption on Monday of the supplies which, by careful husbandry, should have lasted till Saturday. The creation of such responsibility is at present held in check by the knowledge that he who creates must also discharge. If this condition be removed, first in one, and then in another direction, it will appear to plain men that we are within sight of a speedy dissolution of society.

But I am well aware that there are many

advocates of State pensions who do not take this extreme view, who think it possible to limit the extension of the principle to old age, and that, thus limited, the removal of the responsibility from the individual to the State will be a salutary change. The view of these, the more influential, but, as I venture to think, less logical, supporters of the State Pension policy, can be gathered most conveniently by a brief history of this agitation.

It began with Mr. Blackley. He observed that a great many people in their old age became destitute, and a charge on the rates. He was of opinion that many, or all of them, ought to have been able to provide for themselves. He, at first, at all events, insisted that old age was a private charge, and of so paramount a nature did he consider it, that the law, he argued, should be called into operation to force men to discharge their duty in this respect. His proposal, therefore, was that before reaching a certain age every one should be compelled to deposit with a public department a sum of money, sufficient to provide him with a pension in old age. A Parliamentary Committee considered this, and a kindred proposal for compulsory sick insurance, and reported that they were not practicable. Their author has so far accepted this verdict that, for the time being, he has joined himself to the supporters of a different proposal, generally known as Mr. Chamberlain's proposal.

This scheme abandons at once the view of Mr. Blackley, that the maintenance of old age is a strictly private charge. It is proposed by an informal Parliamentary Committee, over which Mr. Chamberlain presided, to pay a subsidy out of the rates and taxes of the country, to assist people to buy deferred annuities. As I understand it, Mr. Chamberlain sees no objection, in principle, to making his insurance scheme compulsory ; but, practically, all parties seem for the present agreed that compulsion is not possible. The argument, I take it, is as follows : It is not possible, as Canon Blackley has proposed, to compel a man "to be kind to his old age"; but if a public insurance department holds out an offer of paying, say 40*s*. for each £1 subscribed, the unwillingness and inability of the submerged classes to join in this form of investment will be removed.

At this point the question is taken up by Mr. Charles Booth and his supporters. They point out that, unless the provision for old age is in some way made universal, it will leave untouched the very class in whose interest this agitation has been raised. If the so-called submerged class will not subscribe to a sick club, by which they become entitled to an immediate benefit in event of sickness, it is not likely they will be induced to subscribe for a benefit which will not become due for forty years, which many of them may never live to enjoy. Mr. Chamberlain's new insurance policies might be taken up by well-to-do members of the middle class, but, in all probability, not at all by the lowest stratum of society.

Mr. Booth, therefore, carries the evolution of the pension theory a step further, and proposes a universal endowment of old age, to the extent of 5s. per week. It is impossible, he urges, in effect, to enforce subscription to an insurance fund ; it is useless to subsidise ; the only way in which our benevolent intentions can be carried out is by endowing every man, when he reaches sixty-five, with a statutory right to an allowance of 5s. per week. To extend this advantage to England and Wales, without any cost of administration, will add, Mr. Booth calculates, a sum of £17,000,000 per annum to our national expenditure. The cost of this proposal, which for the United Kingdom would probably not be less than £30,000,000 per annum, has frightened some of Mr. Booth's most competent allies.

Mr. T. E. Young and Mr. R. P. Hardy are well-known actuaries. They regard Mr. Chamberlain's scheme as unworkable on an actuarial basis, and they approve of the philanthropic principle which, they conceive, underlies Mr. Booth's universal

N

endowment, but they recoil from the expense which it involves. They add, therefore, a condition of their own to this effect: none are to have the benefit of Mr. Booth's endowment unless they are persons of good character, and actually in want. Mr. Booth has also made a concession in this direction. One of the last additions to his plan is a proposal to exclude from pension those who have been in receipt of poor law relief within ten years of reaching the age of sixty-five. Mr. Booth insists throughout that the question of inclusion or exclusion must not be left to the haphazard discrimination of a board. At first, he was in favour of universal inclusion—no one was to be excluded—and now the only exclusion he will sanction is an exclusion that shall be determined automatically, and not by the fiat of any board or committee. This condition has separated Mr. Booth from another of his supporters—Mr. Frome Wilkinson. An article by this gentleman, in the *New Review* for January, 1893, brings us back to the *status quo ante* by proposing that guardians shall give every old person an allowance of 4*s.* or 5*s.* a week out-relief. This last proposal is not a proposal for pensions, but for a wider extension of the facilities for entering the ranks of pauperism throughout the country.

The circle is thus complete. We start from the poor law and we return to the poor law.

I have dwelt on this boxing of the compass of opinion because it seems to me to show that the State-pension party has not quite made up its mind as to the grounds on which it asks us to make a very considerable change in our social arrangements. In truth there are several State-pension parties, and their opinions are mutually destructive the one of the other. In polite controversy one must always assume that opponents have carefully thought out the bearings of their position. I gladly extended this courtesy of debate to our State-pension friends, for I think it entitles me to remark that if these distinguished gentlemen were to be locked up like a jury they would starve rather than agree upon a verdict.

We must examine these proposals in some detail. Mr. Blackley's scheme need not detain us long ; it is left derelict by its author, and I fear no one else is likely to adopt this orphan. If any one doubts the wisdom of this abandonment, I would ask him to attend a meeting of unemployed on Tower Hill, and then to explain to us how he proposes to get a deposit of £10, or whatever the sum may be, from the many young fellows who are there agitating their grievances, or from the young men of the class there represented.

Though I do not believe that Mr. Blackley's scheme is either desirable or practicable, as an amateur in social panaceas, I very much regret that Mr. Blackley has abandoned his very original contention that every man should provide for his own old age. It gave his scheme an air of Athanasian boldness and a value altogether unique in the history of latter day " movements."

While on this question of compulsion, I may be permitted to point out, that though it may not be possible to compel men by law to discharge the duty of providing for old age, there yet remains, though we have nearly legislated it out of existence, a certain amount of natural compulsion urging a man in that direction. There is an old maxim of the poor law, that it is undesirable to make the condition of the pauper superior to that of the independent labourer. The maxim has been largely disregarded, as far as old age is concerned, by those who are responsible for poor law administration. Everywhere, with only a few exceptions, the aged and improvident person has been given relief at his own home, and thus put in a superior position to the independent aged person, who has been obliged to practise much self-denial in order to preserve his independence. When this is the condition of the law, it is not to be wondered, if a large number of the poorer classes regard their old age as a thing to be provided for by the law. Over a considerable part of England that is the view taken, not only by the poor, who cannot be blamed for their attitude, but by the administrators of the law.

Guardians sometimes talk as if they were proud of the number of poor people who have been induced to rely on this provision for their old age. I am afraid, however, that in the rural districts a more selfish motive is often at the bottom of their action. The knowledge that a lavish system of out-relief reduces the farmer's labour bill has had its influence in this matter. If the employer can get old men and widows, partially supported by the rates, to do even a portion of his work for him, he has less work to give to the able-bodied.

This aspect of the question is important, for, if we sympathise, as I have no doubt many of us do, with Mr. Blackley, in his desire to see every man meeting his own responsibilities, we cannot, I think, avoid the conclusion that the independence of the poor in old age is to be achieved, not by the artificial compulsion which Mr. Blackley himself admits to be impracticable, but by that natural compulsion which urges all men to habits of self-preservation. If such be our view, it is obvious how closely this problem is interwoven with the administration of the poor law. If we must rely on compulsion, the only practicable form of compulsion is a natural compulsion. This natural instinct of self-preservation exists in every man's breast, ready to urge him along the path of social and economic virtue, if we do not defeat its power by a lavish and ill-considered administration of the poor law.

To pass to the next phase of the question, viz. to the proposal for assisted insurance against old age. Now the difficulties of the poor are very numerous ; old age is not the only risk which they have to meet ; and I have never been able to understand why these philanthropic gentlemen have fixed on this one particular risk, old age after sixty-five, as the one which they are going to subsidise. Is it quite certain that old age is the most pitiable and helpless condition of mankind ? In such a matter as this, the practice of boards of guardians is a very fair test of the average opinion of the world. Now, there are some boards of guardians which give out-relief to widows with children, but refuse it to the aged, on the ground that the destitute condition of a widow is more helpless and involuntary than that of persons who presumably have had forty years of working life, and, therefore, some opportunity to prepare for the inevitable approach of old age.

Again, one asks, why fix on sixty-five as the age at which a man is entitled to become partially dependent on the rates and taxes ? There are no official statistics available to show what proportion of old-age paupers over sixty-five have been paupers from an earlier period of life; but it would appear, from a calculation made by Mr. Loch, on figures supplied by the relieving-officer of Stepney to Mr. C. Booth, that, of the paupers over sixty-five in the Union of Stepney, nearly one-half—forty-four per cent., in fact—became chargeable before they reached the age of sixty-five.[1] It is obvious, therefore, that the proposed subsidy, even if accepted largely by the poor, would not abolish old age pauperism. Moreover, it is not possible for one moment to contend that it would be accepted largely by the present pauper class. It is probable that the annuities —if, by reason of gratuitous subsidies, they were made what is called in the city "good things"— would be taken up by the prudent, investing middle class, as, indeed, has been the case in France and other foreign countries, where subsidised deferred annuities exist. As far as the submerged are concerned, the result would inevitably be disappointment; indeed, the whole proposal shows, I venture to think, some ignorance or disregard of the condition of the class which these insurance proposals are intended to benefit.

The pauper class in this country is very much what the poor law has made it. I am not going

[1] Loch: "Poor Law Conference Papers," No. 3, for 1892.

to say that they are a vicious class, or that they are less "deserving," to use a question-begging phrase, than their more fortunate neighbours. For my own part, I believe, that all men are equally undeserving, but I do affirm, and that without any fear of contradiction, that the pauper class is an irresponsible class. To this point, however, I propose to return. I only here wish to say that every one who has any practical knowledge of the subject will agree with Mr. Booth, and the other critics of Mr. Chamberlain's scheme, that no amount of gratuity short of a free gift will have any influence whatsoever on this class, in the way of inducing them to subscribe for deferred annuities. Old age is not the risk which the responsible poor find it most difficult to meet, and the proposed insurance will have absolutely no effect on the irresponsible.

The next point with regard to this scheme to which I wish to draw your attention is the nature of the investment which it seeks to popularise. It is a proposal to subsidise, not all forms of saving, but only the purchase of a deferred annuity. Now if the choice of old age as the risk of life to be made a charge on the rates seemed to us an arbitrary choice, what shall we say of the selection of this one particular instrument of meeting it?

It is extremely probable that there is not a single person in this room who began at the age of twenty-five to purchase an annuity to become payable at the age of sixty-five. The Post-Office has most elaborate arrangements for facilitating the purchase of deferred annuities. They have been a complete failure. From April 17, 1865, to December 31, 1889, 540 contracts were opened for deferred annuities, money not returnable ; and 1067, money returnable (*see* 37th Report of Postmaster-General); and with regard to these last, the money returnable is very often returned, and the contract is not persevered in as a deferred annuity.

The great Friendly Societies, the Foresters and the Manchester Unity of Oddfellows, started schemes of old age pensions on this principle ; after some years' trial it was found that only three or four had availed themselves of the facilities offered.[1] Mr. Bartley, the successful manager of the National Penny Bank, wrote some time ago, in the *Standard*, that he does not remember to have come across a single instance of a man saving by means of a deferred annuity. I had the advantage of discussing this question with Miss Octavia Hill some little time ago. She could not call to mind

[1] The Friendly Societies are making great efforts to popularise different forms of deferred annuities. It is very possible that they will be successful. I sincerely hope so, but I submit that no power on earth will ever make a *pure* deferred annuity or pension a popular investment, and it will be no reflection on the Friendly Societies if they fail. They will succeed, I am persuaded, only by making the proposed investment less and less of a deferred annuity, and more and more of a pure savings bank account, withdrawable at will.

a single instance of a deferred annuity purchaser. She knew a great many people who were in the habit of saving in various ways ; some put money in banks, others—unskilled labourers perhaps— made sacrifice, and brought up their children to a trade. She felt strongly the impertinence involved in prying into these poor people's affairs, and she only knew what they chose to tell her ; but she knew enough about them to give her every reason to hope that those people who were really in earnest about saving would not come upon the parish in their old age. I could multiply such evidence as this indefinitely. I will add one small item of official evidence.

The statement is often made that the Friendly Society man is very frequently forced to come on the rates in his old age. If this is really so, it might seem to throw some discredit on the view expressed by Miss Hill, for the member of a genuine Friendly Society is emphatically a person in earnest about saving. But what are the facts ? A certain Parliamentary return, known as Lord Lymington's return, professes to give the number of persons in workhouses who declare that at some period of their life they have been members of some sort of provident society. The list does not exclude members of the Christmas sharing-out club, or persons who have been a few weeks in some publican's goose club, and the figures are without doubt largely exaggerated and certainly unverified, yet the late Chief Registrar informs us that the return for 1881 only shows a proportion of one in-door pauper to every 354 of the adult membership of the Friendly Society, or if the calculation is based, as it should be, on the number of those who attributed their pauperism to the breaking-up of their club, the tale of in-door paupers did not amount to one in 1000—a striking proof, I venture to think, of the substantial accuracy of Miss Hill's remark.[1] Even if we make a very

---

[1] A similar return has been made for 1891. On this the Majority Report of the Royal Commission on the Aged Poor remarks as follows—" In commenting on this return, Mr. Brabrook points out that if it were correct it would show that for every 10,000 members now in registered Friendly Societies there are in work-houses twenty-six persons who have left their societies, and twelve whose societies had broken up. He thinks, however, that even these low figures give a misleading impression : first, because the answers of paupers on such a matter are untrustworthy, and they may use the words Friendly Society very loosely ; and secondly, because societies very often break up for reasons other than financial failure ; while, as we have seen, lapses very generally take place a year or so after admission. We agree with Mr. Brabrook and Mr. Wilkinson that this return is very far from showing, as the former tells us it is often used to show, 'a failure of Friendly Societies to fulfil their duties to their members ' : on the contrary, it seems to us to furnish strong testimony to the success of their efforts in reducing pauperism." The same authority comments on the evidence of Mr. T. Ballan Stead, Permanent Secretary of the Ancient Order of Foresters. "He tells us," says the Report, " that, out of 526,000 English members, to whom the returns he has received relate, 490 only have applied for poor relief during the past five years, an average of under 100 per annum ; while in Wales, out of 23,000 members, 8 only sought relief in the whole five years. Mr. Stead thinks that even these figures do not fully

liberal allowance for the number of Friendly Society members receiving out-relief, I think we may safely assume that the proportion of genuine Friendly Society members who become paupers is very small. The people who become paupers are those irresponsible beings who carefully avoid the Friendly Society and all its works.

Mr. Brabrook, the Chief Registrar of Friendly Societies, told the Labour Commission that his department had cognisance of over £200,000,000 sterling, representing for the most part savings of the working class.

I have made a rough calculation, from the last Statistical Abstract and other available sources, as to the more obvious institutions where working class savings are deposited.

I find that, of a total of £220,000,000, only about £31,000,000 are ear-marked for one particular purpose. The rest is free, and available to be used for old age or any other incident that may arise. Of these £31,000,000, £20,000,000 belong to the

show the extent to which members have kept themselves independent of the Poor Law, as the courts and lodges from which he received no reply had presumably no cases to report. . . . There can be no doubt," the Report remarks, "that in general, as Mr. Brabrook says, 'The man who practises providence in one direction, and becomes a member of a Friendly Society, is not an improvident man in any other sense of the word, and he looks forward to old age as well as to sickness, and endeavours to provide against it by opportunities independently of his membership of the Friendly Society.'"

Friendly Societies, which, in many cases, do make an allowance in old age.

Present Time, say 1891.

[1] Post-office Savings Bank, 1891 .	£71,608,000
[1] Trustee Savings Banks, 1891 . .	42,875,000
[1] Government Stock standing in name of depositors at Post-Office, 1891 .	5,087,000
[1] Government Stock standing in name of depositors at Trustee Banks, 1891 .	1,282,000
	120,852,000
[1] Building Societies, 1890	52,482,000
[1] Industrial and Provident (Co-operative) Societies, 1890	15,261,000
[1] Industrial Insurance Companies, 1890 8,873,000	
[2] Friendly Societies 20,167,000	
[3] Collecting Friendly Societies, 1889 . 2,565,000	
	31,605,000
	£220,200,000

In order that some idea may be given of the rate at which these investments are growing, I have made out a second list, showing the state of affairs during the past fifteen years :—

[1] Post-Office Savings Bank, 1877 .	£28,740,000
[1] Trustee Savings Banks, 1877 . .	44,238,000
[1] Government Stock standing in name of depositors at Post-Office, 1881 (no earlier figures given) . . .	738,000
[1] Government Stock standing in name of depositors at Trustee Banks, 1881 (no earlier dates given) . . .	124,000
	73,840,000
Carried forward . .	£73,840,000

[1] Statistical Abstract, 1877 to 1891, 39th number.
[2] Rev. T. Frome Wilkinson, "Mutual Thrift" (Estimated), p. 191.
[3] *Ibid.*, p. 194.

Brought forward	. .	£73,840,000
[1] Building Societies, 1876		20,854,000
[1] Industrial and Provident (Co-operative) Societies, 1876		6,224,000
[1] Industrial Insurance Companies, 1880 (no earlier figures given)		1,476,000
Friendly Societies, 1876 (as estimated by Mr. Ludlow's "Chief-Registrar's Report," 1890, Part A, p. 9)		9,336,000
		£111,730,000

These figures give you a very fair indication of what the humbler classes of society have been doing with their savings during the last fifteen years. Probably not more than a few thousands have been devoted to deferred annuities.

Mr. Chamberlain and his friends very soon were confronted with this difficulty, that no reasonable man of his own accord ever began at the age of twenty-five to put money away beyond his control which would be lost to him entirely if he did not survive to sixty-five. A reasonable man may see fit to insure himself against the uncertain risk of excessive sickness and premature death, but the risk of old age is of a totally different nature. When a man has insured against sickness and death, he very naturally says to himself, " I cannot afford to ear-mark any more of my savings, certainly not, at all events, for a fund which I may never live to enjoy, in which my widow and family cannot participate. Rather than do this I will save what I can ; possibly I shall have a chance of investing

[1] Statistical Abstract, 1877 to 1891, 39th number.

it in a profitable business. I will take a share or shares in a co-operative society, I will buy a house through a building society. I will subscribe for an endowment policy of insurance, to become due at death or on my reaching a given age, and if when I reach the age at which it becomes due, I am a lone man with no one dependent on me, I will consider whether I will not buy an immediate annuity. Generally I will bring up my family well, see that the boys are put into trades, and in other ways do what I can to consolidate and improve my position in life. The risk of a destitute old age, if I am spared health and strength to carry out even a part of these plans, does not disturb me. If I am not spared, my little savings will go to those I love, and I shall die thankful that I 'have not been selfish enough to waste my money on one of these absurd deferred annuities."

Such a view of the question is obvious enough, and after a period it made itself felt in the voluntary Parliamentary Committee, and necessitated a change of front.

At first it had been proposed to pay a benefit in old age only. This, as we have seen, would not do; it was, therefore, determined to make the scheme more acceptable by adding a variety of multifarious benefits to widows and children and nearest representatives. This change threw the whole scheme into inextricable confusion, from which, as far as I can make out, it has never emerged. Let me explain.

It is an easy task for an actuary to draw up a set of tables for deferred annuities, but it is, I believe, an impossible task for any one to calculate the liability incurred by an institution which contracts to give not only an allowance in old age, but in addition to give an allowance during a more or less lengthened period to widows and children (if any). This is not insurance, but a proposal to establish a charitable fund. It is the essence of insurance that each insurer shall pay a premium carefully calculated to cover the risk which he insures. To insure a man, and possibly his widow, as well as an indeterminate number of children yet unborn, in this wholesale manner, for one inclusive capitation fee, is manifestly inequitable to unmarried men and to men with small families, and imports into the contract an element of speculation altogether at variance with common sense and sound economical progress.

In the earlier stages of the deliberations of the informal Parliamentary Committee there were frequent references to the labours of the committee's actuary, but I notice that their subsequent utterances contain no reference to this gentleman, for whose difficult position we must all feel much sympathy. Actuaries, however, have given opinions on this proposal; as a specimen, here is what

Mr. T. E. Young, a Vice-President of the Society of Actuaries, says of the matter :—

" I am confident, looking to the want of existing and appropriate data, that the incorporation of the element of a pension allowance to widows and children is essentially of the nature of guess-work. . . . It may safely be affirmed that the scheme is doomed to failure."

To sum up, then, the objections which we have taken to this proposal of assisted deferred annuities—

(1) There is no principle in selecting old age at sixty-five, as the estate of life to which State subsidy is to be given.

(2) Nearly half the old age pauperism of this country probably commences before sixty-five.

(3) The proposed scheme will not touch the lowest class of the population.

(4) The method of deferred annuities is not that which commends itself to the good sense of the labouring population.

(5) The attempt to meet this objection by throwing in a number of additional benefits is not business, and deprives the fund of any claim to be called insurance.

One last objection which I have not noticed, though happily it is of more practical importance than all others, is that the scheme is opposed unanimously by the Friendly Society interest.

O

Mr. Chamberlain and other promoters have admitted that if the Friendly Societies continue their opposition, this measure can never be carried.[1]

Mr. C. J. Radley, High Chief Ranger of the Ancient Order of Foresters, in 1891, in his presidential address, referred to the scheme as an offer of " unsolicited assistance."

I would beg you to note the words—*unsolicited assistance.* The situation is a curious one. The philanthropists insist that the working-class shall partake of a dole from the rates. Mr. Radley, a man who, in virtue of his office, was as well entitled to speak on behalf of the labouring class on such a subject as any other man in England, rejected the offer without hesitation. "The assistance is unsolicited." Yet the agitation takes its course.

I am somewhat surprised to see that in his latest contribution to this question, Mr. Chamberlain has seen fit to make complaint in the following terms :—

" Apparently, however, the officials of the great societies have made up their minds to allow no other solution of the old age problem than one which is entirely in their own hands ; " and he goes on—" it seems a pity that the officials of these great and valuable organisations . . . should warn off as intruders on their preserves the fellow-workers who are striving to increase

---

[1] I have already quoted, on p. 165, a specimen of the Friendly Society criticism of this proposal, and it need not be repeated here.

the inducements to thrift." — *Nineteenth Century,* Nov. 1892.

Such criticism, I venture to think, is unjust. I do not think that the opposition of the Friendly Societies to Mr. Chamberlain's proposal can be attributed to such petty jealousy. Their aim and object is to maintain the absolute independence of their members at all periods of life ; and, as the quotation from Mr. Radley's speech amply shows, they—rightly or wrongly—regard Mr. Chamberlain's overtures to them, not as the assistance of a fellow-worker, but as an attempt to substitute a hybrid form of pauperism for that absolute and complete independence which they prize.[1]

Let us pass now to a consideration of the last of

[1] I have in the text avoided any discussion of proposals for a revision of poor law methods for the relief of old age. I avail myself of a note to mention a Bill introduced into the last Parliament by Mr. Bartley, with a view of giving to the *provident* poor preferential terms of pauperism. Mr. Bartley's view of the subject involves two important admissions :—(1) That the relief of any class of persons from the rates is of the essence of poor law relief, and is not a pension ; (2) that " provident " is a term which cannot be confined to members of Friendly Societies, but must be extended to all who have saved in any way whatsoever. A mere statement of this last proposition is sufficient to show the impracticable nature of the proposal. How is it possible to decide what portion of a man's possessions is the result of providence ! A scheme to set a premium on inadequate saving can never afford a solution of this question. There is no halfway house between dependence and independence.

these proposals, the universal endowment of old age, advocated by Mr. Booth.

Mr. Booth proposes that every one who has not been chargeable to the poor rate for ten years, shall, at the age of sixty-five, become entitled to have 5*s.* a-week.

The merits of this scheme are said to be—

1. That it will be instrumental in abolishing pauperism.

2. That it overcomes the difficulty of compelling the submerged classes of the community.

3. That it will be an incentive to thrift, for the hope of receiving a gift of 5*s.* in old age will make it worth a man's while to save during his earlier life.

As to its influence on pauperism, if the figures already quoted from Stepney are at all representative of the rest of the country—and from inquiries I have made, and from what I know of the strict administration of the law there and of the lax administration elsewhere, I am sure that the Stepney proportion is under rather than over the average—then, by one stroke of the pen, by the introduction of his ten-year limit, nearly one-half of our present pauperism is deprived of benefit under his scheme.

Again, will a pension of 5*s.* a-week, even if it be paid weekly (some of the advocates of pension schemes urge quarterly payments, with a view of

keeping down management charges), be effectual
in keeping people off the rates? I recently discussed this proposition with one of the most
experienced poor law officials in the kingdom,
Mr. Vallance, the clerk to the guardians at
Whitechapel. In the first place, he confirmed
my conviction that a large proportion of the
old age paupers over sixty-five had been paupers
before that age ; secondly, he said he had been
in consultation with the master and matron of
the workhouse, and they had agreed that a very
small proportion of the old persons under their
charge would be kept out of the workhouse even
if they had 5s. a-week. This, I may say, was in a
union where no out-door relief is given, so this
opinion covers all the old age pauperism of the
union. A large number of them were friendless
and infirm, and were perfectly comfortable in the
workhouse ; the rest were of that class that cannot
go to sleep as long as they have any money in
their pocket.

This, I believe, is a key to the whole problem—
pauperism is not a question of poverty, but rather
of habit and character. Time after time, those
who observe these matters closely have seen two
men starting life in exactly the same conditions,
even among the very poorest class of agricultural
labourers. One man will maintain his independence,
and bring up his family respectably, and the other

will laugh at his responsibilities, and end his days as a pauper.

May I remind you of one of Charles Lamb's delightful papers?—I hope the digression will be pardoned, for the point it illustrates is strictly relevant to our subject. "The human species," he says, "according to the best theory I can form of it, is composed of two distinct races—the men who borrow, and the men who lend. The borrowers are the *great race.* The lender is born degraded, 'he shall serve his brethren.' There is something in the air of one of this caste (the lender) lean and suspicious, contrasting with the open, trusting, generous manners of the other. What contempt for money, accounting it (yours, and mine especially) no better than dross."

These reflections recall to our author his friend Ralph Bigod, Esq., a prince of borrowers, fit to compare with the great borrowers of antiquity— Alcibiades, Falstaff, Sir Richard Steel, and "our late incomparable Brinsley." "Ralph Bigod was, in youth, invested with ample revenue, and in borrowing had an undeniable way; mankind at large was his tributary. Like Cæsar Augustus, he ordered all to come up and be taxed. With such sources, it was a wonder how he contrived to keep his treasury always empty. He managed it, however, by force of an aphorism which he had often in his mouth, that 'Money kept longer

than three days stinks.' So he made use of it
while it was fresh. A good part he drank away
(for he was an excellent toss-pot); some he gave
away; the rest he threw away . . . out away from
him it must go, like Hagar's offspring, into the
wilderness, while it was sweet. He never missed
it; the streams were perennial which fed his fisc."

It is a picture to the life. Sad havoc this affable
spendthrift must often have made in poor Elia's
slender store of guineas. Yet with what delightful
tolerant irony he delineates the character.

It expresses to the letter what I have to say
about the pauper. The pauper is your Ralph
Bigod, Esq., in humble life, and this is the reason
that 5s. a-week will not suffice to keep him off
the rates.

His principal tributary is the poor law, but he
will condescend at times to borrow of his neighbours. I am told, on excellent authority, that the
publicity given to saving by the posting of a
savings bank book is much dreaded by the thrifty
poor, because of the Ralph Bigods of their
acquaintance, and many of them have gladly
availed themselves of my informant's permission
to have their bank books sent to her private
address.

We all have a sneaking affection for these Ralph
Bigods, and I think middle-class philanthropists
are mistaken in attributing excessive turpitude

to the pauper class. They are, though in their humble way, members of the great race, and take their toll from a tributary poor law.

Another error we sometimes make is, that we are inclined to attribute to the poor an excessive unhappiness in their poverty. I do not know that it is a matter for congratulation or regret, but I think the poor have very little fear of poverty. Over and over again one has seen a poor widow spend the whole, or nearly the whole, of £10 or £20 insurance money in funeral and mourning, although next day she was absolutely destitute, and obliged to apply for poor law or charitable relief. To give a particular instance of this happy-go-lucky sort of disposition, if I may use the term without offence—a clergyman, some time ago, told me of a woman who, as he believes, was entirely dependent on a temporary allowance paid to her by him. At the time a small parish excursion was being organised, tickets 3s., etc. ; to my friend's surprise, this woman applied for a ticket, and, on inquiry, he found that she felt her poverty so lightly that she looked forward to buying a happy day in the country with what was practically the last shot in the locker.

One more illustration. Some eighteen years ago out-door relief was given in St. George-in-the-East, and just outside the relief-office there was a well-known public-house, and on pay-day there was a perpetual stream of paupers through its portals. The average allowance was in those days 1*s*. per week per pauper. I do not suggest that these people drank to excess, but I think the circumstance shows that they estimated very lightly the fact that this unnecessary expenditure would probably leave them very short of the bare necessaries of life towards the end of the week. The owner of this public-house was an active member of the Board, and one of the strongest opponents of the restriction or abolition of out-door relief which took place at that time. He was actuated, no doubt, by motives of a pure but, as I believe, mistaken philanthropy; still at the time it was freely admitted that the change would mean to him a considerable pecuniary loss.

I trust that these anecdotes may not appear irrelevant; they seem to me to throw light on the nature of the character with which we have to deal in our attempts to improve the condition of the pauper.

An ingenious acquaintance of mine, lately returned from the tropics, unfolded to me recently a brand new plan for solving the problem of pauperism. "Emigration," he began. "Ah, yes," I interrupted, "we have heard of that before, but paupers will not make good emigrants, and people who can get on in the colonies can, as a rule, get on at home." My friend, however, was none of your ordinary panacea-mongers. "Mine is not an ordinary emigration scheme at all," he said. "I have come from a place where bananas grow wild ; the native basks all day in the sun, and feeds on bananas. Now that is the climate we want for some of our failures at home. It is no good sending them to Canada, but we will set them down under those banana trees, and they will live happily ever after." Whether my friend is founding a society for the purpose of giving effect to his views, I do not know. I only mention the incident for the purpose of expressing my belief that our pauper class already have their banana trees in the shape of a tributary poor law and a philanthropic public. Consider the temptations to live down to an irresponsible level that lie in the path of an easy, jovial spirit, with a natural aptitude for playing the part of one of the great race. His children are educated for him ; if he is sick, he can go to an admirable infirmary, or, if he prefers it, he can very often get relieved at his own home. If he dies, his wife will get the usual widow's allowance of out-door relief; he has no occasion to violate his favourite aphorism on her account ; and when he grows old he can reckon with tolerable certainty on getting an allowance from the parish equal in amount to what can be saved by that lean suspicious race which he so justly despises. All this he gets from the law of the land, and if any of his remaining burdens are irksome to him, he can readily catch a tributary or two on the preserves of the philanthropic public.

These wild bananas, as I venture to call them (though they are not really wild, but in many cases raised on the privations of the poorer rate-payers), do not satisfy Mr. Booth. The out-door relief allowance in old age is not given with sufficient acclamation and applause, let it therefore be called a pension, and given to every one, whether he requires it or not.

This plan, Mr. Booth would have us believe, will be an encouragement to thrift. He speaks, and I am sure thinks, respectfully of the virtue of thrift, for he has not reached the point of view of the Continental Socialist who declares himself "opposed to all institutions of thrift which merely encourage labourers to new privations," or who asks, "What is this doctrine of personal responsibility? It is economy, it is thrift, that is to say, a doctrine most absurd, for every economy is a crime."

Mr. Booth does not adopt this language, but surely he takes a strange method of showing his respect for the economic virtue of thrift, viz. by seeking to render it even less necessary than it is already.

Is it the experience of men of the world that to give a man 5s. is an encouragement to him to save another 5s. ? I have always been told, on the contrary, that it is an encouragement to him to ask for the gift of a second 5*s.* when his occasions require it. As yet the poorer classes of the country have not solicited this assistance, but, on the contrary, have strenuously protested against it. The politician, however, has been very busy in his offers of service ; already, in the last Parliament, some of those who differ from Mr. Chamberlain about the Irish question, in order not to be outdone, have given notice of bills giving more liberal allowances than Mr. Chamberlain offered.

But the proposition that a pension will not necessarily keep a man out of the workhouse is not mere matter of theory ; from inquiries that I have made from guardians here and elsewhere, I am able to say that there are a considerable number of army pensioners in workhouses. Their allowance is generally, I believe, 1*s.* 5*d.* per diem. If the guardians know of this pension, it is their duty to attach it. Some of these people are no doubt friendless and infirm, and find themselves most comfortable in the workhouse. As a rule, I understand, their pensions more than pay for their maintenance, so that at the end of each quarter a balance is paid over to the pauper. Many of them go out and have a "good time" for a day or two, and then return to the workhouse.

In some instances, the guardians do not know of these pensions, and then the man gets his pension and his maintenance as well. I accidentally heard of one such case within the last few days.

These remarks refer to men in the body of the workhouse or infirmary ;[1] but, beyond this, it has always been a mystery to some of us to know what are the attractions of the casual ward. Possibly, this has something to do with it. There are in the casual wards every night a considerable number of ex-soldiers, pensioned or unpensioned ; it is not possible to say how many, for the casual paupers go in and out of the wards without question ; no one asks what their profession is, and there is, therefore, no danger of their pensions being attached. They, therefore, to use what I believe

---

[1] Since this was written, Mr. Campbell-Bannerman, replying to a question in the House of Commons, stated that the number of army pensioners, whose pensions were attached by the poor law authorities, was very small. It will be seen that this covers a very small portion of my argument. I am inclined to believe that numbers of army pensioners avoid the workhouse and infirmary and confine themselves to the casual wards, for the very reason that no questions are asked. Of the chargeability of this class the War Office cannot possibly have any knowledge. The whole question of casual wards is extremely unsatisfactory. The very phrase so familiar to us, "lunatics and vagrants not included," shows that this class is excluded both from statistical and philanthropic consideration. My suspicion that the casual wards are largely recruited by old soldiers is confirmed by an inquiry made by Mr. Pyddoke, of Toynbee Hall, into the Whitechapel Casual Ward. He says, "As many as 22 per cent.—119 out of 550—have admitted being in the army at one time or another ; and the real proportion is said to be more like 70 per cent."—Report of Whitechapel Board of Guardians, Lady-Day, 1895.

is a technical term, "tumble to," and adapt themselves to the life of a casual ward.

I had an interview with the superintendent of a London casual ward a few days ago. In answer to my inquiry, he told me that there were certainly a considerable number of army pensioners in the habit of coming to his wards. One, whose name he gave me, was in receipt of a pension of 2*s*. per diem. As quarter time drew near, he heard in the wards talk and gossip on the subject, and, immediately after the quarter day, there was a sensible diminution of the numbers in the wards.

Now, if 14*s*. or 9*s*. 11*d*. a-week do not keep a man off the rates, what can we say about 5*s*. a-week? These facts, I confess, have only recently come to my notice, and I do not know whether the pauperism of these pensioners can be proven to any very considerable extent; but I have learnt enough to tempt me to hazard the hypothesis that, to the character undisciplined in the habits of saving, and the frugal living which this necessitates, these pensions, coming as a sort of windfall, are as likely to be an incentive of riot as of thrift.

My argument is, that pauperism is much less a question of poverty than we generally suppose. But what, some one will ask, is to be said about the agricultural labourer and his miserable wages? In the first place, I question if the agricultural labourer is really so much worse off than his urban neighbours. His nominal wages are low indeed, but he has extra wages at harvest time; he has a cottage, as a rule, at a less rent than the town labourer pays for a single room, and he has a garden, and, in many cases, an allotment.

I was told, a few days ago, of a Shropshire labourer, receiving 15*s.* a-week, who migrated to the town and got a situation, first at 18*s.*, and then at 22*s.* a-week; but after some experience he voluntarily gave up his place and returned to 15*s.* a-week as an agricultural labourer.

Still, wages in the country are low; but are pensions any remedy for low wages? Let me quote to you what the Chief Registrar of Friendly Societies says in his Report of 1891 :—

" I do not understand how any plan for relieving the working man of that which ought to be a charge upon his wages, can be other than a disadvantage to him, by leading him to refrain from claiming and enforcing his right to such wages as will enable him to meet the charge. It is for his Friendly Society to fix what he ought to pay, and for his trade union to see that he has the means of paying it. It is better for the State, that is, the general body of tax-payers, that he should be paid suitable wages for such services as he renders, than that it should be made up to him for a deficiency of wages by doles of any kind."

There can, I think, be no doubt as to the justice of this view. A system of pensions would certainly tend to reduce wages, and for the reason given by

Mr. Brabrook.   Whatever view we take of the theory of wages, it is certain that the standard of comfort aimed at by the labourer has much to do with the rate of his remuneration.   If a provision for old age is made no part of his standard of comfort, his wages will tend to be proportionately lower.   To supply to him, out of the rates, the necessaries of life which ought to form a portion of his standard of comfort, is to condemn him to a permanence of inadequate wages.   A principal cause of low wages in the past has been the grants in aid of wages, sanctioned by the old poor law ; a principal cause at the present time is an administration of the poor law which deludes the labourer into resting content that his old age shall be supported by the rates, and not by the adequate wages to which his manhood is entitled.

Those who have followed with attention recent controversies on poor law administration, will bear me out when I say that the most remarkable successes in rescuing populations from pauperism have occurred not in towns, nor in places where wages are exceptionally high, but in agricultural districts where low wages prevail.   I allude, of course, to such remarkable reformation as has taken place in the rural Union of Bradfield. Poverty, alas ! has not been eradicated, but a first step in that direction has been taken : independence has been restored.   The pauperism of the Union has been reduced from over 1200 in 1871, to about 120 at the present time. And how has this been accomplished? Not by any great rise in wages, not by any system of pensions, but by resisting the beginnings of that irresponsible spirit which is the cause of pauperism. Medical relief, the first step in the descent to the Avernus of pauperism, is not given except on loan, and the borrower is not allowed to put himself in a better position than his more self-respecting neighbour. What is the result? That no one now wants to borrow, and, with hardly an exception, every family in the Union is a member of a medical club. Further, out-relief is not given when the breadwinner of the family is sick. What is the result? That the breadwinners are members of Friendly Societies, and they and their families remain independent.

And what has this reformation cost the poor inhabitants of Bradfield? I venture to say very little more than the price of a few pots of beer, and in exchange they have gained, and are gaining, disciplined habits of frugality and independence, which are the only sure foundations of future progress.

The problem of old age is not pressing at Bradfield. While the old pauperism over 60 in some 26 unions selected by Canon Blackley is 42 per cent. of the estimated population over 60, in

Bradfield it is only 4 per cent. The disease is arrested in its early stages, and the problem will grow easier each succeeding year. And all this, mind you, despite the proverbial poverty of an agricultural union!

The cause of pauperism is not poverty, the cause of pauperism is State relief, more especially as it is administered in the form of out-door relief. We shall not get rid of pauperism by extending the sphere of State relief, as proposed in this pension scheme of Mr. Booth. On the contrary, its adoption would increase our pauperism, for, as is often said, we can have exactly as many paupers as the country chooses to pay for.

In the last pages of the volume of "Life and Labour of the People," published in 1891, Mr. Booth stated that he was preparing to equip himself for a practical discussion of the poor law. This admission of inexperience in the practical work of administering relief is characteristic of Mr. Booth's candour. I read and noted it at the time, and I confess that I was somewhat surprised to see that, before the year was out, Mr. Booth had come forward with a stupendous scheme for the revolution of our poor law, involving an expenditure of not less than £30,000,000 a year. I trust it is not hypercritical to remark that the gravity of the matter in hand might have warranted a greater show of deliberation. One other consideration I ask leave to place before you.

There is probably no institution of which the working classes and the country are more justly proud than the Friendly Society. It is a unique Anglo-Saxon institution, of purely working-class origin.

Now, if some Mr. Booth of fifty years ago had induced the Legislature to say that sickness was to be an honourable public charge, would these admirable institutions have ever reached their present splendid and impregnable position?

Who is it that will say, "Thus far and no further," to the onward march of working-class independence? Is it Utopian to believe that in resolutely grappling with the problem of age there will be given to the wage-earners of this country a new accession of strength and of resolute, independent character, which will carry them forward along the path of progress? If this be our hope, we must summon up courage to say to the poorer classes of this country, "These are your responsibilities, do not let any specious counsels filch away from you your right to overcome them. They are the ladders by which you will rise to higher things."

It is very possible, as some tell us, that we shall be worse before we are better. The new ruling classes of this country must buy experience at some cost, but, in the long run, truth and common sense will win; and I do not believe that the working class is likely to ruin itself and the country, by proclaiming a universal cessation of personal responsibility.

In the mean time, we must have our poor law—it is an inevitable evil—but, to justify its existence, it must perpetually be making war on the irresponsibility which is the main cause of pauperism ; it must, in fact, be so administered that it tends to throw the people more and more on their own resources, to diminish, and not increase, the number of those permanently dependent.

To insist on the view which I have endeavoured to present in this article is, at the present day, an ungrateful and unpopular duty. All that I will say, in conclusion, is, that I shall be glad if I have succeeded in doing so without offence.

V.

THE ABUSE OF STATISTICS.[1]

" MANY of us suppose that when we have got into statistics we have got away from cheap fancy and sentimentalism. Never was any opinion more delusive. The arithmetical fancy, the passion for calculation and results, is one of the commonest forms of a superficial imagination, and exercises a mysterious influence over half-educated minds. The temptation to calculate rather than to analyse, to fly at once to a mechanical process rather than pause for one which is laborious and demands original research, is active in many of the sciences, and, within the limits of a working hypothesis, it may have results of a certain very restricted value. . . . The pages of the late Professor de Morgan are full of examples that show how readily the handling of figures becomes the organ of the crudest superstition. The general principle which governs all argument by calculation is this—that figures, being only very mutilated abbreviations of fact, are wholly insignificant, except to those who by concrete experience know precisely and completely for what facts they stand." [2]

[1] Republished from the *Quarterly Review*, No. 358, October, 1894.
[2] "The Civilisation of Christendom, and other Studies." By Bernard Bosanquet, formerly Fellow of University College, Oxford.

This criticism, at once trenchant and precise, from the pen of so thoughtful a writer as Mr. Bosanquet, gives cause to fear that the legitimate value of statistics is in danger of being discredited by the extravagances of some of its votaries, more especially in their manner of applying this method to the elucidation of social problems. A competent authority, the author of the article on Statistics in the "Encyclopædia Britannica," expresses himself to the same effect in more technical language :—

"The statistical method," he says, "is essentially a mathematical procedure, attempting to give a quantitative expression to certain facts, and the resolution of differences of quality into differences of quantity has not yet been effected, even in chemical science. In sociological science the importance of differences of quality is enormous, and the effect of these differences on the conclusions to be drawn from figures is sometimes neglected, or insufficiently recognised even by men of unquestionable ability and good faith. The majority of politicians, social 'reformers,' and amateur handlers of statistics generally are in the habit of drawing the conclusions that seem good to them from such figures as they may obtain, merely by treating as homogeneous, quantities which are heterogeneous, and, as comparable, quantities which are not comparable."

So long as statistical inquiry is confined to questions of pure science, its method and its primary figures are subjected to the criticism of experts, and the danger of error is inconsiderable. When, however, we pass into the burning region of "Sociological Science," the atmosphere is altogether changed. Sociological Science is akin to politics, and politics is the business of the democracy and all its organs. Here the arithmetical fancy luxuriates, and a passion for definite results urges the statistician himself, and still more his less critical audience, to include in one category facts which in their nature are essentially different, to distinguish and classify according to appearances which are only incidental, to mistake coincidence for cause and cause for coincidence. In such a subject-matter valuable results can only be obtained by the most careful analysis, guided by the teaching of experience, for which no mechanical dexterity in the manipulation of figures can be a substitute.

We propose in this article to draw attention to several statistical works bearing on a question of great practical importance, and it may be well before proceeding further to say something of their history, and of the controversy on which they purport to throw light.

Mr. Booth is evidently a born demographist, not easily to be restrained from the manipulation and decimal-pointing of all figures within his reach. He does not claim to have any practical experience of the administration of public relief.

He set out, obviously, with no preconceived opinions, but, as we venture to think, without realising the elusive complexity and heterogeneous nature of the phenomena which he seeks to subject to his statistical processes.   His good faith is above suspicion—a fact that was the more readily acknowledged when it appeared that his first book [1] was designed to prove nothing in particular, and that the author had no views of his own.   Mr. Booth's self-restraint did not, however, last for long.   In the interval between his first and second [2] works his imagination appears to have been captured by some plausible panaceamonger (we are putting our own gloss on Mr. Booth's sudden change of method), and his established reputation as an industrious and impartial investigator has given unexpected currency to a proposal for universal pensions, which has no obvious connection with his statistical inquiry, and as to the merits of which an astronomer or a chemist is as well fitted to judge as a statistician.   The desire to make all men happy by some deft stroke of legislation has to certain minds all the fascination which the squaring of the circle had for the " paradoxers," whose fame Professor de Morgan has embalmed in his " Budget of Paradox."   It

[1] " Labour and Life of the People."   Edited by Charles Booth. 3 vols.   London, 1889–1891.

[2] " Pauperism and the Endowment of Old Age."   Charles Booth. London, 1892.

must always be matter of regret that Mr. Booth has allowed himself to be put forward as the advocate of this utterly impracticable proposal. In his last volume[1] Mr. Booth returns to his statistics, but, unless we are mistaken, he cannot lay aside the attitude of advocacy which he has now assumed. He promises us more books and more practical suggestions. It is time, therefore, to examine the foundations on which this superstructure rests.

There are other types of statisticians whose efforts we shall have occasion to notice in the course of our criticism. The attitude which they have taken up is more controversial than that of Mr. Booth in the earlier stages, at all events, of his various publications. Their position is best made clear by a short historical recital. A long succession of poor law administrators has up to the present time endeavoured to carry out to their logical conclusion the maxims laid down by the Poor Law Commissioners of 1832. It has been their endeavour—to state the matter shortly—to render the influence of the poor law centrifugal rather than centripetal. In other words, it has been sought by a strict and careful administration to give the stream of pauperism a movement away from the poor law toward the more honourable condition of independence. The more advanced

[1] "The Aged Poor : Condition." London, 1894.

school of administrators have tried to attain this
end by a restriction, in some cases by an abolition,
of out-door relief; that is, the relief given to
people at their own homes. The opposite policy
has been adopted in a few isolated cases; but
though some unions may have moved in the
opposite direction, the average shows that the
general practice of guardians is tending toward
the stricter system. Now, it is obvious that the
adoption of this policy must necessarily reduce
the number of persons receiving relief. The
assertion of those who point out that, in any given
union, the restriction of out-door relief must reduce
the number of paupers within that union, is
incontestable.

This admission of course is a very small point
in the general controversy. Guardians may and
do refuse their consent to the proposition that this
restrictive policy is just, and humane, and impartial.
The scruples of such dissentients ought to receive
the utmost deference. Their argument is a
perfectly honest and straightforward one. They
say in effect, " We may pay too high a price for
the independence of the poor, we may inflict too
great hardship if we hurry too fast the withdrawal
of these facilities for relief." For many years this
controversy has gone on, outside the atmosphere
of practical politics. The contention, self-evident
as it is—that a restriction or abolition of out-door

relief will reduce the number of paupers—had practically been conceded. A subsidiary and less important controversy as to the relative cost of the two systems seemed also to be settled. The erection of improved poor law establishments might in some cases make a temporary increase of cost ; but inasmuch as out-relief is eagerly sought for, when obtainable, and in-door relief only accepted when absolutely necessary, it was being practically conceded that in the long run the in-door system was also the cheapest. The question of cost has never been felt to be of much moment, for the advocates of the strict system—with the consent, we may hope, of all reasonable men—argued that the cost was of secondary importance. Pauperism is a social evil, and society should be ready, if necessary, to pay highly for an instrument that would reduce its dimensions. Or, expressing it in figures, we should prefer, so the argument goes, to pay a thousand pounds for a system which would reduce our pauperism to one, rather than a hundred pounds for the maintenance of ten. The controversy whether the strict policy is just and humane remained and remains. Unions where the strict system has been adopted have been closely watched, and the success of the plan has been confidently asserted. Poor law literature and poor law conferences for the last twenty years have dealt with very little else. The authority of the Local Government Board inspectors, with almost complete unanimity, has supported the stricter school. The text-books and the historians of the poor law are, we believe, absolutely unanimous on the same side. The London Charity Organisation Society has, from the outset of its career, and of late years with many signs of increasing conviction, used its influence in support of this view ; and, by its practical work, it has enforced the argument that such relief as can be judiciously given to applicants at their own homes, is best given from voluntary sources and private charity. Of recent years the advance of these opinions has been indubitable. Though all did not absolutely agree as to the exact measure of restriction to be used, those in favour of restriction of some kind included, it may be said without exaggeration, every one who had ever seriously and impartially considered the subject.

The situation is now changed. The problem of the administration of the poor law is being dragged into the vortex of practical politics. It is all too evident that the rate devoted to the relief of the poor can be made an admirable electioneering fund. The *débâcle* has already begun. The poor law electorate before Mr. Fowler's Bill was by no means perfect. Electors who were not direct ratepayers abounded, but the anomaly was met to some extent by a counter-anomaly which gave a plural vote to the larger ratepayers, who in many unions were the only *bona fide* contributors to the poor rate. By a barefaced disregard of every principle of constitutional government, the public purse has been put at the disposal of a local electorate, the majority of which is in many cases financially irresponsible. Attempts have been freely made from both sides of the House to purchase the Friendly Society vote by offering preferential terms of pauperism to members of these associations. On what grounds the man who has invested his savings in a Friendly Society, as distinguished from a depositor in a Savings Bank, should have this unsought-for privilege thrust upon him, does not appear. There is, however, a politician who does not argue. His idea of statesmanship is confined to attempts to win the support of different sections of the community by proposals for looting the rates in their interest. The demoralisation is proceeding at an accelerated pace. The temptation to make political capital by advocacy of an out-door relief policy is growing irresistible, though hitherto it has seemed too thoroughly disreputable even for the latter-day politician.

At this juncture, therefore, it would be a godsend to a party on the look-out for a good political cry, if a man would come forward with argument and statistics, and his hand on his heart, to show that out-door relief was an electioneering card that an

honest man could play. The psychology of
political conviction is inscrutable. Men find
salvation in many ways. Far be it from us to
say that Mr. Hunter[1] and the author of an
anonymous pamphlet, entitled, "Plain Words on
Out-Relief,"[2] are not honestly persuaded that a
cry in favour of out-relief is not only not disreputable, but, on the contrary, the highest statesmanship. Every subject must have its "paradoxers,"
and at another time the line they have taken
would have been a harmless eccentricity. As
it is, Mr. Hunter's figures will be used to give
a cloak of decency to electioneering devices from
which respectable politicians have hitherto stood
aloof. Already the London Reform Union has
more or less adopted Mr. Hunter's policy for the
abolition of workhouses. At a recent meeting
convened by the Union, Mr. Stansfield, who, as
a former President of the Local Government Board,
knows something of the subject, got so far as to
speak "very sympathetically" of this new idea,
and expressed a hope that some one would one
day discover a test of destitution other than the
offer of relief within a poor law establishment.
In progressive circles to express a hope is equivalent
to complete achievement of the thing desired.

---

[1] "Out-Door Relief," by W. A. Hunter, M.P. : *Contemporary Review*, March, 1894.
[2] "Plain Words on Out-Relief." Knight & Co. London, *n.d.*

Mr. Stansfield knows something of the subject and will not talk absolute nonsense, but the London Reform Union is a less judicially minded body. It is chiefly remarkable for its fantastic optimism, and its exuberant belief in the power of sentimentality to advance the millennium. Many of its members, we are sure, will quite honestly believe that Mr. Hunter has succeeded in showing that no test is necessary to protect the rates from those who desire an addition to their income, and that an out-door system is cheaper and more repressive of pauperism than an in-door system. It is the honest simplicity and enthusiasm of the "paradoxer" and his dupes that constitute them a danger to society.

Lastly, we have certain statistics prepared by Mr. Loch,[1] in defence of what we may call the common-sense view against the attack of Mr. Hunter and the author of "Plain Words," and incidentally also traversing some of the conclusions of Mr. Booth. Mr. Loch's position, however, is somewhat different from that of the other contributors to this controversy. His opinions on the problems of poor law administration have been arrived at independently of statistics. He has adopted the view of the poor law experts which is based on administrative experience, and on a careful

[1] "The Statistics of Metropolitan Pauperism," by Charles S. Loch. London, 1894.

analysis of human motive. Hitherto it has not been thought necessary to defend the position by elaborate statistics. The interest of the discussion lay elsewhere. The reduction of pauperism by means of the strict system seemed unquestionable, and the only matters on which argument seemed possible were the justice and humanity of the course pursued. The new attack, however, leaves these aspects of the question comparatively in the background, and produces a number of figures which traverse the commonly received opinion. If the received opinion is to stand, these figures must be refuted or explained. To this task Mr. Loch applies himself.[1]

Such in brief outline has been the course of this controversy. We have thought it convenient to take this preliminary survey before proceeding to an appreciation of the figures and methods which have been used. To this part of our subject we now turn.

"My object," says Mr. Booth,[2] "has been to attempt to show the numerical relation which *poverty, misery, and depravity* bear *to regular earnings and comparative comfort,* and to describe the general conditions under which each class lives."

Throughout Mr. Booth treats his readers with

---

[1] Since this was written, an elaborate and conclusive vindication of the common-sense view, by means of statistics, has been published by Mr. W. Chance, Hon. Sec. to the Central Poor Law Conference, in the *National Review*, July, 1895.

[2] "Life and Labour of the People," vol. i. p. 6.

entire frankness; if an importance altogether
unwarranted has been attached to Mr. Booth's
calculations, the censure should fall, not on him,
but on those who are responsible for the uncritical
way in which his figures and conclusions have
been received. In the above quotation and elsewhere we have put into italics words of his own
which seem to govern the whole of his procedure.
Here and throughout Mr. Booth treats poverty,
misery, and depravity as three forms of one and the
same identical quality, and he contrasts them not
with absence of poverty, but with the appearance
of comparative comfort. This is not a mere verbal
quibble, it is essential to a proper understanding
of Mr. Booth's method. On p. 33 Mr. Booth
describes the eight classes into which he divides
the population of London. They are as follows :—

" A. The lowest class of occasional labourers, loafers,
    and semi-criminals.
  B. Casual earnings—"very poor."
  C. Intermittent earnings ⎫
  D. Small regular earnings ⎬ together "the poor."
  E. Regular standard earnings—above the line of
    poverty.
  F. Higher class labour.
  G. Lower middle class.
  H. Upper middle class."

We were warned of the assumption made. It
is this; where misery and depravity are obvious,
the terms "poor" and "very poor" are applied;

Q

where comparative comfort is apparent, there the absence of poverty is assumed. "Poor" is further defined to mean those "who have a sufficiently regular though bare income, such as 18s. to 21s. per week, for a *moderate family;* and by 'very poor' those who *for any cause* fall much below this standard." In his second volume (p. 18), he remarks, "A good many families have been reported as poor, *who though they are poor, are so without any economic necessity.*" Now Mr. Booth's classification is not a mere division of the population into manual and non-manual labourers, a distinction which might be successfully made by a cursory inspection of a man's dress and appearance, but an elaborate subdivision of manual labourers into at least six classes, with reference to a condition for which the most varying definitions have been given. First, poverty is identified with the visible signs of misery and depravity. Next, it is made to turn on the possession of a definite income ; but such precision as this implies is at once destroyed by the quali-fication "for a moderate family," while a still further uncertainty arises from the admission that the poverty chronicled is not an economic condition, but merely an enumeration of persons in the humbler ranks of life who have families and other occasions of expenditure, in their own or Mr. Booth's opinion, immoderate relatively to the amount of their income. No complaint is made of the introduction of these considerations. They are, each and all, important and determining, but how is it possible to give to them quantitative expression? All who know the poor are well aware that comparative comfort is not incompatible with low wages if combined with moderate ambitions, and *vice versâ* that high wages are not necessarily exclusive of misery and depravity. If poverty is not a definite economic condition, but a want of equilibrium between a man's habits and his income, we are clearly embarked upon an inquiry of an extremely vague nature : it is honeycombed by the ambiguity of these hypothetical definitions. The earning of 18*s*. or 21*s*. a week is a definite fact, and, if we had any means of discovering the number of those in that position, we could express it in terms of quantitative value. No attempt has been made, or could have been made by Mr. Booth, to ascertain the earnings of the enumerated population. In place of this we have the opinions of a large number of anonymous persons, mostly School Board visitors, on a long series of controversial subjects. These cannot be taken as a statistical product from which trustworthy conclusions are to be drawn.

The justice of the foregoing criticism will be confirmed by an inspection of the specimen entries of the note-books given in vol. i. pp. 7–24.

On page 13 :
　　Labourer, 3 school children, is put in Class E.
　　　　do.　　2　　do.　　　　do.　　A.
　　Lazy, drunken vagabond, etc.

Here the classification is by degree of depravity. There is no evidence as to earnings.

On pp. 14, 15 :

　　Bootmaker, 3 school children, 1 baby, 2 boys over
　　　　　school age, is put in Class B.
　　Good workman, but cantankerous.
　　Bootmaker, 1 child, 1 baby, is put in Class E.

Here, unless a bad mark is given to No. 1 for being cantankerous, the classification is apparently by degree of responsibility, though whether allowance is made for the earnings of the boys over age does not appear.

Page 16 :

　　Smelter, 3 children, 1 baby, is put in Class B.
　　Earns good money, but both drink, etc.

Classification by alleged depravity, income being disregarded.

Page 17 :

　　Washerwoman, 1 child, is put in Class D.
　　　　do.　　3 children,　　do.　　B.
　　1 boy at work ; has parish relief.

Here, notwithstanding the addition to income from

boy's earnings and from parish, the "immoderate" family apparently determines the classification.

Page 21 :

Foreman dung-carts, 2 school children, 1 baby,
is put in Class E.
Pleads poverty, but should do well.

This last note shows an attempt to grapple with the uncertainty of all this hearsay evidence, but in the majority of cases such discrimination was impracticable. Indeed, the whole process reminds one of the children's game of Russian scandal. One visitor is credulous, and makes himself a conduit for any gossip that reaches him ; another discounts all pleas of poverty. This brings us to the important question how far the vague impressions of School Board visitors, noted down not for the purposes of Mr. Booth's inquiry, but as memoranda to assist them in their own duties, can form a trustworthy foundation for the superstructure which has been based on them.

The principal business of the School Board visitor is to get the children to go to school. His measure of mankind, *mutatis mutandis,* is not different from that of Punch's dustman, who divided society according to its ability to fill dustbins. The School Board visitor judges his constituents according to their appreciation of the benefits provided by the School Board for their

children.   An argumentative shoemaker may very
well be of opinion that his boy is better employed
helping him at his work than earning a grant for
his school by displaying proficiency in the higher .
standards, and there would be nothing very
wonderful if (as in the case quoted above) the
father was put down as lazy because he wanted
his boy to help him, and cantankerous because he
had freely expressed the opinion that the law and
possibly its representative "was a hass."   Further,
both with regard to fee-paying and half-time
arrangements, it was to the interest of the poor
to make out a plea for poverty.   Such a plea is
detected and remorselessly pilloried if made by such
an exalted personage as a foreman of dung-carts,
but the same bias is present in the mind of every
single person interrogated.   Again, every one who
knows anything of the more unskilled labouring
class in London, is well aware of the extreme
vagueness of the term "labourer," and of the
general looseness of statement with regard to
occupation.   The School Board visitor rarely
crosses the threshold of the door, and his inter-
views are, as a rule, with the women of the family.
The trade of the head of the family and the
amount of his earnings are quite immaterial to
the main purpose of the visitor's errand.   In his
classification Mr. Booth is obviously much guided
by the trade assigned to the head of the family,

yet we cannot avoid a suspicion that the information on this head is very liable to error. Again, no two men take exactly the same view of social phenomena, and there is no means of bringing their impression to any common standard. It is true that general inquiries were made of the local clergy, and that Mr. Booth or one of his assistants inspected the various localities ; and if the division was merely between those who are manual labourers and those who are not, we might be willing to admit that a fairly accurate conclusion had been reached. In his second volume Mr. Booth wisely abandons the division between classes C and D, mainly on the ground that the trade of the head of the family has not been obtained, and it would have been wiser if this affectation of minute accuracy had been avoided altogether.

It is of course impossible to say what amount of inaccuracy has been introduced into the primary figures from these and other considerations ; but, in one or two other similar inquiries, accident has made it possible to show how large a source of error they will prove in a subject of this controversial nature.

In March, 1887, Mr. Ritchie directed an inquiry to be made as to the number of the unemployed in certain poor districts of the Metropolis. Of this return Dr. Ogle, the official responsible for the work, remarked, "The tabulation is a tabulation of

statements, not of facts. . . . I have come to the
conclusion that these returns are of a very small
statistical value." Yet want of employment, unlike
poverty, is a definite condition, and the inquiry was
made *ad rem.* Again, Mr. Booth and his assistants
have tabulated what they imagine to be the causes
of pauperism in one country and in two London
unions. The estimates assign drink as the cause
of from 12·6 per cent. to 21·9 per cent. of the
pauperism of these unions. Mr. MacDougall, a
gentleman well known as an active guardian in
Manchester, calculates that drink is the cause of
pauperism in 52 per cent. of the pauperism of his
union. It is not likely that this great difference is
warranted by the greater prevalence of drunkenness in Manchester; it is much more likely that it
is due to the extremely vague nature of the phrase
"cause of pauperism," and to the varying attitude
of different temperaments toward the vice of
drunkenness.

Again, with regard to questions of poverty, it is
notorious that many well-meaning men permit
themselves great latitude of expression. An
extreme case is that of a reverend witness before
a recent Royal Commission, who asserted that
many persons in his union had been "done to
death" owing to the neglect of the guardians in
giving relief. Naturally members of the Commission
pressed for chapter and verse. On inquiry it turned

out that some of those who, it was alleged, had been "done to death" were still alive and well, and apparently the term "done to death" was a mere *façon de parler*. This is an extreme case, for only the most hysterical controversialist will fail to distinguish between the living and the dead. Still, if excellent persons can be found to confuse the living and the dead, much more will they fail to be accurate over a matter so difficult to define as the relative degrees of poverty. Again, if we proceed beyond the bare fact of death and attempt to tabulate causes of death, the temperament of those charged with the enumeration plays us sad tricks. In a paper read to the Economic Section of the British Association of 1892, Mr. Loch drew attention to the fact that in the central division of London there were seventy-six deaths in 1873 of which the cause was alleged to be starvation, while in each of the years 1874 and 1875 there were only seven. A new coroner seems to have been appointed in 1874, and Mr. Loch is probably correct in suggesting that the difference is caused by a different interpretation of the term "starvation." Yet starvation is a more definite conception than poverty, and, though "Crowner's Quest Law" is not impeccable, the verdicts are arrived at with all the solemnity of judicial procedure. Indeed, the longer we look into the matter, the more certain does it become that the primary figures on which the whole inquiry turns are unverified and unverifiable. Occasionally attempts have been made to verify by an independent investigation, and, as might have been expected, no two enumerators have produced the same results. Each fresh inquiry brings out an answer not only absolutely different, but showing great relative differences between the various subdivisions. Mr. Loch tells us that, being struck with what appeared to him unduly high percentages of poverty in certain districts as given by Mr. Booth, he caused an independent inquiry to be made. In three areas in Marylebone Mr. Booth's figures were 60·2, 39·9, and 52·5. Mr. Loch's informants, who included the relieving officers, were unanimous that the poverty of the middle district was markedly greater than that of the first district, and that both were poorer than the third district. Similar results attended similar inquiries made in Clerkenwell, and in Haggerston and Hoxton.

We have no wish to press the accuracy of Mr. Loch's informants as against Mr. Booth's; though possibly it might be argued that a relieving officer is a better judge of the poverty of a neighbourhood than a School Board visitor. All we desire to urge is, that no two persons, however impartial, are likely to agree in their manner of arranging the minute subdivisions attempted by Mr. Booth.

The untrustworthy nature of the whole inquiry becomes more apparent when we turn to one of the postulates which Mr. Booth asks us to concede. The classification according to poverty, based on the notes of School Board visitors, covers only the portion of the population who have children of school age ; that is, about half the population. Mr. Booth asks us to concede that the remainder, *i.e.* the portion who have no children of school age, may be distributed, among the several classes of poverty, in the same proportions as those who have children of school age. Surely this is a most inconsistent demand. The moderateness or immoderateness of a man's family has, as we have seen, been a governing consideration in Mr. Booth's classification according to poverty. Let us suppose that a naturalist wished to classify animals according to their possession of a certain quality x. His observation extends over half the animals in a given area. He makes a discovery, which when once pointed out is indubitable ; namely, that the possession of quality x is largely dependent on the size and power of the tail ; and in absence of definite observation of the presence of the quality x, he has been guided largely by the size of the tail while classifying animals according to their possession of quality x. He then wishes to classify the other unobserved half of the animals. These, however, possess no tails, and one of his principal guides to their classification is therefore absent. Now, if the statistical argument of Mr. Booth is to be admitted, it would be safe to argue that the unknown and tailless half may be classified relatively to x in the same proportions as the known and tail-bearing section of the animals under consideration. Nowhere, we imagine, except in the exact science of statistics, would such a method be allowed to pass.

In his first work Mr. Booth made no practical suggestions. There was a vague reference to the advisability of "harrying" the poor into a more satisfactory way of life. It was not possible to suppose that Mr. Booth was in favour of penal legislation against poverty, and this ambiguous phrase was interpreted, by some at all events, to mean that the poor should be allowed to retain the privilege of confronting and overcoming their own responsibilities. At the end of the second volume of "Life and Labour," he leaves us with the assurance: "To the proposals for a revision of the poor law I shall return, but not until I am better equipped for its practical discussion." This not altogether precise announcement seemed to imply that Mr. Booth was going to give up his statistics for a season, in order to gain some practical experience of poor law administration. Both these interpretations proved to be erroneous, for, within a year, Mr. Booth's second work, on the "Endowment of Old Age," made its appearance. This contains proposals for amending the law for the relief of the poor in the most revolutionary manner. The responsibility of the poor for their old age is to be removed by a universal pension scheme. Under the guise of a benefit, this may prove, as some assert, a great injustice to the poor, but it is an abuse of language to describe it as "harrying." Either Mr. Booth under some new influence had changed his opinion, or his earlier language was singularly inappropriate.

In his second work Mr. Booth lays aside the office of statistician and becomes the advocate of limited and experimental socialism. Before leaving the statistical portion of Mr. Booth's labour, we may record our conviction that he has made a very gallant attempt to solve the insoluble. He has, in our opinion rightly, declined to consider poverty as a mere question of income. He has rightly treated it as a question of character and habit, but in so doing he has amplified the limits of his subject and carried it into regions altogether beyond the ken of the statistical method. Further, even if we could believe that some accuracy had been attained in spite of the difficulties of the inquiry, it is obvious that the results obtained are of no practical value whatsoever. If poverty were purely a question of income, we might say that by doubling every one's income, poverty would be made to cease out of the land, but the poverty chronicled by Mr. Booth is not economic poverty, but a much more complex thing, and we must consider it as affected by the standard of life current in different classes and even in different families, and by the multiform and often incomprehensible motives which govern the conduct of men. These problems remain, when our tabulation is accurate and complete, just as difficult and insoluble as they were at the outset.

Over the special method employed in this second work we may pass somewhat lightly. The descent of ladies with notebooks and pencils into various rural villages has produced much varied and interesting information ; but when reduced to percentages and decimal points, we hardly suppose that any serious person will attach much value to it. Here and in his last volume, " The Aged Poor : Condition," Mr. Booth relies mainly on the official returns. In this he is followed by Mr. Hunter and the author of " Plain Words."

Admitting for the sake of argument the substantial accuracy of the half-yearly returns and of Mr. Burt's return,[1] we still have the difficulty of interpreting these documents. For this purpose it is necessary to have a very full knowledge of the facts for which these figures stand, and here not unfrequently our statistical

---

[1] " Boards of Guardians : Persons in Receipt of Relief," No. 36. December 9, 1890. A return showing number, age, and sex of persons over sixty chargeable to the Poor Rate, etc.

friends will be found to fail. To take the most important example. In common sense, and presumably in statistical inquiry, a totally different value must be given to out-door and in-door pauperism. In many unions out-door relief is to be got by the aged for the asking; there is no strong feeling against claiming it among the poor themselves; it is a pension paid to the poor persons at their own homes, an addition to their all too limited incomes which it requires some strength of mind to decline. In-door pauperism, on the other hand, represents in most unions (with the exception of London, to be presently explained) the irreducible minimum of helpless and friendless old people. Throughout this inquiry, however, statisticians have been apt to treat all pauperism, whether out-door or in-door, as if it were of the same material. Yet in the view put forward by the most experienced poor law administrators the solution of this whole difficulty turns on the distinction between these two forms of pauperism. Thus, according to Mr. Burt's return, there were on August 1, 1890, 286,867 paupers over sixty years of age; of these 218,743 were out-door and 68,124 in-door. In reply to those who say that this total is excessive and that heroic remedies are necessary, the experts point to the administration of the Union of Bradfield, Berks. A very potent cause of pauperism,

they argue, is the offer of out-door relief. If this
is removed, both in-door and out-door relief will
be reduced. In 1871 there were in Bradfield 1258
paupers, 999 out-door and 259 in-door. In 1871
the policy of restriction began, and in 1893 the
pauperism had fallen to 121,—of these 99 were
in-door and 22 out-door, the latter being all old
people, whose vested interest in the allowances
given them under the old system has not been
disturbed. Very similar results have been obtained
elsewhere, wherever this policy has been applied.
It is argued, then, that if the country really wishes
to reduce its old age pauperism, the numbers can
be brought down by an application of the Bradfield
system from 280,000 to 60,000. On the merits of
this controversy, statistics, except so far as they
are involved in the elementary facts here stated,
can throw no manner of light, and yet it is obviously most important. As already remarked,
it is self-evident that if a union ceases to give
out-door relief, it will have fewer paupers, and
there remains only one question of interest : Is
this a humane and justifiable course to follow ?
Mr. Hunter and the author of "Plain Words"
have ignored the obvious strategical advantages
which a joining of this issue offers to the advocates
of out-relief, for, in this connection at all events,
sentiment is often a stronger force than logic, and
they attempt to show that increased facilities for

obtaining relief do not increase the number of those who accept it. Space does not permit us to follow them into all the arguments by which they support this paradox. One or two instances will suffice to show that the desired answer can only be obtained by an utter neglect of the facts for which the figures purport to stand.

Mr. Hunter divides the London unions into what he calls out-door and in-door unions. More than the average amount of out-door relief is given by thirteen unions, while seventeen give less and are classed as in-door. Now, every one who has the most superficial knowledge of the administration of the poor law in London is aware that the Guardians of Bethnal Green rarely refuse out-door relief. It is a matter of surprise, therefore, to find Bethnal Green among the in-door unions. The explanation is simple and instructive, and obvious to any honest inquirer who is not a perfervid statistician. The policy of Bethnal Green is neither in-door nor out-door, but simply a policy of allowing every man to choose for himself. During nineteen consecutive weeks (Jan. to May, 1894), 1767 admissions to the Bethnal Green Workhouse were recorded; of these only 162 went in on an order of a relief committee of the Board. The rest (1605) applied direct to the relieving officer, and became in-door paupers because presumably they preferred in-door to

R

out-door relief, though the last can be obtained for the asking by the settled poor. This is the more remarkable, because the Guardians of Bethnal Green have lived for many years in a perpetual state of controversy with the Local Government Board, by reason of the very inadequate equipment of their in-door establishments. If therefore the poor, of their own free will, enter the Bethnal Green Workhouse—which, though popular because of the general laxity of discipline, is still much below the average of comfort to be found in the London workhouses—it would follow that the same is done in unions where there are good infirmaries and clean accommodation. From inquiries made, we have no doubt that this is the case.

Mr. Hunter's contention that in London it is the refusal of out-door relief which drives the poor into the workhouse is obviously erroneous. As a matter of fact the comparatively high percentage of in-door to out-door relief in London is due, not to the restrictive policy of the guardians, but to other causes. With the exception of one or two unions, the policy of the London guardians is not one in favour of the restriction of out-door relief. The high rate of in-door pauperism is due to two causes: (1) the great improvement in the infirmaries and workhouse accommodation generally, in virtue of the provisions of the Metropolitan

Poor Law Act of 1867; (2) the large number of homeless poor who avail themselves of shelters and casual wards while they are well, and who crowd into the infirmaries when they are ill. Mr. Loch discusses the first cause at considerable length : he shows that the change in the law and its administration followed on the revelations of an inquiry known as the Lancet Commission, which had exposed serious shortcomings in our poor law establishments. He proves conclusively that the greatly increased expenditure which followed the Act of 1867 was due, not to a desire to restrict relief, but to a wish to make relief, more particularly relief to the sick and infirm, more adequate and more humane. As we have seen in the case of Bethnal Green, the poor are not unwilling to avail themselves of the relief offered in a workhouse. Secondly, the great numbers of the vagrant class are often overlooked by our statistical enthusiasts. It is assumed that a man who enters a workhouse or infirmary is torn from his home and family. In the great majority of cases nothing can be further from the truth. The facts revealed by the following extract from a return prepared for the Stepney Board, showing the number of persons admitted into the workhouse of the Union, is an interesting comment on this assumption.

ADMISSION CLASSIFICATION.

Return for Half-years.	Resident Poor.	Admissions from Shelters or Homeless.	Percentage of recent Arrivals in London on Total Admissions from Shelters.
	Per cent.	Per cent.	Per cent.
Ending Michaelmas, 1891	67·9	32·1	42·9
Ending Lady Day, 1892	59·3	40·7	46·5
Ending Michaelmas, 1892	59·3	40·7	42·2

A tabulation even more remarkable is the following from the Report of the Whitechapel Guardians for year ending Lady Day, 1895.

Whence admitted.	Workhouse.		Infirmary.		Total.	
		Per cent.		Per cent.		Per cent.
From their own or friends' homes ...	145.	2·7	726.	16·8	871.	9·1
Homeless or from institutions	1658.	31·5	320.	7·4	1978.	20·6
From lodging-houses	1945.	37·0	2088.	48·3	4033.	42·1
From shelters... ...	1156.	22·0	926.	21·4	2082.	21·7
From casual wards ...	153.	2·9	144.	3·4	297.	3·1
Remands from police-courts	205.	3·9			205.	2·2
Born in infirmary ...			118.	2·7	118.	1·2
Totals	5262.		4322.		9584.	

The strict London Unions—Whitechapel, Stepney, and St. George-in-the-East—in order to put aside the reproach of inflicting hardship, have

expended much money and care on their infirmaries and workhouses ; and on this very
account, as well as owing to the character of the
neighbourhood, these East-end unions collect more
than their share of this vagrant population.[1] In
unions where out-door relief is freely given,

[1] As proof of this invasion of the Union of Whitechapel by
Shelters, and its effect on poor law statistics, the following table
is quoted from the Whitechapel Guardians' Report, Lady Day, 1895.

Shelters.	No. of Admission Orders given by District Medical Officers.
Salvation Army Shelter for men, 272, Whitechapel Road	294
Salvation Army Shelter for women, 194, Hanbury Street	279
Salvation Army Shelter for men, Quaker Street	83
Salvation Army Shelter for men, Royal Mint Street	55
Church Army Shelter for men, 83, Whitechapel Road	11
Jewish Shelter, 84, Leman Street ...	2
Barnardo's Shelter for women, 12, Dock Street	30
Barnardo's Shelter for women, 81, Commercial Road...	54
Tenter Street East Philanthropic Shelter	22
Wood Street Church Army Home	—
Working Lads' Institute, 137, White-chapel Road	—
Pelham House, Spital Square ...	—
Total ...	830

workhouse accommodation is still, to a section of paupers, more attractive than out-door relief. Naturally in such places the rate of pauperism does not rapidly diminish. The author of "Plain Words" devotes a section of his pamphlet to showing: "Why 1852–1853 should be taken for purposes of comparison with 1892–1893." We need not trouble the reader with his reasons. The insuperable objection to this procedure is that previous to 1867 there was no attractive in-door accommodation. Now, the workhouse, the infirmary, and the schools have their attractions; and, except in one or two instances, the guardians are almost as lavish of out-relief as ever they were.

To proceed with our indictment of Mr. Hunter's method. Having grouped together Bethnal Green and Whitechapel, which represent the opposite extremes of poor law policy, he uses the figures obtained from this incongruous classification to point a moral against the administration pursued in Whitechapel. Let us next consider the tests which he and the author of "Plain Words" use in judging between different methods of administration. They have relied chiefly for the purpose of these comparisons on (1) the number of paupers per head of population; (2) the cost per head of pauper. Now, if it can be shown that these tests are clearly fallacious in one instance, it is obvious that they are not trustworthy in any, unless supplemented by information which is not statistical. Mr. Loch has pointed out that in 1871 the population of West Ham Union was 99,143, and its pauperism was high, 59·5 per 1000. In 1891 its population was 365,130, and its pauperism seemed to be low, 21·8 per 1000. The policy of the Union has not been changed in the interval. It is and always has been an out-relief Union. The actual number of paupers was 5904 in 1871. In 1891 it was 7964. The addition to the population was mainly due to the immigration of able-bodied artisans altogether above the pauper class. Yet by the test proposed, the decreased rate of pauperism per head of population would be used as an argument in defence of the method of administration followed at West Ham. The administration may be good or may be bad, but this is not the way to prove it. In poor and central parts of London the fluctuation of population is all in the other direction. In St. George-in-the-East the population is decreasing, owing largely to the emigration of the more prosperous and adventurous labourers. These considerations demonstrate the fallacy of this method of direct comparison.

The cost per head of paupers is put forward as the next test. Again we take our disproof of its efficacy from Mr. Loch. An inspection of the following table will be enough.

	Population.	Total Relief.	No. of Paupers.	Cost per Head of Paupers.		
		£		£	s.	d.
Bishop's Stortford (Herts)	21,513	12,798	1,275	10	0	9
St. Neot's (Hunts)	15,238	3,803	253	15	0	7

Mr. Hunter argues that unions where the cost per pauper is low, have an advantage over unions where it is higher. The above instance clearly shows the worthlessness of the test. A large number of paupers inadequately relieved would by this method of judgment be preferred to a small number adequately relieved. The author of "Plain Words" ingeniously goes out of his way to complain that the official statement of the cost of in-door and out-door maintenance takes no account of sums spent on "workhouse and other loans repaid and interest thereon, on salaries, rations, and of officers, assistants, and servants," and on "other expenses of or immediately connected with relief." This, he thinks, should be added to the cost of in-door maintenance as officially stated. But we have seen that the policy of improved and more costly in-door management has no necessary connection with the policy of restricting out-door relief, and in many instances it has been adopted without any departure from the old plan of giving out-door relief to all who press for it.

We now return to Mr. Booth's latest volume, "The Aged Poor : Condition." In the first pages he explains that the demand for "trustworthy official statistics" has been satisfied by the production of Mr. Ritchie's Return (No. 265). This shows, classified according to age, *the number of paupers relieved on January* 1, 1892, *and the total number relieved during the year ended at Lady-day*, 1892. This return, Mr. Booth contends, confirms his own calculations ; and Canon Blackley, who also deals largely in estimates, wrote to *The Times* of May 22, 1894, to claim a like confirmation of his own figures. He specially bases his reputation for correctness on the return furnished by St. Saviour's, Southwark, where the rate of pauperism among the population of those over sixty-five years of age is alleged to be eighty-four per cent.

Now, it is not often that an answer in figures bears its own refutation on the face of it. This return of Mr. Ritchie's, however, seems to be one of these few exceptions. In the preliminary memorandum we are informed of some of the difficulties that stood in the way of getting a correct yearly census of pauperism. In one London union the calculation took six weeks of continuous work. First, there were the duplicates for the two half-years to be eliminated, then the duplicate entries in each separate establishment, then the duplicates arising from paupers who have been in more than one part of the workhouse. It has been frankly admitted by not a few clerks to the unions, that the yearly census portion of the return is altogether untrustworthy. Among others, the clerk to St. Saviour's Board has admitted in a letter, quoted publicly by Mr. Loch, that the duplicates were not rigorously excluded in his Union. One difficulty, it may be pointed out, is quite insuperable. We have it on the authority of one union clerk that a certain pauper, who at the time of the return was in the infirmary of a London union, declared that he had left Darlington fourteen weeks earlier in the year, and during the interval he had been in the following workhouses (not casual wards) : Northallerton, Knaresborough, Birmingham, Burton-on-Trent, Market Harborough, Leicester, Bedford, Luton, Barnet, Holborn, Strand, and several others on the road which he had forgotten ; say, roughly, fourteen different workhouses in as many weeks, or fifty in a year. Such a man is in himself a perfect stage army of paupers.[1] The absurdity of the affair reaches a climax when we take the figures recorded of St. George-in-the-East. Here the number of paupers over sixty-five years of age during the year is alleged to be 2863 ; but as

---

[1] According to Mr. Pyddoke (Report of Whitechapel Board, 1895), the casual ward population " is made up for the greater part of the same men coming back again and again, and can only include a few thousands for the whole of London." A few thousand men will make a very imposing stage army, if they are counted often enough.

the estimated population of that age is only 1600, these figures proved too much even for the most omnivorous statistician. On p. 96, Mr. Booth puts down the percentage of old age pauperism in this Union at 66 per cent. of the population of that age. He has evidently used a different set of figures, which we understand has been supplied privately to the Royal Commission on the Aged Poor by the authorities of St. George-in-the-East. One glaring error has thus been detected and admitted, but there is no evidence that the remainder of the figures are more accurate, and we have positive evidence with regard to Southwark that they are quite untrustworthy. Surely in this affair the statisticians are hoist with their own petard.

On p. 100, Mr. Booth remarks that "the results attained are chiefly negative." Yet, on the next page, certainly in very obscure language, he suggests a solution of a controversy which, as we have already shown, is probably the most important in all this matter. He sums it up again on p. 423, in these words : "Remarkable instances of successful administration are to be found with any proportion of out-relief from over 80 to under 7 per cent." The statement and the argument are full of ambiguities and of unwarranted assumptions, such as could only be made by one who is stubbornly blind to the heterogeneous nature of the figures which he manipulates. "Successful administration" is assumed to mean an administration which yields a low rate of pauperism irrespective of the population with which it deals. He therefore compares without flinching Wharfedale with Bradfield, Oxford with Bridlington, Manchester with Dunmow. It would be instructive to analyse the different character of the pauperism and of the population in all these unions, but space obliges us to confine ourselves briefly to one instance. Let us take at random Fylde and Bradfield, the first and last names of the list on p. 101. Fylde, according to Mr. Booth, gives 65 per cent. of its relief out of doors, and has 2·2 per cent. of pauperism. Bradfield gives 18 per cent. out of doors, and has 1·7 per cent. of pauperism. Here Mr. Booth has struck out a new line of error for himself. Contrary to the usual custom, he has, in reckoning the percentage of out-door to total pauperism, taken the cost and not the numbers of out-door pauperism,— a method which, as already shown, must in the case of inadequate out-door relief prove quite untrustworthy as a true test of policy. Thus Bradfield gives 18 per cent. of its relief to 22 old persons, or an average of 3s. 1d. per person per week. Fylde gives 65 per cent. of its relief to 374 persons, of whom 170 are children, *i.e.* about 1s. 7d. per week each. The method used in this comparison obscures the different nature of the pauperism in the two unions.

Next, as to the population. Fylde is a Union

where there has never been a high rate of pauperism. It contains a rapidly growing and flourish-
ing watering-place, Blackpool. An immigrant
population is not one in which much pauperism
is to be found. The rural parts of the Union have
been described in some detail by Mr. Wilson Fox
for the Royal Commission of Agriculture. "There
are few labourers' cottages, . . . because many of
the farmers employ no labour, and those who do
usually have hired men who live and board in
the farmhouses. . . . These are unmarried men."
Bradfield, on the other hand, up to 1871, was
administered on the policy which now prevails in
Fylde, and had, as already stated, a high rate of
pauperism. This has been reduced to a low percentage by a change of administration. Bradfield
is a rural district, with a stationary population ;
wages are low ; there is a large number of labourers'
cottages, and the small farmer cultivating his land
with assistance from his family and without hired
labour is almost unknown. There is no inducement
to the labourer to defer marriage in the hope of
acquiring a farm, as in Fylde. The conditions of
tenure and labour are thus totally different. Mr.
Booth's procedure entirely evades the point of the
experts' argument. If in a union where pauperism
is naturally high, it can by administration be
reduced to the low percentage shown at Bradfield,
much more, they argue, could the naturally low

pauperism of Fylde be reduced to vanishing point by an adoption of the Bradfield system. The argument may be answerable, but Mr. Booth neither answers nor attempts to answer it.

No candid student of the subject can fail to see the fallacy of these promiscuous comparisons.

On p. 103 (and here we are glad to agree with him) Mr. Booth refers to the desirability of having some test by which the general poverty of one district can be compared with another. He suggests density of population, but this gives no sort of indication of prosperity or adversity except in the few places which are clearly overcrowded, and it assists us not at all with the rural districts. What we really want is to get some measure of the relative proneness to pauperism in various districts. We very much question if this is possible. Mr. Loch has suggested a method of correcting the recorded rates of pauperism in such a way as to make it possible to compare union with union; but his device, though ingenious, only professes to remove the uncertainty arising from a fluctuating population. This, we have seen, is only a small part of the problem. Differences of race, of land tenure, of industry, depressions of local trade either permanent or temporary, are matters with which the most highly trained arithmetical fancy must fail to deal. We cannot devise any substitute for experience, common sense, and detailed analysis.

To one other of Mr. Booth's conclusions drawn from his "negative results" we think it necessary to draw attention. On p. 422 he writes :—

"The improvement shown in the decade 1881–1891 is greatest in Wales and the West. Wales on the whole represents an out-door, and the border counties an in-door, policy. In both divisions the rate of improvement is the same, thus suggesting that it is the result of causes other than policy of administration."

No one, so far as we are aware, has ever argued that administration is the sole cause of the rise and fall of pauperism ; but it is idle to maintain that the varying degrees of facility with which relief is administered can fail to have an effect on the numbers who receive it.

On p. 505 we get some indication of the way in which the above conclusion is reached. "In Wales itself out-relief is given very freely, but among the border counties the original example of Sir Baldwin Leighton's administration of Atcham has had a great effect." This, as far as we can judge, is the only argument used to show that the border counties pursue an in-door policy. The union with which Sir Baldwin Leighton was officially connected was the Atcham Union. Here, on January 1, 1893, the proportion of out-door paupers to in-door was as 1 to 6·7. The unions of the border counties selected by Mr. Booth as illustrations of the policy of the late Sir Baldwin

Leighton show, according to his own statement, a proportion of out-door to in-door paupers of nearly 4 to 1. They are, in fact, illustrations of the result of a policy exactly the opposite of that advocated by the late chairman of the Atcham Union. Of course, if we permit ourselves to classify according to our view of what might be, but evidently is not, the sphere of influence of a gentleman who has been dead for twenty-three years, whose estate lay partly in Wales and partly on the Welsh border of Shropshire, who was therefore no more responsible for the unions of the border counties (other than Atcham) than for those of the Welsh counties which were nearer his home, there need be no limit to the conclusions to be drawn even from negative results. This may be statistics, but it is not common sense.

The history of the Union of Atcham contains a singular episode. In 1871 the urban Union of Shrewsbury, with a population of 25,753, was thrown into the rural Union of Atcham, with a population of 18,313. Up to this date Shrewsbury had been an out-relief Union, with a comparatively high rate of pauperism. After the amalgamation the stricter policy of Atcham prevailed, and in 1873—within, that is, two years—the pauperism of Shrewsbury fell to the level of that of Atcham, and has continued to fall ever since. The following figures are exclusive of lunatics and vagrants:—

	Out-door.	In-door.	Total.	Percentage of Out-door to Total Paupers.	Percentage of Paupers on Population.
Jan. 1, 1871. Atcham	129	138	267	48·3	1·4
Shrewsbury ... ... (Still separate unions.)	638	188	826	77·2	3·0
Combined Totals	767	326	1093	70·1	2·3
Jan. 1, 1873. Atcham (now including Shrewsbury) ...	264	283	547	48·2	1·2
Jan. 1, 1881. Atcham (now including Shrewsbury) ...	88	373	461	19·0	0·94
Jan. 1, 1893. Atcham (now including Shrewsbury) ...	52	352	404	12·0	0·83

It is difficult to avoid the conclusion that under the old system Shrewsbury had a maximum of pauperism, which under the policy followed after the amalgamation was speedily reduced to a minimum.

This last classification of unions by Mr. Booth can only be explained on the hypothesis that, no doubt quite unconsciously, he holds a brief for the party which, in its advocacy of State Pensions, argues that a reduction of pauperism is impossible by a careful administration of the poor law. Of

S

Mr. Booth's desire to be fair we have already spoken. But this last argument, bearing proof of its irrelevancy on the face of it, fairly takes our breath away. Is such reasoning due to the keenness of the advocate, or to the fact that Mr. Booth does not know, from concrete and practical experience, for what facts his figures stand? It is impossible not to admire the industry, public spirit, and good faith of Mr. Booth. At the same time the subject at issue has assumed national importance; and Mr. Booth is the last man to complain if those who distrust his figures and dispute his conclusions decline to swell the uncritical chorus of adulation which has accompanied all his efforts.

VI

THE POOR LAW AND CHARITY.[1]

ALL agencies for the relief of the poor should have two objects in view: (1) The relief of distress; (2) The removal of the causes of distress. It is sometimes said that the Charity Organisation Society concerns itself too exclusively with the prevention of pauperism, and that it is indifferent to the cause of abundant and adequate relief. On this criticism I will only remark that the bitterest element in the distress of the poor arises,

[1] A paper read at the fourth meeting of the Charity Organisation Conferences, London, May 17, 1893, on the "Co-operation of Charitable Agencies with the Poor Law." An apology may be thought necessary, for republishing a paper addressed to one particular form of society, without some attempt to enlarge its scope, and make it applicable to charitable societies generally. The answer is that as far as the author is aware, no other society has attempted to co-operate with the poor law, to the same large extent as the London Charity Organisation Society. Certainly no Society has done so much to attract public attention to this aspect of the question. It is, therefore, impossible to discuss co-operation of charitable agencies with the poor law without repeated mention of the Charity Organisation Society.

not from mere poverty, but from the feeling of
dependence which must of necessity be an
ingredient in every measure of public relief.
This feeling cannot be removed, but is rather
intensified by liberal measures of public relief.
This fact might in itself be justification for those
who would say, " The object of our efforts is not
only the relief of the poor, but their independence."
There is a section of the well-to-do classes of
society who, unfortunately, limit their conception
of their duty to their poorer neighbours to relief,
and plenty of it, from legal or from voluntary
sources. It is in their view the ransom due from
those who are well to do in this world's goods.
There is a section also among the poorer classes
who have a vague feeling of some injustice which
depresses them. It is foreign to the purpose of
this paper to discuss how far this feeling of resent-
ment is justified. It is mentioned only to remark
that this feeling sometimes makes itself felt by
demands on the poor law for forms of relief which
have been already tried and condemned in the
experience of the past. It is worth notice that
such demands, as a rule, are for " work, not
charity," and that among the poor themselves little
or no support has been given to a mere policy
of extensive relief, such as making the old age
maintenance of the community a charge on the
rates. What the poor want, they say, are better

wages and better conditions of life. Controversy, of course, rages as to what is the best course for the poor to follow in this quest. The Society, unpopular though it may be with the working class, can yet distinctly claim to have them on its side in this matter. Its business is to insist, in the hearing of all men, that independence is a nobler ideal than any form of dependence, however adequately and abundantly relieved.

As a further justification of the practical wisdom of its attitude in aiming at the independence as well as the relief of the poor, it may point to the fact that during the fifteen years covered by the last report of the Statistical Abstract, 1877–91, the invested savings of the working class have risen from 111 millions to 220 millions.[1] Here is a new creation of wealth, not arising out of the confiscation of other men's goods, but owned and acquired in accordance with the laws of our country and the principles of private property. Surely a process is here disclosed from which we can justly hope for the spread of the blessing of independence among our labouring class. Contrast this with the vague hopes held out that some species of common property will yet be devised which will make the acquisition of private property by the poor an unnecessary thing. I will not carry this controversy into other fields,

[1] For further particulars, see p. 189.

but in the province which it has made its own
the Society protests against the futile assumption
that the progress of the poor can be advanced
by inducing them to rely on the common property
which can be derived from the voluntary bene-
factions of the rich, or from the enforced contributions of the taxpayer.

The Society has, however, taken up no
doctrinaire position; its subject matter is the
charitable effort of the community at large, and
if it can be shown that there is no adequate
provision made for a certain form of distress,
the Society, as is shown by its recent report on
the condition of the feeble-minded and epileptic,
is ready to advocate an extension of charitable
effort.   In the case cited, a certain form of
co-operation between the poor law and voluntary
effort is recommended.   It is suggested that
charitable agencies shall establish and manage
the necessary institutions for these unfortunates,
and that the guardians shall be permitted to send
patients there and pay for them out of the rates.
Under certain restrictions this form of co-operation
already exists, but I think I am right in saying,
that in every instance the persons in whose favour
this exceptional provision is made are, so to speak,
marked out and separated from the rest of the
community automatically or, as it is sometimes put,
by the "act of God."

By reason of this condition, it is obvious that we get rid of some very familiar difficulties in poor law administration; the capricious discrimination of guardians and the rankling feeling of injustice to which it gives rise; and, secondly, that deterioration of character which results when the poor are tempted, as they are by out-door relief, to qualify themselves for pauperism by presenting themselves in a real or feigned condition of destitution. It is the absence of these dangers that warrants the Society in urging that from one source or another ample provision should be made for this class.

Let us go a step further, and attempt to apply this automatic principle as a dividing line between two classes of pauperism :—

(1) Those who become paupers by fulfilling or accepting an automatic test. (*a*) Those afflicted by some congenital disabling disease, *e.g.* epilepsy, deficient intellect ; (*b*) those who accept in some shape or another the workhouse test.

(2) Those who are selected arbitrarily by guardians for out-door relief, and who in many cases (it is impossible to say how many) have been brought to their present condition by the attraction of a maintenance to be obtained without effort.

With regard to the first class of paupers—those determined by an automatic test—there is a very large field for the work of charitable volunteers.

As recommended in the Society's report already mentioned, charitable bodies may establish and manage institutions to which paupers may be sent. Volunteers may with great advantage visit the poor law institutions, schools, infirmaries, workhouses ; may organise employment for the old and infirm on the lines of the Brabazon experiment ; may take steps to help inmates of the workhouse to make a new start in life ; may by judicious interposition save young people from lives of pauperism ; and do a variety of kindly actions which it is impossible to enumerate.

Here the poor law and charitable agencies combine to assist the same person, and for the sake of clearness I will term this form of action *co-operation proper.*

A totally different account, and a totally different recommendation, is to be given in regard to the second class of pauper.

Those who have paid most attention to the question condemn the state of the law which permits a man to receive from the rates an addition to his income to be used in exactly the same way as a similar sum derived from wages or savings, on the sole condition that he can succeed in persuading guardians that he is destitute. It has been shown over and over again that relief given under these conditions is rarely adequate and is always demoralising.

Those, therefore, who wish well to the poor are anxious to reduce the evil results of the present law to the smallest dimensions. Their recommendation is simple. They say to guardians, Cease to give this demoralising form of relief, and allow such relief as may be required by people at their own homes to be administered by voluntary agencies. This form of co-operation I will call *the subdivision of labour* as between the poor law and voluntary agencies.

By this division of labour there will result, they argue, a great diminution in the burden borne by the poor law, and a great diminution also in the burden borne by charitable institutions, for a third agency will be called into existence, viz. the successful effort of the poor themselves. If these expectations are realised, if, by this policy, sickness, old age, premature death, and the ordinary risks of life are more and more provided against by the provident associations of the poor, it is obvious that the demand both on compulsory and voluntary funds will be a diminishing quantity.

For this reason there is a disposition to argue, by those who hold this view, that we should not commit ourselves irrevocably to the pro-position that the feeble-minded and the imbecile should be relegated to the care of the law and made a burden on ratepayers; for it is maintained that in the future—in the not very distant future, let us hope—the ordinary risks of life will be so fully provided for by the thrift associations of the poor, that the contributions of the charitable will be set free for extraordinary occasions of distress such as arise from epilepsy and deficient intellect.

This condition of affairs has not arrived. It is my task to show that this prospect of reformation is not Utopian. I will endeavour to do this by a brief reference to the past and present history of the subject. And at the outset let me insist on one point which I believe to be the governing truth in all this controversy. Reformation will not come from any jerrymandering of the poor law or charitable funds, but from the development of the poor man's capacity for a life of independence. All our administration of legal and voluntary relief should be made subservient to this idea, provided always that adequate relief is not thereby withheld.

The most serious crisis of poor law administration which this country has ever experienced was that previous to the Poor Law Amendment Act of 1834. The idea that an able-bodied working man could support himself and his family was regarded as chimerical. Every man received an allowance from the rates in proportion to the number of his children, and the employer obtained his services at a nominal wage. The single man or the man without a family was not employed, because the farmer or manufacturer had to pay his wages in full. The poorer classes of the country lived in a state of discontent and open rebellion ; land went out of cultivation because its produce was not sufficient to pay the rate. The country was brought to the verge of ruin. The Poor Law Commissioners inquired and reported on this state of affairs. Now what was their recommendation ? It was simple enough. Stop, they said, all out-door relief to the able-bodied. Throw the poor man absolutely on his own resources, and do not fear for the result. Their advice was carried into legislation, and, as all now admit, with the happiest results. It is hardly an exaggeration to say that we have got rid of the able-bodied pauper—or, to be more correct, and the distinction is important, we have got rid of those economic conditions which condemned the able-bodied man of that day to pauperism and dependence. Poor law reform does not war against the person of the pauper, but against the economic conditions which arise when the poor are encouraged to look to rates rather than to wages and savings for their maintenance, and against the formation of the parasitic habits of dependence, the necessary correlatives to this economic condition.

But to return. We have got rid of able-bodied

pauperism, but we are still struggling with a pauperism that is not able-bodied.

Let us review the situation briefly. Throughout a great part of the country, more especially in the rural districts, there is still a perfectly unbroken tradition of pauperism handed on from generation to generation. It is assumed that the labourer must become a pauper in his old age, in his time of temporary sickness ; that his widow and children must at his death become pensioners on the rates.

Is it possible for us, without inflicting undue hardship, to break this tradition ? and if so, how is it to be done ? Time does not permit me to elaborate all the detail of the argument. I will state, however, in baldest outline, the policy which I think has now become an integral part of the theory of those who support the Charity Organisation Society.

In the first place, we rely with absolute confidence on the precedent of the abolition of able-bodied pauperism. The only way in which the legislator or the administrator can promote the reduction of pauperism is by abolishing or restricting the legal endowments provided for pauperism. The country can have, there is no doubt of it, exactly as many paupers as it chooses to pay for. Abolish or restrict that endowment, or the more acceptable form of that endowment

—I mean, of course, out-door relief—and new agencies are called into activity, man's natural capacity for independence, the natural ties of relationship and friendship, and under this head I would include private as distinguished from public charity, for private charity in any real sense of the word is not a virtue practised toward a stranger, but arises out of the natural affection of neighbours, and proceeds on the gospel rule of seventy times seven, rather than on any pedantic weighing of merit and demerit. By the action of these forces pauperism, so to speak, evaporates.

I insist on this aspect of the question, for I think it is apt to be overlooked. The abolition or limitation of out-door relief is urged not merely because out-door relief can be best administered by voluntary agencies, but because its abolition restores men to their independence.

There are many subsidiary reasons why it is desirable that the poor law should confine itself to giving relief within the walls of some one of its institutions, and leave the relief to be given at people's homes to voluntary agencies; but I venture to think that the reason I have given is the paramount reason, viz. that this policy more than any other calls out the successful effort of the poor themselves. Every other consideration, though some of them are of great force,[1] is relatively trivial.

[1] To one of these other considerations I am conscious that I have

Now let me meet the objection which is at once raised to this. It is often said, but I think only by persons who have no practical experience of such matters, that there is no difference brought about by transferring the duty of giving out-door relief from a legal to a voluntary agency, and seeing no difference they ask what is the necessity for this. If we could secure really good boards of guardians, Professor Marshall has argued,[1] they would administer out-relief with quite as much discrimination as any Charity Organisation Society. This argument evades the whole point of our contention. We do not rely on the greater discrimination used by a voluntary agency. We

not, in the text, or perhaps elsewhere in this volume, done full justice. It is that the remedial power of personal sympathy is the only force which can counteract the enervating influence inseparable from all methods of relieving distress. Obviously this personal element cannot exist in a system of legal relief, nor is it easy to preserve its healing virtue in large schemes of public charity. This aspect of the question has been insisted on with great earnestness in the teaching and example of Miss Octavia Hill and many other devoted friends of the poor, and, in theory, at all events, its truth is fully recognised. Of the immense amount of good that is being done by quiet, indefatigable, personal effort, I am deeply conscious; if I have said less about it than it deserves, it is because my argument has been chiefly concerned to show the vast amount of harm that may be done by systems of legal and public relief, from which the element of personal sympathy is necessarily absent, and, as a consequence, more attention has been bestowed on proving the need of reform in a system of relief which creates distress, than on setting out the details of admirable and devoted work done in the relief of unavoidable and unmerited suffering.

[1] Nos. 5 and 6 of the *Economic Journal.*

rely on a much more efficacious protection, viz. the greater moderation of the poor in making claim on a charitable fund.

Legal relief seems to be, indeed is, the right of all the poor equally. All are "poor," that is, have an insufficient income ; application for relief, therefore, is made by all, or at all events by many more than will apply to a charitable fund.

The success which has attended the administration of the poor law in Bradfield and Whitechapel is often, and no doubt with justice, ascribed to administration, but it can never sufficiently be insisted on that the action of the poor law is purely negative—it is restriction, abolition ; the positive element in the reform is the quickened development of the spirit of independence among the poor themselves. This quickened development, again, rests on the fact (too often ignored by the mere theorist) that the moderation of the poor is such that they will not, except in case of necessity, apply for in-door relief, or for relief from the funds of a charitable society, if those funds are protected by a very slight exercise of discrimination and inquiry.

I am not merely theorising as to the existence of this moderation of the poor in pressing demands on charitable funds, as the following facts will show : In St. George-in-the-East the out-door relief

administered by the guardians in 1871 was £8916 ;
in 1874, £4391.   It is now a merely nominal sum,
and the local Charity Organisation Society is
giving relief at the rate of about £600 per annum.
The clergy of the Union are firm supporters of
the Society, and the indiscriminate almsgiving
is probably less now than in the old out-relief
days. As a matter of fact, moreover, the committee does not refuse many cases. The trade
of the Union is, on the whole, less prosperous
than in old days, owing to the decline of the
shipbuilding and sugar industries.   To what, then,
are we to attribute the fact that the Society
(which, I may add, has never refused a case for
lack of funds) has had to meet a demand so
comparatively slight?   They have never been
so absurd as to pretend that the diminution is
due solely to their greater industry in investigation
and discrimination. Far from it. It is due much
more to what I have termed the moderation of
the poor.

It has frequently been pointed out that it is
necessary to restrain the acceptance of poor law
relief by deterrent conditions.   There is something
repugnant to our feelings in this. I would have
it observed, therefore, that by relegating the
duty of giving relief to people at their homes to
voluntary agencies, the condition of deterrence
is replaced effectually by a much more honourable

and salutary safeguard—I mean the moderation of the poor themselves.

The offer of institutional relief, to which legal relief is by our proposal confined, will be said by some to be inhumanly deterrent. Such an opinion requires some qualification. It is urged by the Poor Law Commissioners, and ratified by common sense, that the condition of the pauper ought to be inferior to that of the poorest independent labourer. Now, the condition of the poorest independent labourer is poor indeed, and attempts to maintain the pauper at his own home, in a still inferior condition, result inevitably in inadequacy of relief. Juries occasionally find verdicts of starvation at inquests on the death of persons in receipt of out-door relief. Such a state of things cannot be thought satisfactory, and it is aggravated by the feeling of injustice which arises because all are not treated alike. There is no union where every one gets out-door relief. Some are everywhere refused. The inferiority of the pauper's condition ought not, on grounds of humanity, to be brought about by inadequacy of relief. What is the alternative? Nothing more than this, that the same measure should be given to all, namely, carefully managed and adequate relief within the walls of some poor law establishment. When the Irish poor law was created it was feared that the scale of maintenance

T

in the workhouse, which, relatively to the standard
of living of the Irish peasant, was ample, even
luxurious, would attract too many applicants.
Those who understood the question insisted that
there was no fear of that. The result proved
that they were right. The dilemma is a simple
enough one. It is desirable that the condition
of the pauper shall be inferior to that of the
poorest independent labourer. Will you effect this
by giving inadequate relief and half-starving the
pauper at his own home? Or will you not rather
import the necessary element of inferiority into
the lot of the pauper by attaching conditions of
restraint and discipline to an adequate and, on
the whole, comfortable maintenance? On grounds
of humanity, quite apart from the fatal influence
of out-door relief on the thrifty habits of the
people, can we have any doubt as to the best
choice in this dilemma?

There is no wish to pursue the pauper with
penalties. His destitution arises from the fact
that, from one reason or another, he has failed to
fit himself into the framework of free economic
society. If there are causes which have brought
him to this pass, removable, without injustice
to others, by legislation, by all means let them
be removed. In the mean time, his condition is a
misfortune; no legislation can reverse this verdict
and convert failure into success. Remedies are

only a choice of evils. Civilised society will not permit the unfit to perish, nor will it ruin itself by permanently fostering failure by giving it all the rewards of success. In a sound administration of the poor law it takes a third course. It gives a maintenance to failure more adequate than that which can be won by those who live on the border line between success and failure ; but, in order that this shall not be a premium on failure, it imposes conditions of discipline and restraint.

To return, however, to our proposed division of labour. Although it is true that the moderation of the poor and their latent capacity for independence will contribute largely to the success of this policy, still it is necessary that schemes of public charity should be conducted with care and discrimination. I can best explain my meaning by an illustration.

The heaviest year our Society ever had in St. George's was 1886, the year of the Mansion House Fund. This fund was raised amid great excitement and boundless advertisement. The idea of relief was in the air, and though some £2000 was expended in the district by the Mansion House Relief Committee, the only result was that a larger demand was made on other agencies. The moderation of the poor was, in this instance, and by the means above mentioned, broken down. The fund was happily only temporary, but its influence while

it lasted was very similar to the state of things
brought about by a permanent system of lavish
out-relief. The poor were kept in a state of
speculative ferment, and during the sittings of
the Mansion House Relief Committee application
for relief was made to it on behalf of about one-
third of the whole population.

Public charities of a permanent character
managed in this manner would, without doubt,
be very nearly as mischievous as out-door relief.
Public charity, therefore, should be administered
without ostentation, and under the safeguard of
full and deliberate investigation. In this way,
and in this way only, can the whole benefit of the
policy now advocated be secured. I use the term
public charity advisedly, for the action of *private*
charity, as already indicated, is not a matter to
be controlled by organisation societies, whose work
lies mainly with funds arising from endowments
and subscriptions, and from the donations of
the rich for persons unknown to them. Private
charity, in the strict sense in which I use the
term, is liable to error. A father may be over-
indulgent to a son, and a friend, by misplaced
liberality, may confirm a friend in unprofitable
habits ; but this is a form of error not to be dealt
with *ex cathedrâ* by any organ of public criticism.

The co-operation of the poor law with charitable
agencies, as carried out in three of the poorest

unions of London—Stepney, Whitechapel, and St. George's—was commended in the report of the Select Committee of the House of Lords, and the experiment is often quoted in poor law discussions. There is, however, one misapprehension on the subject which I should like to correct. The reform of the poor law in these three unions was begun and carried out before our system of organised charity had taken root in the soil. The poor law reform in Whitechapel and Stepney began in 1870–71. The first report of the Tower Hamlets Pension Committee is dated 1878. In 1879, the Whitechapel and St. George's Committees had not even separate offices, and at an earlier date there was only one Committee for the whole of the Tower Hamlets, which used to meet in a little room in Philpot Street.[1] We have been enabled to extend and consolidate our operations because the poor law guardians have taken the

[1] The following note has been supplied to me by Mr. Loch with reference to the early history of the Society in the East End :—

The East End Inquiry Committee was opened in February, 1871, and continued to be the only office for five of the East London poor law divisions (viz. Whitechapel, St. George-in-the-East, Poplar, Stepney, Mile End Old Town) till February, 1873, when the joint Whitechapel and St. George-in-the-East Committee and the Poplar Committee were formed. The East End Inquiry Committee became in April, 1873, the Stepney and Mile End Old Town Inquiry Committee. In March, 1875, separate Committees were formed at Whitechapel and St. George-in-the-East, and they continued to make use of only one office. In April, 1875, separate Committees were formed in Stepney and Mile End Old Town.

first step and confined themselves to giving in-door relief only.

It is impossible to make any subdivision of labour till the more powerful party to the agreement has become satisfied of its necessity. I argue, therefore, that poor law guardians must take the first step, under a profound conviction that, whether there be an organisation of charitable agencies, or whether there be none, they have no right to withhold from their union the benefit of sound administration. As a matter of fact, there can be no doubt that, if guardians have the courage and disinterestedness to face this reform, there will also be found among them men of sufficient position and energy to organise the charitable agencies; but I confess there seems to me to be very little to be done till the policy of guardians is animated by a profound conviction of the necessity of reform.

At the same time, though I must insist that the initiative lies with the poor law authorities, I think that our organisation of charity has been of service in strengthening the party of reform on the various boards. Guardians are able to say that provision has been made to deal with exceptional cases, and they have not been deterred from continuing to the union the enormous benefit of a sound administration. They have never (and this is a danger to which I desire to draw attention) asserted a right to choose our applicants for us, or to override our decisions. The two bodies are entirely distinct, and there is no publicly ratified compact between us. The only bond between us is that we both believe that by the tactics pursued the poor are learning to do without the help of either of us.

The proposal of Professor Marshall, that Charity Organisation Societies should be recognised as a part of the legal machinery of public relief, would, therefore, be fatal to our usefulness. The co-operation which we advocate is, therefore, more a division of labour than co-operation pure and simple. It consists in this, that the poor law should confine itself to institutional relief; as a result the greater part of the out-door legal relief now given will be rendered unnecessary by reason of the increased independence of the poor, and the remainder is so small in amount that it can be dealt with by voluntary charity.

The administration of the poor law and of voluntary relief should go hand in hand, animated by the common purpose not only to relieve adequately, but, as it has been well put, to make the influence of our relief system centrifugal, and not centripetal. When this purpose is not present in the minds of administrators, the most senseless and disastrous competition between the poor law and charity is set up.

The City of London is a contiguous Union to Whitechapel. At the time of the Lords' Select Committee the pauperism of Whitechapel was 16 per 1000. In the City it was 62 per 1000. A few years ago I made some remarks on this contrast, and I was taken to task by an influential City paper. This gentleman, it was said, is very badly informed about the City union. "Many poor persons have come into the City for the small charities which have hitherto been obtainable in different parishes, and it is hardly fair to compare the City" with other places. How far this is an exculpation of the City guardians I do not stop to inquire, but it does confirm my view that, where no definite division of labour exists, the larger and more numerous the charitable institutions, the greater the burden on the poor law. In the chaos here delineated both legal and voluntary relief act with an overpowering centripetal force, so much so that their warmest defenders can only excuse the authorities by saying, "What can they do? The place is a nursery for paupers."

Let me say a few words on the experience of those country unions which have reformed their poor law administration. In none of them, as far as I know, has there been established any Charity Organisation Society. The contrary is often asserted, but without foundation. A charity organisation society is very desirable, nay, even necessary, where there are a number of public charities and a large mass of population, but there is much less necessity for it in a sparsely populated rural district. The squire and the parson and the charitable persons of the neighbourhood ought to exercise their common sense, and if there be many of them there is no reason why, if they choose, they should not meet in a committee, but neither at Bradfield nor at Brixworth has this been found practicable or desirable. The late Mr. Bland-Garland told a friend of mine, who has repeated it to me, that when he became responsible for the administration at Bradfield he put aside a certain annual sum—£100, I think—which he was prepared to give away, in order to make the transition to a stricter system more easy. He added that in the first year the demand on his purse did not reach half that sum, and that in subsequent years it became gradually less.

Very similar is the information given to me by Mr. Bury, Chairman of the Brixworth Board. He has from his own resources, and from moneys entrusted to him, a small fund which he has used much in the way described by Mr. Bland-Garland. He is definitely of opinion that he would much rather not have any organisation society. It is not—there, at all events—necessary. I do not think I misinterpret Mr. Bury's opinion if I say

that he does not regard the reform of administration at Brixworth as a mere transition from
dependence on poor law relief to a dependence
on charitable funds, but rather that under the
administration for which he is responsible the poor
are successfully learning to achieve an absolute
independence for themselves. This desirable
result would be endangered if a charitable
committee were established permanently and
prominently before the eyes of the people. I
mention Mr. Bury's opinion and experience—
even though it may seem to show that co-
operation with charity is not necessary—because
it emphasises what I have already stated, viz. that
the *positive element* of reform in all this matter
is neither charity nor the poor law, but the spirit
of independence in the people themselves.

In the foregoing remarks I have advisedly
avoided going into detail. The first step in reform
is to convince the majority of a board of guardians
of the necessity of reform. The details of the
methods taken to give effect to the principle
must differ widely in each district and with each
board. It would be very desirable, I think, that
the Society should publish one or two statements
similar to the late Mr. Bland-Garland's paper,
"From Pauperism to Manliness." It would be
interesting to have an account of the success of
the cross-visiting system pursued in Manchester;

of the method of reducing pauperism by rigid investigation, as in Paddington; of the successful establishment of a provident medical society covering the whole union, as at Milton in Kent; of the history of efforts to affiliate provident societies to hospitals, with a view of making our hospital system the auxiliary, and not the hostile competitor, of friendly societies and doctors' clubs; of the efforts for the improvement and better management of the in-door establishments in Whitechapel and elsewhere, and a thousand other matters which will readily occur to you all. I hope this meeting may encourage both the London and the Provincial Societies in collecting and circulating in a readable form information on such points.

If time had permitted I should have liked to say a good deal on these matters of detail, but I hope I shall not be blamed for confining myself on this occasion to the larger aspect of the question. I have presented to you an ambitious programme—the reformation of public opinion on this whole question.

I do not disguise from you the difficulties, but to some minds its attractiveness is its difficulty, the splendid opportunity that it offers for being unpopular in a good cause. My reading of poor law literature has discovered to me one little bit of sentiment. It is where Sir G. Nicholls, to

whom as much as to any man the country owes
the reform of 1834, relates how, on his return
to his old home at Southwell, he was met in the
market place by a party of labourers, who shook
him warmly by the hand and thanked him for
having been their best friend. In a momentary
lapse from the dry, unemotional language of a
public official, he bids us imagine how "gratifying"
the incident must have been to one whose conscientious discharge of his duty had for years
made him one of the best abused men in England.

There is one element of encouragement which
I think worth mention ; there is no subject in
which there is a more complete unanimity of
opinion among persons who have made any
intelligent study of the question. Among the
recognised authorities there is absolute conformity.
The enemy in this case is ignorance and inexperience. There has been a disposition in the
past to relegate this matter to the "loose ends"
of society—to the unemployed busybody of the
leisure class. But the question is becoming urgent
—it is becoming a question for statesmen—and,
with the hour, let us hope there will come the
men of courage and insight. Hitherto the
politician has not helped us much, but rather
the reverse. Legislation of various kinds is
proposed, most of it of a mischievous character ;
but the debate is only just begun, and those who

have for years made study of this question must
not be silent. I confidently believe that we shall
be able to defeat the pessimism of those who
assume that inadequacy of wages and spendthrift
habits are ineradicable incidents in the life of the
labourer. We, at all events, cannot admit that
the only solution of this question is to be found
in conferring easy terms of pauperism on those
who were born for independence and freedom.

VII

PEOPLE'S BANKS.[1]

MR. H. W. WOLFF has recently put within the reach of English readers a most interesting account of the history and constitution of Co-operative Banks in Germany and Italy.[2] For fuller information on this subject the reader is referred to this excellent work. The object of the following pages is merely to discuss how far these institutions of popular credit are fitted to take a place among the provident associations of the poorer classes of this country.

Before considering any proposal for the establishment of popular credit, there is a preliminary question to be asked. What is the function of Credit in the wealth-producing mechanism of industrial society? No English writer seems to me to have apprehended this matter so profoundly, and at the same time explained it so lucidly, as Mr. H. D. Macleod, in his various works on the theory of banking and credit. Briefly, Credit is Capital. By means

---

[1] Reprinted from *The National Review*, January, 1894.
[2] " People's Banks." By H. W. Wolff. Longmans, 1893.

of credit a man is enabled to pass into currency as capital his mere promise to pay. The value of such a promise to pay rests on the trustworthiness and industry of the promiser, and on the general proposition that human effort properly applied is productive of harvest sufficient to reward all who contribute to the result. A man, therefore, who possesses credit capitalises his reputation, and acquires thereby a better equipment for the enterprise in which he is engaged. If the operation is successful, a solid addition to the wealth of the community is made; if it is unsuccessful, a certain amount of loss is sustained; but, as far as the country at large is concerned, it is immaterial whether the capital consisted in hard cash or material actually hoarded by the operator, or in credit advanced to him by other tradesmen, or by credit associations. Credit, and the vast addition to the national wealth thereby created, can only arise in a settled state of society. It is based on the general trustworthiness and the mutual confidence of the persons who avail themselves of its assistance. It depends on the general law that the punctual performance of contract is the rule and not the exception. A farmer trusts his seed to the ground in the assurance that the natural sequence of seed-time and harvest will be maintained. So the granting of credit in the ordinary business of the world is based on the assumption

that, if the industry of men of character and intelligence can be set in motion, a harvest of profit
will be reaped for all concerned—for consumer,
for labourer, and for capitalist. Human energy,
which in a highly-developed state of industry
can only be set in motion with the assistance of
capital (and in many cases the capital will take
the form of credit), is just as prolific a source of
profit or harvest as the action of the seasons in
agriculture.

The illustration most frequently given of the
beneficial results of a well-organised system of
credit is the banking system of Scotland. Mr.
Macleod has pointed out that 150 years ago Scotland was perhaps the most backward country in
Europe. She owes her advance from this state of
barbarism, in part at all events, to her judicious
use of the instrument of credit. The broad fields,
which are now the scene of the most scientific
farming in the world, were then many of them
barren heath and swamp. The men were there
and the land was there ; but there was no realised
capital for the development of the country. At
this juncture the banking system of Scotland
stepped in, and by supplying the first instalments
of capital in the form of credit, laid a permanent
foundation for the agricultural industry of Scotland. Agriculture was, as the event has proved, a
field in which there was profitable employment for

labour and capital. Even at the present day the Scotch farmer receives a considerable amount of assistance from the bank on what is known as the "Cash Credit" system, and the additional capital so imported into the industry is without doubt an advantage to all concerned. In contemplating the finished result of this effort we must not overlook the fact that progress has advanced gradually in the wake of successful experiment. The beginnings were small, and the originators of the system had little thought of the vast possibilities of the business which they were founding. Every advance has been tentative, till proved successful by experiment. The actual process may be briefly described. In the rural districts of Scotland there was no capital available to carry on agriculture on improved methods. A bank agent appeared on the scene, the emissary of some great corporation with head offices in Edinburgh. A box of bank-notes was sent down to him from the capital. The notes were of the value of £1, and were repayable in gold on demand. The farmer went to the bank agent with such security as he could command: his lease (according to the Scottish custom) of nineteen years, the guarantee of a friend, or merely with his reputation as an honest man. The bank accepted the security, and put a sum at the "Cash Credit" of the farmer. Against this he drew cheques which were paid to him in notes ; with these he paid

U

for wages, machinery, manure, and the apparatus of agriculture. If this form of enterprise had been unsuccessful the banks would have withdrawn their assistance after a few experiments and with a trifling loss. Obviously, therefore, the real security for this most important development of credit has been, not the technical security obtainable in each case, but the probability, which, in process of time, grew to a certainty, that in nine cases out of ten a competent, trustworthy man could, under given conditions employ capital profitably. It is the business of a dealer in credit to study these conditions scientifically. Naturally, experiment is his chief source of knowledge, and he discovered, *ambulando*, that credit or capital could be advantageously advanced to trustworthy persons engaged in agriculture.

The dealings of Scottish banks with the farmer have admittedly been of great service to the country, and justify Mr. Macleod's comparison of them to the fertilising waters of the Nile. Through their instrumentality men who would otherwise have remained labourers or farmers, struggling vainly against a climate and soil by no means naturally productive, have been given the means of turning a wilderness into a fruitful land. Apart from the economical aspect of the question, it is worthy of note that, when the banks found they could do sound business by advancing money to farmers of skill and trustworthiness, there arose a demand for men of that stamp. It would be curious, and perhaps profitable, to inquire how far the premium thus set upon character has been conducive to creating that solid trustworthiness which is the proverbial possession of the Scots middle-class. There is very little in the earlier annals of Scotland to lead one to expect that the character of her people would be developed so conspicuously in this direction, and one is tempted to hazard the conjecture that here is one of those harmonies of social adjustment which ever follow on freedom of enterprise and freedom of trade.

The Scottish system of banking, however, has not succeeded in putting credit at the disposal of the mere labourer. Are we, therefore, to conclude that there is no form of industry in which the labourer can use capital so as to preserve his capital intact, and in addition earn enough to pay wages and interest? This is the problem which Mr. Wolff's interesting volume invites us to consider. It is his contention that People's Banks as they are organised in Italy and Germany have taken a very important step forward in the solution of this difficulty.

We need not complicate the comparatively simple issue now before us by discussing the right of banks to issue notes. This is a very important question; but it is not immediately relevant to our present purpose. The Italian and German popular banks have not, as I understand, any right of note-issue. The credit which they themselves require in order to give assistance to their humble constituents is obtained from larger banking institutions, and this practically comes to much the same thing.

The popular banks operate principally among the peasant proprietors. There are no peasant proprietors in this country, and, as we have seen in the case of Scotland, agricultural credit is duly provided by our commercial banks. As far as agriculture is concerned there has been in our own country no very crying evil to amend. It has been otherwise in Germany ; and in inventing a remedy men appear to have hit upon an expedient which will prove useful over a far larger area than that in which it was originally intended to serve. The following quotation from Mr. Wolff will best describe the crisis :—

"Under this oppressive system," he writes, "in 1846–1847 the 'Jews' were making hay. Among the poor peasantry the distress was great. And the peasants' distress was the Jews' opportunity. Every little wattle-cottage and tumbledown house was mortgaged ; most of the peasants' cattle belonged to the Jews . . . famine and ruin stared the poor inhabitants in the face. There was no one to turn to for help but the Jews. The whole district accordingly was converted to a usurer's hell. Naturally, Herr Raiffeisen's heart was touched at the sight of so much misery . . . he promptly resolved to take up cudgels for the poor oppressed peasants, and declared relentless war against the plague of usury."

After one or two minor experiments Herr Raiffeisen determined to establish a credit association.

" With a balance of the £300 which, in all, he had succeeded in raising with a good deal of trouble, in 1849 he set up his first Loan Bank, and offered the peasantry who would subscribe to his rules to supply them with money for their needs."

Briefly the " Rules " or principle on which this most successful enterprise is extending itself through Germany and Italy is the Co-operative principle, in its most elementary form. The maxim *Natura non facit saltum* has a very special application in matters of social economy. The proper use of credit is not learnt intuitively, but only by practise and experiment. To set up elaborate People's Banks, as was done by Proudhon and his associates at the Revolution of 1848, without first laying the foundations of mutual confidence and trustworthiness, was, as the result proved, to invite disaster. The Raiffeisen Co-operative Banks, like our own Friendly Societies, are not only business institutions: they actually create the feeling of mutual responsibility, to which alone they owe their success. All associated life is co-operation, though the fact may occasionally be concealed from our view. In ordinary commercial business the co-operation is automatic and unconscious. Lending and borrowing, for the purpose of bringing capital to bear upon production, can be equitably conducted when the parties thereto have learnt the true social or co-operative lesson, namely, that the whole system rests on the punctual fulfilment of contract.

When attempt is made to use the commercial principle between those who have not learnt this lesson many evils arise. This truth is exemplified by the strained relations which exist between the money-lender and the small cultivator, whether it be in Germany, Ireland, or India, by the failure of ambitious attempts such as that of Proudhon in 1848, and by the disinclination of the higher finance (*e.g.* the Scotch banks) to organise credit for the proletariat. In this last case the disinclination is due partly, no doubt, to the fact that full employment for banking resources in earlier times was to be found in lending to the upper and middle classes, and the organisation of petty credit has been neglected. From this neglect a certain degree of repulsion has arisen between the dealer in credit and the small borrower. There has been comparatively little competition, and a usurious, monopolist lender has begotten an evasive and untrustworthy borrower.

To some extent these difficulties have been overcome by the elementary co-operative system adopted by Herr Raiffeisen. The constituents who form his banks are set to learn the lesson of mutual confidence and personal responsibility, line upon line and precept upon precept. A few peasants bring together a portion of their savings. The mere fact of their combination under the Raiffeisen system entitles them to credit with larger financial institutions. Practically they have command of ample capital for their requirements. Loans are made to members of the association, the terms are ratified by all the solemnity of mutual agreement, and every unit of the association is morally and financially interested in the punctual performance of the contract. Great care is therefore taken that only honest and industrious men are admitted to membership, that loans are made only to those who are engaged in a reasonable enterprise, and that, when the loan is made, it is properly applied. Every nerve is strained to enforce these conditions, and the whole institution makes for the establishment of that mutual confidence which allows men to co-operate freely, with no capital more material than hope, in turning poverty into wealth. The mainspring in all the enterprise thus set in motion is a belief in the fruitfulness of human endeavour and the inviolability of contract.

If we may believe Mr. Wolff, some 150 millions sterling are circulated yearly by the Co-operative Banks in Germany alone, every penny of it used productively, and, for the most part, under the control of the poor man and for the benefit of his labour.

There is an analogy, worth remarking, between the success of this co-operative banking and the success of the Friendly Society movement in this country. It may not be necessary to assume that co-operation on the ordinary automatic principle of free exchange must always fail in dealing with the poor man in credit or in sick insurance; but at present it appears to be impossible for a money-lender to escape ruin if he lends at low interest, or for a commercial insurance company to survive the claims of malingerers if it undertakes to insure against sickness. It is well known that various highly-successful Life Insurance Associations have tried to undertake sickness risks, but have one and all abandoned the attempt as hopeless. The experience of sickness in the Centralised Friendly Societies, again, is considerably in excess of the experience in the Affiliated Orders, where the local supervision of claims is much more close and effective. It is no reflection on human nature to say that most men's desire to make their word as good as their bond is much assisted by the mutual supervision and advice which is the essence of co-operation in its narrower, and, as I contend, its more elementary form.

To sum up : There is much human enterprise, in its result most beneficial, which is set to work entirely in the hope of future profit. Credit is the essence of such operations. It is proved by our Scotch banking system that a desert can be converted into a fruitful land by a judicious extension of credit to a comparatively humble class, and that German peasants can be rescued from the hands of the money-lender by co-operative banking. It will be conceded that, *if possible*, similar facilities for advancing his position in life should be given to the artisan and to the agricultural labourer. The possibility is to some extent proved by the German and Italian experience, and I propose now to consider briefly such indications as seem to me to warrant the presumption that a development of credit associations would prove useful in English industrial life.

The precedents of foreign countries, as well as a certain natural fitness of things, point to agriculture as the most suitable field for an extension of popular credit. In the Report of the Royal Commission on Labour of Mr. W. E. Bear, Assistant-Commissioner, on the condition of the agricultural labourer in certain selected districts, some interesting details are given as to cottage-gardens and allotments.

"Small holdings under fifty acres are most numerous in proportion to population in the Union of Southwell, and next so in that of Melton. . . . The most prosperous small holders apparently are the makers of Stilton cheese in the Melton Union, and I am disposed to place next the few growers of fruit in a favoured part of the Thakenham Union, on the greensand. . . . On good soil for vegetables many occupiers of ten or more acres in the neighbourhood of St. Neots get a living, though they complain of hard times. . . . In the Hampshire district the small holders for the most part are said to pay their way."

Mr. Wilkinson, another Assistant-Commissioner, states that "allotments are generally plentiful, or, rather, the supply is generally equal to the demand." There is general testimony that this is the case all over the country. The main objection in the mind of the landlord is the greater difficulty which there is in obtaining fulfilment of contract with small men who do not, as a class, realise the sanctity of such engagements as fully as might be wished. The following sentence from Mr. Bear's Report is fuller of promise for the extension of small holdings than many Acts of Parliament.[1] Speaking of St. Neots, he says :—

[1] Under the old poor law it was usual for a certain class of speculator to build cottages and then to obtain a pauper tenant, for whom the overseers were directed to pay the rent. The system was liable to great abuse, and naturally made building for pauper tenants a safer speculation than building for independent labourers. Unless I am misinformed, a somewhat similar result has already, in some

"Twelve or fourteen years ago there were hardly any in St. Neots. When agricultural depression set in allotments increased. 'Could not let at £1 to farmers, so let at £3 to labourers.' This was the complaint. . . . That this complaint is natural will be admitted generally, although they do not make sufficient allowance for the value of land in a town. A rent of £3 to £4 an acre for good land close to the populous parts of a town— and it is excellent land round St. Neots — is not excessive."

Elsewhere Mr. Bear remarks that the rents of allotments at Basingstoke and St. Neots are very high, "while they are enormous near the town of Melton," where, as already stated, there is a profitable industry in cheese-making. Now, if a labourer can pay £3 an acre for land for which a farmer can only pay £1, it is to the interest of all parties that free trade should prevail. It means, in this, no doubt, exaggerated instance, that the production per acre in the hands of the labourer is 200 per cent. in excess of what it would be in the hands of the farmer. Exaggeration apart, it appears evident that there is a considerable impulse now being given to the

places, arisen with regard to allotments. Under the influence of the open market, landlords were more or less eager to let allotments to suitable tenants. There is a disposition now on the part of some landlords to decline this risk on the ground that their rents will be safer, if they let to the public authority, and allow it to bear the risk of sub-letting. The allotment acts are not easily put in motion, and the result, in some places, has been a check on the extension of the small holding system.

industry of cultivating allotments, and if a well-organised system of credit has been of service to the German peasant, there is no reason to suppose that it will be useless to the English labourer, who is engaged in a similar industry. An extension of credit associations would tend, moreover, to put the industry on a sound business footing. Allotments will never prosper if they have to rely on the protection of Parliament or the whim of philanthropic landlords. A man who means to fulfil his contract must scrutinise it before he engages, and in doing so it will be to his advantage to have the assistance and advice of a body of experts assembled in the parlour of the Co-operative Bank.

The opportunities of the labourer are not, however, confined to allotment. The profitable cultivation of a garden, which is, as a rule, an adjunct to a cottage let at a very low rent, could be very greatly aided by reasonable facilities for credit. It is precisely these small interests which the Co-operative Banks have been so successful in fostering. In parts of England, allotments *sub hoc nomine* are not given, but labourers acquire holdings under the less dignified name of cow-grass. On one particular estate in Shropshire the granting of cow-grass to labourers who are thrifty enough to save money to buy a cow has obtained with excellent, and in some cases astonishing,

results for more than one generation of proprietors.[1]

If there is ever to be a change in the set of
migration to the towns it must be caused by a
development of the opportunities for small men
to rise in life. At present all chances of advancement seem to be confined to the towns. There is
no reason to suppose that our large system of
cultivation will ever give way to a general adoption
of small holdings. Still, there is room for every
variety ; and, if small industry had the assistance
of a properly-organised system of credit, a new
career would be opened to talent which in time
would prove a very potent influence in staying
the tide of rural emigration.

There is perhaps less to be said with regard to
other branches of industrial life. Still, very considerable changes are coming about in the ownership of industrial property. Manufacture is now
organised on so gigantic a scale that ownership
on some joint-stock principle is becoming more
and more a necessity. The most useful application of the principle of credit is the setting of
otherwise idle men to work in the creation of
new wealth out of poverty. Still, credit may
play a legitimate part in helping to transfer

[1] See a remarkable table given by Mr. Cecil Chapmun, Assistant-
Commissioner, in his Report to the Labour Commission, headed,
" Particulars of Small Holdings supplied by Sir Baldwyn Leighton,
from his Estate at Loton." Appendix v., p. 141.

industrial property from one class to another. Some very interesting evidence was given by Mr. Hardern to the Labour Commission, on behalf of the working-class associations known as the "Oldham Limiteds." For some reasons these associations, which are joint-stock companies pure and simple, have been generally classed as part of the so-called co-operative movement. The only way in which an "Oldham Limited" differs from an ordinary joint-stock company consists in the fact that its shares are owned by working men —generally by working men who are engaged in other industries, and not by those who are in the company's service. I am informed that local banks have at times rendered considerable assistance in the financing of these working-class associations. Indeed, one of the objections alleged against these companies is the facility with which they obtain capital and the reckless competition thus engendered. The pecuniary interest of the officials and managers of these companies, it has been remarked, is principally their salaries. They are, therefore, less careful in some instances than they might be of the safety and profitable employment of the capital entrusted to them. It is their interest to carry on the business on any terms, rather than wind it up in the interest of shareholders whose capital is being diminished, and it is the interest of the banker, whose loan is more or less fully secured, to side with the manager rather than the shareholder. The result is reckless trading at a loss.

This, even if it be true, is a danger incidental to all joint-stock trading, and might form the ground of an indictment of the joint-stock company system ; but it contains no valid objection to the proper use of credit as an assistance to poor men towards creating or acquiring industrial property. If working men can, with the assistance of banking credit, establish mills at Oldham, and work them successfully, there is no reason why they should not do so elsewhere. If, as is alleged, the present state of the law as to joint-stock companies is unsatisfactory, by all means let us alter it, and put all trading on the same reasonable footing of responsibility, based on freedom of trade and freedom for all lawful forms of contract. It would undoubtedly be conducive to a better tone of commercial morality, if the advantage of credit were obtainable, not merely on the faith of material securities, and, in the last resort, legal remedies, but that in addition the financial association should, as in the case of the co-operative banks described, rely on the reasonable nature of the enterprise in which the borrower is engaged, and on his good faith and ability to carry it to a successful issue. The paradox that personal security, properly understood, and fortified by the responsibility bred from a truly co-operative system, can be made the very highest security of all, will prove a hard saying to the ordinary man of business. It has, however, commended itself as a profound truth to an economist as little given over to illusions as M. Léon Say, who lays it down that the best form of credit for banking purposes is purely "personal credit"—"*le crédit tout court sans phrase.*" "*Le crédit sur gage n'a jamais été que l'enfance du crédit.*"

Leaving the question of the large industry and the part which credit may play in transferring property from the manufacturer to the labourer, a few words may be said on the opportunities for petty trade, which are probably much more frequent than is generally supposed. I have before me an account of a Costermongers' Co-operative Loan Association, which appears to transact a considerable loan business every year with little or no loss. Many of my readers can, I have no doubt, supply other illustrations from their own observation of the advantage of credit judiciously employed in aid of men of small means. It was remarked to me by a gentleman who has an unrivalled experience in savings bank business, that over and over again depositors have come to him and said that the £5 or £10 which they saved in his bank had been the foundation of their fortune.

So much impressed was he with the apparent frequency of these openings for the profitable investment of small savings, that he had drawn the perhaps somewhat large conclusion that it was better for a workman to deposit his savings in a bank, in preference to sinking them beyond his control in a sick benefit club or other insurance association. Now, if the thrifty character represented by the £5 or £10 thus saved could command not only that sum, but in addition a credit of perhaps a similar amount, together with the advice, supervision, and assistance of a co-operative credit association, is it not obvious that a wider door of advancement is opened to talent and a new element of hopefulness brought to bear on the humble ambitions of working-class life?

A practical question still remains. If it be conceded that the establishment of popular banks is an experiment worth trying, who are the persons to whom this most promising enterprise can be most fitly entrusted? Is it possible that existing savings banks can take any part in making the savings of the poor reproductive?

A very interesting controversy has for some years been carried on in France by M. Eugène Rostand, the president of the Savings Bank of Marseilles, with a view of getting the Government Banks to do something toward promoting popular credit. The savings bank system of France is

X

very similar to our own. The money collected by the banks finds its way into the Caisse des Dépôts et Consignations, just as with us the savings of the poor are placed in the hands of the Commissioners for the Reduction of the National Debt. ·The money so gathered is used to purchase government securities, consols, exchequer bills, and, in France, the "rentes" of the Republican Government. Such employment is, of course, the very negation of the useful fertilising application of petty savings which is the essence of the Co-operative Bank, or of the commercial bank pure and simple. M. Rostand has conceived the idea that, if he can obtain for the rural and provincial banks leave to employ their funds more freely, a certain advance will be made. He has been at pains to show that in every civilised country in the world (England alone excepted) the authorities of savings banks have greater liberty of investment than in France. His crusade is very interesting to us because, practically, France stands in the same position to this question as we do ourselves. Both countries have a savings bank system, admirable as far as the safe custody of funds is concerned, but otherwise entirely sterile. Neither country has a supplemental service of popular banks of credit. No one can fail to have great sympathy with M. Rostand in his energetic crusade; but it appears to me to be an error to

mix up the question of co-operative banking with
that of the savings bank pure and simple. Without presuming to speak for the possibilities of the
matter in France, it would be, in my opinion, an
entirely hopeless endeavour to seek aid from the
Post Office Savings Bank in establishing popular
credit. If the Government accepts the responsibility of safeguarding the deposits of the poor,
it must be ruled by the most rigid system of red
tape. To guarantee deposits, and at the same
time to allow more or less speculative investment
to be made locally, *without the assistance of mutual
co-operative supervision,* would be to invite certain
financial disaster. M. Rostand, as I understand
it, would reply to this objection that there is
available—in France, at any rate—á large amount
of philanthropic and civic enthusiasm. Persons
animated by this spirit would, he believes, be
forthcoming to manage gratuitously the business
of popular banking. Now, without seeking to
disparage either philanthropic or civic enthusiasm,
it is enough to say that this idea is altogether
foreign to the habits of the English working class.
All their successful institutions are self-managed.
They may not always attain the ideal heights of
wisdom, but they are schools of experience in
which wisdom is being perfected. The self-
management of a Co-operative Bank by its
members is a school, not only of wisdom, but of

that mutual rectitude of conduct on which its success depends. To build popular credit without this foundation would be to build in vain. M. Rostand is far too acute a man not to perceive this danger. All he asks is that the banks controlled by Government may be allowed to follow the example of the German and Italian banks, and give credit to the smaller Co-operative Banks. With us, however, the difficulty is that these smaller banks do not as yet exist. Co-operative banking has yet to win the confidence of the country. It has done so in Italy and Germany, and the higher finance is eager to offer it every legitimate assistance. When success is assured by laborious effort in detail, the Government Banks will no doubt be found willing to encumber it with their patronage.

Mr. Wolff, whose view of the subject seems to me to be entirely judicious, points out that in many places where Government savings banks exist side-by-side with popular banks, the people prefer their own institutions. They very soon realise that the savings bank pure and simple is merely the apotheosis of the old stocking, and that the best use of savings is the reproductive use of them in the service of those who have gathered them. It is to be hoped that this matter will attract the attention of the Friendly Society and Co-operative leaders. They are, of all men, the most competent to lay the foundation of a new departure in the cause of thrift. They have withstood all the blandishments of State pensions, and, by putting their hand to this new enterprise, they will give yet another practical illustration of their steadfast faith in the value of personal responsibility ; they will found another school of character, just as effective as the great Friendly Society movement itself ; and they will confer a great and lasting benefit on the whole nation, to which it is difficult to see any limit.

To one other class of persons this matter ought to have more than a passing interest. No one questions the fact that there is much that is unsatisfactory in our social arrangements. No one maintains that this is the best of all possible worlds. There are, however, many whose fortune or misfortune it has been to be able to perceive nothing but evil in many of the proposals for social amelioration which from time to time are made by well-meaning enthusiasts. Such people have been called " Gradgrinds " and other ill-sounding names. These flowers of controversy are, of course, very welcome from critics whose praise would set us seriously questioning the sanity of our opinions. Still, those of us who believe in personal responsibility and in the freedom of private initiative, should be glad to welcome this new illustration of the truth of our principles.

Here is a successful movement, based on honest human endeavour, involving neither the robbery of the rich nor the degradation of the poor. Based on the principle of freedom, and independent of patronage, it puts a new weapon in the hands of the poor man, and opens a career to industry and intelligence which at present is closed.

To those who, like myself, regard increased facilities for poor law relief and State pensions as merely devices to sink the poor more deeply in the slough of dependence, I recommend a study of this question. They will find in Mr. Wolff's book a guide at once entertaining and instructive.

VIII

FREEDOM OF EXCHANGE

v.

THE "COLLECTIVE BARGAIN."

IN social controversies generally, there seems to me to be a singular misuse of terms. A "socialist" is a person who believes not in Society, but in the coercion of Society by the State. An "individualist" is a person who believes not in that inconceivable abstraction, the individual man, but in the harmonising power of a free society. So a collective bargain in the mouth of certain controversialists appears to mean an arrangement which is not a bargain at all. This last proposition, however, requires fuller explanation.

According to recent presentments of the case, trade unionism is part of the collectivist movement. Mr. and Mrs. Webb, in their "History of Trade Unionism," declare that the sovereignty of the trade union, in their opinion, rests on the same basis as the sovereignty of the City or State. The trade union, therefore, for the members of each trade, is, or, in the opinion of these authors, ought to be a compulsory, all-embracing association.   In this event, admittedly, individual workmen are denied their right to bargain, and it is for the union to arrange the terms on which its members shall work.

It may be said, however, that the bargain, such as it is, is made between the trade union or monopoly of labour, and the combined employers or monopoly of capital.   It must then be asked, Can two monopolists, in arranging for an exchange of services, be said, in the ordinary sense of the term, to bargain?   The question is, perhaps, an idle one, for, except in a case like that of Robinson Crusoe and his man Friday, in these days of foreign competition such a condition of things is utterly unknown.   Let us, however, admit, for the sake of argument, that rigid monopolies of labour and capital have been established.   Even in this case, a closer examination of the collectivist trade union theory will show at once that, in the arrangement proposed, there is nothing in the nature of a bargain.   According to the doctrine of the " living wage," which is a necessary complement of the theory, it is the business of the union to fix a minimum rate of wages; then, if employers cannot or will not accept the proffered terms, their monopoly of employment will be taken from them, and the State, imperial and municipal, will become the universal employer, and regulate industry on the basis of the living wage. This solution of the question cannot be called a bargain.

The account of the matter given by the eulogists of the new trade unionism is somewhat as follows. The older trade unionists, they tell us, involved themselves in a controversy with the economists as to whether trade unionism was an advantage to workmen and to society at large, and with the moralists as to how far its methods were consistent with justice. Taking advantage of the prevalence of free trade opinions, they insisted

"on the right of every Englishman to bargain for the sale of his labour in the manner he thought most conducive to his own interests" (Webb, p. 278). "When," however, our authors continue (p. 279), "they" (*i.e.* the old trade unionists) "contended that the union should be as free to bargain as the individual, they had not the slightest intention of permitting the individual to bargain freely if they could prevent him."

Mr. Howell, the historian of the old unionism, expressly denies this imputation; but, it is necessary to add, the facts, to some extent, at all events, support the view of Mr. and Mrs. Webb. The old trade unionist occasionally acted coercively, but he either denied or palliated the offence, he had not the effrontery to defend it directly.

"No trade unionist can deny," Mr. and Mrs. Webb sum the matter up, "that without some method of enforcing the decision of the majority, effective trade combination is impossible" (Webb, p. 281).

According to these authors, therefore, the central idea of trade unionism is not a bargain of any kind, but a right to use coercion, to replace Free Exchange, and the laws of demand and supply by an artificial regimentation of all industry. According to this ideal, there will be no bargaining in the market; but for wages, as at present understood, will be substituted an arbitrary scale of maintenance called a "living wage," an amount varying in different trades, and fixed apparently by the combined labourers themselves. This scale of remuneration, further, will be enforced by the allied forces of trade unionism and municipal socialism.

Giving evidence before the Labour Commission [Q. 4501, Minutes of Evidence, Commission sitting as a whole], Mr. Webb used the following words :—

"What appears to me is that piece-work is apt to be very prejudicial to the standard wage, unless there can be some kind of price list or standard list to maintain that collective bargaining which is the essence of trade unionism."

As I understand it, this means that all bargains

should be subject to revision by reference to a standard that is not arrived at by bargaining. Mr. Webb does not like piece-work, especially when reference to an ideal standard is difficult, because essentially it does involve a bargain.

It is not worth while to quarrel about words, but by collective bargaining it is clear that Mr. Webb does not mean that voluntary arrangement which most men understand by the word bargain. The use of the term may be due to a confusion of ideas, or it may be part of the exoteric doctrine of Socialism adopted for the sake of his allies among law-abiding academic economists and for the sake of the weaker brethren generally.

It is not of much importance, but it would probably be an injustice to the intelligence of the new unionists, as represented by Mr. and Mrs. Webb, to suppose that they have any belief in the collective bargain or any other sort of bargain. The old unionists believed in it, but, by the lips of Mr. Howell, they admit the immorality of the methods deemed necessary, by Mr. and Mrs. Webb and the new unionists, for its attainment.

The view of the scholastic economists is not easily ascertained. In their hands the enunciation of general principles has been so overlaid with exceptions and qualifications that it is very difficult to understand their precise position. Still, amid much that to the plain man appears a mere darkening of counsel, it may be gathered that the new economists do cherish a belief that the labourer, in the sale of his labour, derives a benefit from the collective bargain.

In the background, throwing a sinister shadow forward, is the Nemesis of that old injustice which denied to the labourer his undoubted right of combination. Persecution even of false doctrine begets enthusiasm. Enthusiasm, even half crazy enthusiasm, has so many attractive aspects, that academic apologists are not wanting. Here, too, as well as elsewhere, the wire-pullers of political intrigue seek to use both the enthusiast and the pedant for their own purposes. These are the elements in which superstition flourishes, prompting a line of conduct detrimental at once to civilisation and progress.

The consequences which follow from an acceptance of the alleged right of coercion are obvious. To realise the trade union ideal, men are not scrupling to resort to intimidation and violence. A mere recital of the methods employed in recent strikes makes it plain to every impartial mind, that even if these methods led to the millennium, they could not for long be supportable by human nature. If our present system scourges us with rods, collectivism, acting through its faithful instrument of trade unionism, would scourge us with scorpions. Mr. and Mrs. Webb's contention that, without coercion, trade unionism, as understood by the new unionists, is impracticable, seems irrefutable, and for that very reason condemnatory of the methods of which they are the apologists. Very few have the hardihood of Mr. and Mrs. Webb, in claiming the right of coercion for trade unions. Most people, apart from the injustice of such a demand, see that it is one which could not be enforced ; they rest the trade union case, therefore, on the advantage which is supposed to accrue to the labourer by means of combination, enforced only by justifiable methods of argument and persuasion. Those who believe in this view of the subject reject or overlook, more or less consciously, Mr. and Mrs. Webb's incontrovertible statement, that on these terms "effective trade combination is impossible." It is this modified assertion of the practicable advantages of trade unionism that I propose to examine.

There are, obviously, many difficulties in bringing this opinion to the proof. Proof in this, as in other matters, must proceed by a reference to the facts of the case, or by the application of a general principle, or preferably by a combination of both these methods. Now, with regard to the facts, it is obviously difficult, not to say impossible, so to isolate the different phenomena, that we can, with any confidence, arrange them in sequence of cause and effect.

Turning to the evidence given before the Royal Commission on Labour, we find, for instance, that one set of witnesses regards the rise which took place in seamen's wages in 1887 as the result of action taken by Mr. J. Havelock Wilson's union; while other witnesses declare that it followed naturally on an expansion of trade due to independent causes. Again, it is pointed out that the wages of women, of agricultural labourers, and of domestic servants have risen, although, in the last-mentioned class, trade unionism has not existed at all, and in the others only fitfully and locally. From this fact one party seeks to draw the conclusion that, when circumstances warrant it, wages rise, quite independently of trade unions; while another party argues that this rise is due to the reflex action of trade unionism in other employments. Again, interpretation of the facts depends a good deal on the difference between real and nominal wages. In an address delivered October 29, 1894, to the Bradford Chamber of Commerce, on the Fall of Prices, Mr. Shaw-Lefevre pointed out that

"it appeared, as the result of the Royal Commission on Labour, that it was now certain, not only that there had been no general fall in the money wages of labour, during the last twenty or twenty-five years, but the reverse—that money wages had risen in most, if not all, trades."

With regard to the purchasing power of their wages, Mr. Shaw-Lefevre sums the matter up as follows :—

" It could scarcely be doubted that the wages of ordinary labourers went from 30 to 40 per cent. further than they did twenty years ago, and those of the artisan classes from 20 to 25 per cent. further. Wheat at 20*s.* a quarter, and sugar at 13*s.* per cwt., and tea at 9*d.* per lb., as compared with 52*s.*, 26*s.*, and 17*d.* twenty years ago, must be an enormous advantage to the labourers of all classes."

Mr. Shaw-Lefevre's address was directed to estimating the fluctuation in the value of gold relatively to the value of other commodities. The gold-value of labour had increased, while the gold-value of most other commodities had fallen. Now, as men do not live on gold, but on the commodities which gold will purchase, it is obvious that the cheapness of most commodities, so long as his labour is not one of them, is of the greatest advantage to the labourer. In any appreciation, therefore, of the advantage of collective bargaining, we ought not only to consider the result of its action on wages, but also its action in raising or lowering the price of commodities.

Further, we cannot confine our inquiry as to

the effect of a collective bargain, to one trade.
If, as has been argued, there is a solidarity of
labour, and a reflex action from one trade to
another, we shall not have got to the bottom of
the matter, even when we discover that collective
bargaining has raised the wages of one particular
industry. Let us take, for example, the case of
miners. The following are some among many of
the possible indirect consequences of a so-called
collective bargain. (1) Miners fix what they call
a living wage, that is, a sum very considerably
in excess of an agricultural labourer's earnings.
When employers urge that an advance is impossible or a reduction necessary, the principles
of trade unionism will not allow other labourers to
improve their position, by accepting wages which
to them would be affluence. By this action miners'
wages are upheld, but other labourers' wages
are kept down. Similarly, just as it is, in this
way, made difficult for all other labourers to
pass from poorly paid callings to more profitable ones, so it is difficult for a coal miner to
pass into any better paid industry which is
protected by a trade union. In any computation,
therefore, we must strike a balance between those
who gain and those who lose by this restrictive
policy. (2) Mr. Pickard, M.P., the well-known
miners' representative, once proclaimed his intention of keeping the price of coal at £2 a ton,

with a view of enabling employers to pay high wages. How many colliers could find a sale for their output at such a figure? How many iron furnaces and kindred industries would have to close? Would the increase of wages secured to some coal miners compensate, on an average, for the loss to other miners and other workmen whose place of employment would be closed? Mr. Pickard's £2 a-ton was not seriously meant, but every artificial rise of price has similar results. How are these to be computed? (3) Would the gain to some miners compensate for the increased cost which all, poor as well as rich, have to pay for coal? Or rather, for it is a much larger question, would the gain in money wages be equal to the loss in purchasing power, if the price of all, or even a large number, of commodities were thus artificially raised?

If we are going to decide this controversy on the facts, it is obvious that all these considerations and many others are material, and that an answer to all these questions must be given in the relentless logic of arithmetic before we can be said to have the facts before us. I venture to say that it is quite impossible to produce these facts. It may be indicated that there are facts, but, in the main, I submit, this discussion must be determined by more general considerations. It will be legitimate to introduce illustration by the way, but

Y

allegations of facts in a matter so entirely hypothetical must be received with considerable caution.

As a first step to answering the question—Does
combination for the purpose of collective bargaining give the labourer an advantage?—we must
consider the nature of the market in which the
bargain has to be made. Here we are met by a
preliminary difficulty. Mr. Howell, in his "Conflicts of Capital and Labour," p. 190, quotes with
approval a somewhat rhetorical passage from an
article written by Mr. Frederic Harrison, in which
he protests against the idea that labour is a commodity. (1) First, because, in Mr. Harrison's interpretation, the term commodity cannot be applied
to a thing of which there is no stock or realised
store. (2) Because the seller of a commodity can
send it or carry it about, because he can send a
sample of it and can treat by correspondence.
The labourer, he argues, has no commodity
to sell. He must himself be present at every
market. He cannot correspond with his employer,
he cannot send a sample of his strength, nor do
employers knock at his cottage door. This is not
a market. (3) And this, says Mr. Harrison, is the
most important point :

"The labourer has not got a commodity to sell ; what
he seeks to do is not to exchange products, but to
combine to produce. . . . The union of capitalists and
labourers is, in the highest sense, a partnership involving

a real equality of duties and powers. . . . Applied to
this noble and intimate relation of life—this grand institution of society—the language of the market or of
barter is a cruel and senseless cant."

Mr. Harrison does not, it may be presumed,
adopt the socialist doctrine that markets must
be abolished and replaced by municipal or com-
munistic regimentation. It is difficult, therefore,
to understand the meaning of this attempted
interruption of a serious argument. The term
commodity is, in this connection, a clumsy but
surely a very innocent synonym for service. Mr.
Harrison's formula does not help us in the very
least to determine the just proportion which ought
to exist between the wages of a haymaker and a
blacksmith. No one has ever maintained that
the sale and hiring of services are precisely the
same thing as the sale and purchase of material
commodities, but it may be as well to take his
objections seriatim. (1) No competent economist
will nowadays argue, that exchange is confined
to material commodities. The greater part of
modern business is the exchange of incorporeal
commodities. Services are exchanged; incorporeal rights, such as debts, credits, etc., are
exchanged, and it is usual to speak of the mechanism by which the exchangers are brought
together, as the market. (2) All markets are not
constituted alike. Land is even more immobile

than Mr. Harrison considers labour to be. A vast amount of the hiring of labour is done by correspondence, advertisement, and by aid of the references of former employers, an agency which has much the same effect as the sending of a sample. In Scotland the hiring fair is still a national institution. Master and man meet in the market and spend the day in negotiation. Readers of that admirable Scottish eclogue, "Johnny Gibb of Gushetneuk," will remember the account of the "feeing market" day at the Kirktown of Pyketillim. Even if we admit, for the sake of smoothing Mr. Harrison's susceptibilities, that his servants and his labourers and the printer's devil are his partners in the "highest sense" of the term, it still remains that the terms of partnership rest ultimately on some economical basis, and that basis, *pace* Mr. Harrison, is conveniently termed the market. (3) The same consideration suggests the answer to Mr. Harrison's third objection. This turns in part on a mere verbal quibble, but incidentally it betrays, I venture to think, an important misconception of the industrial mechanism of society. It is based on the mistaken notion of certain economists that production is a process to be distinguished from distribution. Fundamentally, all our industrial actions are exchanges, and, as a condition of our treating them as economic phenomena, they must be expressed or considered as phenomena of exchange. Mr. Harrison seems to admit that the sale of products, (in his vocabulary, products mean material products,) is a process of exchange, he does not appear to realise that all our economic actions are likewise processes of exchange. Thus a man deposits coins in a bank; he parts with his money, and receives in exchange a right to require payment of an equal sum on demand or at a date agreed, and, in some instances, to receive interest in the mean time at a stipulated rate. If a man enters into a partnership, it is still a process of exchange; he exchanges his capital, or promises his services, for a share in the stock and credits of the business, coupled with a right to receive profit and an obligation to share losses on terms agreed. If, as Mr. Harrison argues, a labourer's contract implies a partnership, it is still subject to the laws of exchange. Nor, as far as I can see, is the dignity of human life, and of labour as its most important manifestation, by any means abated, because, in every industrial community, services as well as commodities are subject to the rules of the market.

In the great majority of labour contracts, services are exchanged against money. By consulting Mr. Schloss's "Methods of Industrial Remuneration," Williams & Norgate (second edition), 1894, the curious may see that there is practically no limit to the variation of terms on which labour is hired. In some contracts, part payment in kind still survives, a house is provided free or under cost price, board is supplied, or a portion of farm produce is allowed in addition to money wages. Further, in every case, more especially in the industries where labour is not a principal part of the cost of production, personal considerations have great weight. Many employers prefer to pay something over the market rate, to secure the permanent services of good-tempered and suitable servants, rather than risk the lottery of the market. On the other hand, domestic servants, farm labourers, and, generally, those whose comfort depends a good deal on their personal relation to their employers, will prefer to take lower wages in a place where they are comfortable and considerately treated, rather than change to a less agreeable employment, where higher wages might be obtainable.

All these circumstances have their weight, but they do not alter the fact that all persons who deal with their neighbours either for services or commodities are necessarily subject to the ordinary laws of the market. The fact that there is a labour market is obvious and requires, I submit, no further demonstration, and the purpose of this article is to discuss the conditions which govern this market, and to inquire, from the point of view of the labourer, what are the comparative merits of a free market and a collective bargain respectively.

A market has been defined to be "the whole of any region in which buyers and sellers are in such free intercourse with one another, that the prices of the same goods tend to equality easily and quickly." Now labour is not all of the same quality, and, of necessity, there is a subdivision of the market. The labour of the skilled artisan commands a higher price than that of the agricultural labourer. Still, there are causes which make for a unification of the market.

First, even adult skilled labour has considerable mobility, or power to pass from one industry to another. Mr. H. Llewellyn Smith, in his very interesting pamphlet on "Modern Changes in the Mobility of Labour" (H. Frowde, London, 1891), has shown most conclusively that the specialisation of industry has increased rather than decreased the mobility of skilled labour. This consideration is of the utmost importance to the subject, but only one or two illustrations can be given in support of this general statement. A woollen-weaver could, says Mr. Smith, become an efficient cotton-weaver in a few days. This initial difficulty of a few days, in normal times, prevents a complete unification of the market, but this "initial friction" is overcome by even a slight disturbance in the conditions of supply and demand. An offer of better wages in one trade would, it may be presumed, be the way in which this "disturbance" would make itself felt in the labour market. It is, according to this authority, in the domestic industries, *i.e.* the industries not carried on in large factories, that immobility is most conspicuous. Thus the hand-made nails of Cradley Heath have been in course of displacement by foreign machine-made nails since 1830. "Mr. Burnett is of opinion that the machine-made nail trade might have taken root in the hand-made trade district and absorbed the displaced labour, 'if the hand-made trade had been carried on in factories ready to adopt new mechanical ideas.'" And in support of this view Mr. Smith relates that—

" In the hand-nail trade at Silsden in the West Riding, the tendency to crowd into a decaying trade seems to have been checked by collecting the nailers into two or three workshops. . . . The new generation now find other outlets . . . so that the hand-nail trade is mostly in the hands of old men and is naturally dying . . . with but little of the acute suffering which has made Cradley Heath notorious."

The tendency of modern industry, we need hardly point out, is towards factory manufacture, and it is satisfactory to learn that this tendency is productive of greater adaptiveness among manual labourers. Again, "among the various textile trades there is almost perfect interchangeability both of weavers and overlookers," subject to the initial friction existing in normal times. At Lord Masham's great mills at Manningham, Mr. Lister, as he then was, substituted in succession the manufacture of velvet for silk, of plush for velvet, and of sealskin for plush, without introducing fresh workmen, although the looms had to be adapted. Further, in some cases men learn more than one trade, *e.g.* painters and plumbers, probably because painting is a seasonal trade. At Kingswood, near Bristol, Mr. Smith informs us that a certain number of men oscillate backwards and forwards between the boot factories and the neighbouring collieries, according to season. The management of steam machinery is obviously an art which opens many varieties of trade to the same workman. Mr. Marshall ("Principles of Economics," p. 318) has drawn attention to the importance of the principle of interchangeable parts in machinery, and, *mutatis mutandis*, and *pace* Mr. Harrison, there is a certain analogy between the animate and inanimate parts of our industrial machinery. They are becoming more interchangeable with great advantage to the labourer himself, and with increased efficiency to our industrial machinery.

A second cause is of much greater importance. The young are, so to speak, the raw material of which the skilled artisan is made, the labour force which may be educated into many forms. Now, it is most important that we should understand the causes which determine the destination of this new labour. Notoriously, for many years, there has been a steady drift of labour away from agricultural industry to the better paid industries, which most usually are carried on in the towns. In the north of England and in Scotland, there is practically a unification of the labour market. In the south, the isolation of rural parishes remote from great centres of trade has retarded this movement ; but even here intelligent young people tend towards the employments which are better paid.   Money wages are not the only point to be considered.   The agricultural labourer has advantages in the shape of a cheap house and garden, and the wages of unskilled labour in town and country are much nearer an equilibrium than is generally supposed.   Mr. Giffen informed the Royal Commission on Labour (Q. 6956, Minutes of Evidence, Commission sitting as a whole) that fifty years ago one half of the working population of the United Kingdom were agricultural labourers or poor Irish ; now, less than one-fifth are of this class, or, taking Great Britain alone, only about one-eighth (see also "Essays in Finance," Second Series, p. 422).   This transference of labour from agriculture to other forms of industry has been con- temporaneous with a great rise in money wages.

Professor Leone Levi calculated that the average yearly earnings of the working class, including men, women, and children, was in 1867 £38 per head, in 1884 £42 14s., and Mr. Giffen puts it at the present time at £48. Further, since 1872 there has been a great fall in prices, from 25 to 30 per cent. in most articles of common necessity, not including, of course, rent. This exception, as we shall hereafter see, is very instructive. In connection with this tendency of labour to pass from the poorly paid agricultural industries to more remunerative work, it has been pointed out by Mr. Giffen and others that the number of income-tax payers has increased in the last fifty years at a much greater rate than the increase of population. Evidently, then, there is an upward movement at the top of the working class, as well as at the bottom, and it is not unreasonable to suppose that this upward tendency is present also throughout the whole intermediate mass. (Giffen, " Essays in Finance," Second Series, p. 427.)

Let us endeavour to follow the actual course of this development. Let us visit in imagination a remote part of rural England, at intervals of ten years, during the past half century. In the earlier decades we should have found labour in a condition not far removed from mediæval servitude, the price of wheat extremely high because we were isolated by protection from foreign markets, and the price of more perishable rural produce very low, because, from difficulties of transit, the local market was shut off from the larger markets of Smithfield and Leadenhall. As we continued our visits, we should remark a tendency towards a unification of markets. We should observe that the young labour each year has gravitated towards new industries, to a neighbouring town, to a brickfield, a cement work, or a colliery. We should find that the wages and condition of the emigrants, and also of those who remained, have improved; that though the cultivation of wheat is discontinued, yet bread is cheaper; that vast imports of cereals from all parts of the world, and of meat from Australia and New Zealand, have put these articles within the reach of the labourer in a way that fifty years ago would have been considered luxurious; that the price of miscellaneous country produce, such as eggs and chickens, has probably risen, for railway communication has united the country with the market of the town. If we extend our observation and follow this produce to the town, we shall find that this country supply has prevented the price of such things from rising to a famine rate. At the same time, the labour which has come in from the country has found profitable employment, and, as the eminent statisticians already quoted have shown us, wages have continued to rise.

Let us consider first the cheapening of production. The French economist Bastiat has dwelt on this aspect of the question with his usual epigrammatic force. *Besoins, efforts, satisfaction, voilà l'homme au point de vue économique.* The whole economical progress of mankind depends on our making the middle term "effort" less onerous and more productive. Some wants are satisfied gratuitously; when we breathe we merely appropriate the air. We are conditioned, however, by the fact that other things cannot be as free as air. Nor need we lament this limitation, for where a maintenance is free owing to the bounty of nature, effort is unnecessary, and a lower civilisation is the result. In our Western civilisation, by means of accumulated knowledge, the result of many centuries of laborious effort, there is year by year a greater approximation to a gratuitous satisfaction of our most necessary wants. According to Bastiat, economical progress consists in the conversion of what he calls *utilités onéreuses* into *utilités gratuites.* Thus, the earnings of capital are being reduced, the price of agricultural produce is continually falling, both tending to a condition which Bastiat has happily termed gratuity. On the other hand, labour is being so distributed that both agricultural and manufacturing wages tend upwards.

Mr. Mallock, in his admirably clear and suggestive

little book, "Labour and the Popular Welfare," has
drawn attention to another aspect of this process
of development. The force which pioneers this
beneficent evolution is, in Mr. Mallock's language,
ability. In other words, it is the free enterprise
of captains of industry, which is constantly moving
the waters of industrial chaos and forming a cosmos
in which common necessaries are given a continuous
tendency towards gratuity, and labour is organised
in an ever-ascending scale of higher remuneration.
Under the successful guidance of the captains of
industry common labour is given almost super-
natural power, and, even if the enterprise to which
it is applied proves unsuccessful, the wages of labour
are paid with exact punctuality. On every ground,
therefore, it is to the interest of labour to give a
free hand to the enterprise of the capitalist. Our
industrial system is a vast exchange, and it is to the
interest of all that each, be he capitalist, organiser,
or simple labourer, shall be permitted freely to take
his services to the best market. The limited aspect
of the subject now under consideration, namely,
the continuous enhancement of the price of labour,
which has attended its transference from agriculture
to other industries, is a necessary corollary of this
larger economic harmony of freedom.

Here, in all probability, an objection will be
raised which, even at the cost of a slight digression,
it is necessary to meet. It will be said that,

although wages have gone up, there is a far larger number of unemployed men than formerly, and that the miserable condition of the unemployed is due to the migration of labour which we have described. This we believe to be a complete misconception. The existence of the unemployed must be assigned to quite different causes. There are many persons whose character and disposition are altogether averse to the yoke of industrial discipline. Nothing but the sternest necessity will induce them to submit to punctual and regulated toil. It is idle to wax indignant over the conduct of these humbler inhabitants of Bohemia. There is no stern necessity driving them to work, and vagabondage is plentifully, nay, as far as quantity and ubiquity are concerned, extravagantly endowed. Casual wards and philanthropic shelters are open everywhere. In the winter this population frequents the towns, and while the summer nights are warm, it wanders into the country. Here is a nucleus for the unemployed problem. Further, we have described the "initial frictions" which, in Mr. Llewellyn Smith's phrase divide one market from another. The activity of trade unionism, in each or many of these separate markets, has magnified these initial frictions and has insisted that no one shall work for less than a certain wage. Employers may be willing to employ men of average efficiency at this price, but they are not willing nor able to find profitable employment for those who, by reason of old age, the inexperience of youth, or lack of skill, fall below this average. These men also must perforce join the unemployed. Further, there are workmen out of work because their trade is seasonal, or because, like the nail-making at Cradley Heath, their trade is decaying. Their misfortune is by no means due to the migration of others, and their remedy must be the adoption of an additional or supplementary trade, or migration to some new industry, a solution which is more or less forbidden by the restrictive tendencies of trade unionism. Again, there are a considerable number of men whose intellects are altogether debauched by their love of political agitation. They live on the earnings of their unfortunate wives and families ; they perhaps honestly believe that their sufferings can be ended by some act of parliament, and politicians give encouragement to a superstition which thus magnifies their own office. These men devote their ample leisure to organising the unemployed. It is singular that women, the most poorly paid part of the community, do not take part in the unemployed agitation, and that, although in previous winters the movement, as a rule, began in October or November, this last year, the winter of 1894–5, nothing was heard of the matter till the School Board,

Guardians, and Vestry elections were over. The spouters and agitators were of course otherwise engaged. Genuine workmen who are out of work, if they are unhappily beguiled into taking part in this agitation, instead of watching for a market where their services are required, are artificially collected together and are mixed up with elements which not only are unemployed but unemployable. They are deluded into coming to London by vestries which undertake the duties of guardians and attempt to find relief work for all comers. The unemployed in this way are driven into hopeless congestion, and their chances of finding their way back into the ranks of industry are destroyed. Their character deteriorates, and their case becomes hopeless.[1] The origin of this ruin is not the freedom of migration, but the restrictions which have been artificially set to their right of free labour. A free organisation of labour would inevitably carry such part of the unemployed, as

[1] Numerous philanthropic attempts have been made to help this class ; but the conditions are such, that the measure of success has not been large. Our principal hope must be that a wiser administration of public relief and a relaxation of trade union restrictions will diminish the artificial creation of this class. Once created and collected in great numbers, it is almost impossible to effect an improvement in its condition. The only chance of reform is to separate them, to allow them to find their way back one by one into the ranks of industrial society, and in the limited number of cases where this is possible, to subject them to wholesome personal influence in a small and carefully supervised training home. The attempt to deal with them in large masses is bound to fail.

was really desirous of working, to a point, where their efforts would be found profitable. It is a mere question of organisation, one portion of the unemployed will become customers for the work of another portion, if a free market is allowed to determine the use to which their efforts should be directed.

The difficulty of the unemployed, then, is by no means caused by the migration of labour from the less to the more profitable, but, for the most part, by the restrictions imposed by trade unions and other similar influences on this beneficent migratory movement.

To return to the improvement in the condition of labour by reason of this continuous migration —where is it possible to find all this scope for expansion? The answer is obvious, in the great growth of some old industries, and in the daily invention of new ones. Even a superficial consideration of this aspect of the question brings into striking relief the solidarity and mutuality of a social organism based on the principle of free exchange. A portion of the labour withdrawn from agriculture has busied itself in making agricultural machinery. An equivalent to the labour which is deserting the poorly paid slop work in the tailoring trade is being employed in making sewing-machines, and the more elaborate machinery proper to a clothing factory. This substitution of machinery for manual labour is going on indefinitely, and when we read of Niagara being harnessed for the service of man, it is difficult to see where we can set a limit to this tendency. Further, old machinery is perpetually being retired in favour of new and improved machinery. Railways have taken the place of stage coaches, and there is every probability that in the immediate future the application of mechanical power to locomotion will be largely increased.

The improved conditions of labour have enabled wage-earners to create new and important industries. Bicycle making, for instance, employs a large staff of skilled and highly-paid workmen, and their products are bought very largely by their own class. Inventions, at first sight of little value, have at times effected important and unexpected revolutions. A toy, like the automatic " penny-in-the-slot " machine, has brought about a most interesting innovation in the method of supplying gas to artisans' dwellings.

The following figures, taken from " Mullhall's Dictionary of Statistics," seem to bear on the matter under consideration.

The total number of persons employed in the United Kingdom were distributed in the following manner at the several dates given, as follows :—

TABLE

SHOWING DISTRIBUTION OF POPULATION IN VARIOUS EMPLOYMENTS

AT INTERVALS OF TEN YEARS.

	Agriculture.	Manufactures.	Commerce.	Professions.	Domestic.	Various.	Total.
1841	3,401,000	3,137,000	684,000	223,000	1,555,900	2,362,000	11,362,000
1851	3,519,000	3,922,000	1,165,000	320,000	1,542,000	2,293,000	12,761,000
1861	3,149,000	4,164,000	1,418,000	363,000	1,914,000	2,552,000	13,560,000
1871	2,808,000	4,377,000	1,712,000	422,000	2,233,000	3,132,000	14,684,000
1881	2,561,000	4,535,000	1,946,000	524,000	2,448,000	3,721,000	15,735,000

The following table presents the same facts from a different point of view :—

RATIO PER THOUSAND.

	1841	1851	1861	1871	1881
Agriculture ...	298	276	233	192	162
Manufactures ...	277	307	307	298	288
Commerce ...	60	92	104	116	124
Mines	22	24	37	38	41
Building	43	46	51	55	61
Professions ...	19	25	26	28	33
Domestics	137	120	141	153	156
Various	144	110	101	120	135
Total	1000	1000	1000	1000	1000

It will be significant to add that among the professions, the principal increases have been under the head of medicine, which has risen from 56,000 in 1841 to 102,000 in 1881, and of education from 76,000 in 1841 to 224,000 in 1881. Among manufacturing industries, the chemical trade employed 7000 in 1841, and 55,000 in 1881. The paper trade, 15,000 in 1841, and 61,000 in 1881. The textile industries show a decrease from 1,481,000 in 1841 to 1,283,000 in 1881, owing largely, no doubt, to the disappearance of the hand-loom weaver. In 1841 there were 234,000 male domestic servants, and 843,000 women. In 1881, the numbers were 292,000 males, and 1,546,000 women. These last figures point to a growth of middle class comfort, rather than to an increase of the richer and larger establishments.

Many interesting particulars as to the redistribution of the population, in the various industries, during the decennium 1881–1891, can be gathered from the *General Report*, issued with the Census of 1891. The natural increase of population averaged 11·7 per cent. All increase, over and above this limit, must be due to other causes, and chief among them must be the attraction of a better market, or, in the case of a decrease, the repulsion of a falling market.

Subject to this qualification, the following increases are recorded, and may be regarded as proof of the growth of the class that can afford to amuse itself:—Musicians, 51 ; actors, 60 ; performers, showmen, etc., 80 ; photographers, 59 per cent. respectively. Significant, also, is the growth of insurance business. In 1891, 31,437 persons were engaged in this employment, twice as many as in 1881, and three times as many as in 1871. Road, railway, and water traffic employs 23 per cent. more than in 1881. The telegraph and telephone service employed 14,955 in 1891, as against only 9442 in 1881. Farmers and agricultural labourers have each decreased 10 per cent., while expansion of a more profitable form of land culture is attested by an increase of no less than 65 per cent. in the number of gardeners, most of them engaged in the industry of market gardening. The increase of " engine and machine makers " was 28 and 29·8 per cent. in the decennia ending 1881 and 1891 respectively. The industrial class, as a whole, increased 15·1 per cent., a percentage which would have been much greater but for the exceptionally small growth in two of the largest groups, namely, the building trades and the textile industries.

A striking instance of the growth of a new industry is afforded in the case of the makers of electrical apparatus, which has risen from 428 in 1871, to 12,604 in 1891. Persons employed in bicycle and tricycle making were, in 1881, returned as 1072, and in 1891 as 11,524.

One or two decreases must now be quoted, they are of even greater interest than the increases. Shirt-makers and seamstresses are returned in 1881 as 83,244. To this we must add machinists (female) 7524 ; total, 90768. In 1891, this group is arranged—seamstresses, 55,096 ; machinists (female), 21,478 ; total, 76,574, or a decrease of 15 per cent. The interesting point to be observed is that the more highly paid labour of manufacturers and workers of sewing-machines is superseding the "gratuitous" labour of the poor needle-woman, while the price of clothing is still tending to "gratuity."

The shoe trade exhibits a different and more forward stage of the same process. In each of the two preceding decennia there had been a decrease in the numbers following this trade.

This was due to the substitution of machinery for hand work, and the process continued till the change was complete. The substitution once made, the numbers of those employed would naturally begin to rise again with the growth of the population. The increase, accordingly, in the last decennium is 11 per cent., corresponding to 11·7, the average increase of population. In Northamptonshire and Leicestershire, the chief home of the machine boot trade, it is noteworthy that there has been a continuous growth in the numbers of employed, in each decennium, since 1861, of 34, 41, and 62 per cent. respectively, the whole decrease having taken place elsewhere among the hand-working operatives.

Allusion has already been made to the industry of hand nail making. It is satisfactory to notice that it shows a very remarkable decline, having fallen from 18,741 to 9943, or 47 per cent., and, further, that this follows on a decline of 18 per cent. in the previous decade.

This list of illustrations could be extended almost indefinitely; but enough, for the purpose, has been said.

The continuous fall of prices, since 1872, is nothing more than the tendency of the common necessaries of life to pass from the list of *satisfactions onéreuses* to the list of *satisfactions gratuites*. The distribution of labour, as illustrated

by these quotations from the census report, follows
a different law. There is a continuous flow of
labour from the less profitable trades, to the more
profitable. Competition, which is perpetually
bringing down the rate of interest and profit, as
well as the price of common necessaries, points
out to the labourer by the unmistakable sign of
a stagnant market, the place where his labour is
tending to gratuity, and by the equally unmistakable sign of a buoyant market, the place
where advantageous employment is to be found.
The harmonious organisation of industrial society
depends entirely on the labourer's ability to read
and obey these signs. To attempt to destroy,
by coercive intimidation, the delicate sensitiveness
of this barometer, viz. the free market, is foolish
and suicidal in the extreme.

Before leaving this aspect of the subject, it may
be well to consider shortly some of the lets and
hindrances which impede the continuity of these
self-adjusting migratory movements of labour.

First and foremost, we should be disposed to
name the disastrous delusion which has taken
possession of the public mind, that the great capitalists, or captains of industry, who enrich themselves by organising services acceptable to the
people, are enemies of society to be cribbed,
cabined, and confined in all their movements. All
value is the result of partial and temporary

monopoly. The only way to counteract monopoly
is by means of that competition which is daily
bringing the common necessities of life nearer to a
condition of "gratuity." The great development of
municipal pretensions has, without doubt, closed
the door to a vast expansion of private enterprise.
There is, we grant, a certain amount of difficulty
in admitting private enterprise to some of these
large undertakings, but the difficulties are exaggerated, and have been elevated into a body of
opinion, which is simply strangling our industrial
life. Private enterprise is being driven out of
many forms of industry. Municipalities in every
quarter lie in wait to confiscate the property of
tramway, water, and gas companies. Railway
companies are harassed, in their beneficent enterprise, by endless interferences and regulations, till
competent authorities tell us that the era of
railway construction is past. The country, it is
said, wants light railways, but such are the
impediments put in the way of private enterprise,
that it seems to be assumed that we can only get
these by means of the rates. The Post-Office
tried to extinguish the telephone companies, and
the district messengers companies, and now black-
mails them. The rich man, who uses capital with
success, is a great benefactor to mankind, but in
the opinion of the democracy, and Sir W.
Harcourt, he is a person to be subjected to

invidious and penalising taxation. The building of artisan dwellings is pursued under circumstances of the greatest difficulty, owing to threats of municipal competition, the exactions of the rate collector, and the utter indifference of the legislature to the necessity of simplifying land tenure and transfer, and so introducing the healthy spirit of private competition. Here is the cause that house rent, almost alone among the common necessities of life, has not shared in the general tendency towards gratuity. Here perhaps also is the cause of the curtailment of employment in the building trades alluded to in our quotations from the census returns.

The same spirit of delusion seems to animate many of our voluntary associations. A volume might be written on the mischievous, ill-considered charities which add to the state endowments of pauperism, and on the vast amount of energy that is wasted in mere political gabble. But among voluntary associations, without doubt, by far the most mischievous is the trade union, as at present conducted. At every turn, the migration of labour to its most profitable place of employment, at every step, the tendency of commodities toward gratuity are thwarted and repressed.

One of the avowed objects of the Miners' Associations is to restrict the output of coal with a view of keeping up prices and of paying high wages to the present number of coal miners. The true solution of course is, that the flow of labour, in the coal mining industry, both in and out, should be un-interrupted. It is the policy of unions, however, to prevent this. They endeavour to enclose themselves in an isolated market, and proceed to violence and intimidation to maintain their monopoly. In the first place, they never succeed for long in doing so, and, in so far as they do succeed, they inflict on all other trades an injury which reacts on themselves, and, most important of all, they destroy the delicate mechanism which regulates, to the advantage of all, the movements of exchange which we have already described. It is esssential to the interest of poorly paid workmen that they shall be allowed to pass freely into higher paid industries ; these have ample compensation for this in the expansion of still higher industries, and in the never-ending discovery of new industries.

The question, Where is the custom to come from for all this expansion? can only proceed from those who are blind to the mutuality of our industrial organisation. The answer is obvious, *solvitur ambulando.* The growth of working-class incomes permits the working class to be its own customer. This, however, is a point on which we shall have something to say later on. The talk of returning the labourer to the land is the purest imbecility. At a time when agricultural produce is tending to gratuity, it is gravely proposed to lead the emancipated labourer back to the soil, and to the gratuitous toil from which he has escaped. As we may see, by glancing at the western farms of America, labour on the soil need not be a gratuitous calling. Nor would it be in this country if the healthy migration set in motion by the call of the market were allowed to exercise its salutary influence. To take the labourer back to the land by any other means than the legitimate attraction of the market, would be a crime against him, and a double crime against the less adventurous spirits, who choose to remain agricultural labourers. Yet this is the principle of artificial restriction which underlies the policy of trade unionism, and the avowed object of empirics of all shades of political opinion. At the risk of over elaboration, let me illustrate this by an imaginary and by a real instance.

One hundred men, let us suppose, are engaged in cheese making. Too much cheese is produced and prices become unremunerative. The trade unionist says, "Keep the hundred men employed, but reduce your out-put of cheese, and endeavour to make the public pay the same price for a smaller amount of cheese." Now with every cheese producing district in the world in telegraphic communication with the English market, this is something like the action of Mrs. Partington and her broom. Even if it is successful, the productive energy of a hundred men is reduced perhaps twenty-five per cent. If this procedure is spread, as unfortunately it is, to some extent, by the action of trade unions, over the whole area of our industries, we see that labour is confined to its least remunerative employment, and the tendency of commodities towards gratuity is reversed.

A charitable society in the east of London has a number of old pensioners, men and women who have striven hard to attain independence. Their small pensions are given to them expressly in recognition of these efforts. During the coal strike, these old people were much distressed by the high price of coal. The society accordingly made an additional allowance. This was based on a rough estimate of the additional expense. During eight weeks some £13 were divided among thirty hearths. The statistical reader, who happens to know the number of hearths that were in the habit of drawing supplies from the area affected by the strike, may work out the sum for himself. It is easy to see that by raising the price of coal the workman's chance of attaining independence and leisure is greatly diminished.

We have described the principle which we believe to be our best guarantee for industrial progress. As far as we have yet seen, trade unionism, as at present conducted, has no conspicuous part to play in the ascent of labour. On the contrary, we have seen that the restrictive policy of trade unionism is one of the chief obstacles at the present time barring the way of progress. Lest the considerations already brought forward appear too general, let us consider again the concrete case of the labourer born in an agricultural district. *Ex hypothesi*, he must either migrate to another field, or the value of his services must be kept up by a return to protection or by a restricted output. As matter of fact, this second solution is not attempted. It is altogether impracticable, and the agricultural labourer does migrate. Now if twenty young men in some rural district find it necessary to seek other than agricultural employment, they do not attempt to bargain collectively, they move off one by one, each, in all probability, to a different place, and a different trade. This migratory ascent of labour is only possible when men are allowed to act singly and independently.

The advocates of the collective bargain confine their view to too narrow a range. They see that the collective bargain, established by the coercive exclusion of other labourers on the one hand, and by the threat of a strike on the other hand, does at times extort from some employer a rise of wages. This, of course, is seen, but it is necessary to consider what is not seen. Either the advance of wages is warranted, or it is not warranted, by the condition of the trade.

In the first case, *ex hypothesi,* the trade was profitable, and in due course fresh capital and enterprise would have been attracted to it, and wages would have risen. The action of the collective bargain, held as a threat over the employer, has antedated the advance by a few days or weeks, and this, as far as we can see, is the only economical advantage derived from attempts at collective bargaining. Even then, it is attended by inconvenience. The continuous fall of prices since 1872 proves conclusively that these attempts to regrate and forestall the market are bound to fail. We must recognise the conditions of the struggle in which we are engaged. In spite of all opposition the cost of the production of common necessaries is tending to gratuity. Labour is an item in this cost of production, and it can only escape from this universal tendency by acquiring sufficient mobility to follow the guidance of its own market. For the permanence of its promotion it must trust to the fact that human wants are inexhaustible, and that the free market guarantees a constantly improving organisation of industry for their continuous satisfaction.

Next, if the rise is not warranted, the advance is gained by forcing employers to take less than the normal rate of profit. In the long run, this cannot fail to prove disastrous to all concerned. For, if there is one thing more certain than another, it is, that, in these days, no industry can prosper and retain its market without repeated and continuous application of fresh capital, and this cannot be obtained if less than the normal rate of profit is earned. If machinery is not kept up to date, the market is supplied from other sources, or, in face of an enhanced, or even stationary price, the demand becomes languid, the trade decays, and the last state of the operative becomes worse than the first. If, on the other hand, a rise in wages is refused, or a reduction accepted, the industry in question retains its market. The lower wages act as a storm signal to keep other labourers away, and, in course of time, equilibrium is restored, the temporary check is removed, and the old level reached or passed. The unity and solidarity of labour is preserved, and each labourer is automatically directed to his most profitable market.

The fall of prices, the tendency towards gratuity, is, we believe, inevitable. Even if the bimetallists had their way, and their promised equilibrium between gold and silver was maintained (a very large assumption), there might be, with the increase of money, a temporary rise in prices, but the tendency towards gratuity would not be checked, it would soon reassert itself. It is a condition

out of which, happily, we cannot contract ourselves.

Here, it may be convenient to notice two
fallacious arguments which prevent, more, perhaps,
than anything else, a right understanding of this
important question. One is the introduction of
the question-begging phrase, "fair wages." This
is based on the assumption that the market rate
of wages is unfair, and that when the market for
capital and enterprise in a particular industry is
good, *i.e.* when interest and profits are high, these
interests and profits should be reduced not by the
competition of capital and enterprise, but by
the coercive action of labour to secure a share
for itself. As the preceding argument has shown,
nothing can be more fatal to the true interest
of labour. Such action destroys the continuity
of the progress of labour, which, as we have seen,
is perfectly secure, without this killing jealousy
of the goose that lays the golden egg. The
natural organisation of the markets is inevitably
tending to a cheapening of production, to a lower
rate of profit and interest, and to the distribution
of labour in the most remunerative forms of
employment. Attempts to make a "corner" for
labour are unnecessary, and have no more moral
justification, or chance of success, than attempts, by
legislation or otherwise, to regrate and to raise the
price of wheat or any other commodity or service.

A second fallacy is based on the assumption that every employer is a rigid combination in himself, and that he derives some advantage from the fact. Now, in so far as this rigidity exists, it is a source of weakness. The employer's plant, contracts, and capital, are hostages to fortune. Notoriously, during long periods, great industries are carried on at a loss. If an employer, in hope of better times, and from an unwillingness to part from his staff of workmen, disregards the falling market, he does so to his own detriment, and to the temporary advantage, at any rate, of his workmen. If he attempts to hold himself unduly rigid against a legitimate rise in the labour market, his best workmen will drop off from him and go elsewhere ; other firms will extend their operations, if they can afford to hold the market, and still give higher wages to labour. Mr. Cree, in his pamphlet on trade unionism, gives an illustration which, I think, very happily reduces the argument *ad absurdum*.

" If Professor Marshall's argument had any force," he says, "then a provision merchant, buying butter from ten farmers and selling to three hundred customers, should be at a great advantage in dealing with both, as he 'represents a perfectly rigid combination,' etc., and it should be necessary, in order to prevent him exploiting the farmers, that they should combine against him, and also that the customers should protect their interests in the same way.　But they do not combine, and provision merchants do not make fortunes; the price of butter rises and falls independently of their will."

Perhaps it will be said, that though the single employer is not master of the situation, yet there is a natural combination between all employers.

Now, this is a mere truism.　There is a natural combination between all men, not to give more in an exchange than the market requires.　That employers succumb to this all-pervading human foible is, of course, true, but it is distinctly untrue that in normal circumstances capitalist employers ever desist for a moment from competition one against another.　Combination is occasionally forced on them, by an instinct of self-preservation, in face of the attacks of the men's trade unions, but even then it is difficult to maintain it for long. Notoriously, the coal-owners' combination, entered into at a moment when they had every inducement to stand together, was broken down during the late English strike by the defection of Colonel Seeley.　The militant Shipping Federation is not an association for the purpose of influencing wages, but is simply a protection society against the domineering tactics of the Seaman's Union, and, but for that union, would never have come into existence.

The great American combinations, of which the Standard Oil Trust is the best known, have never,

so far as I am aware, been accused of endeavouring
to use their power to keep down wages. On the
contrary, according to a Foreign Office Report,
1890, No. 174, "the number of workmen" (in
the employment of the Standard Oil Trust)
"receiving average wages has increased, with a
chance of each individual workman to rise. The
better class of workmen are employed, and strikes
are unknown." Whether the consuming public
has a grievance is another question ; but it seems
to be conceded that the Standard Oil Trust is
by no means a monopoly, nor has it prevented,
or tried to prevent, a great decrease in the price
of oil. Its permanency is due to its moderation,
and the report of a committee of the House of
Representatives is probably not wrong in declaring
that "Every combination dangerous to the public
interest carries within itself its own destruction."

It will be admitted of course that some employers are closer and more arbitrary than others,
but these men, whether in the Scotch farm-
servants' feeing fair, or in the less formally
organised market, are avoided and worse served
than more liberal employers. Beyond this, no
employer, or combination of employers, can over-
bear the market, and the proof of this is, that they
never attempt to do it. If a workman asks for
a rise of wages, the firm may give it or refuse it,
but we never heard of an instance where a

combination of employers attempted to prevent him from exchanging his services at a more profitable rate elsewhere. The nearest approach to such a state of things has been the futile complaint of some old-fashioned maiden lady of straitened means that her favourite maid-servant has been decoyed away from her by an offer of higher wages.

The weakness of the employer's situation, somewhat inconsistently, is at times urged by the Socialists. His capital, they say, cannot run away, but they add to this an exaggeration of their own. Fixed plant cannot easily leave the country ; spoil it, and rob it, and tax it to extinction, is the statesmanlike maxim of this school. The most superficial knowledge of modern industry, however, should apprise them that credit (not corporeal commodities) constitutes the main instrument of commerce. Credit is based simply on our appreciation of the chances of reaping where we sow. We have seen how vastly important it is that new and miscellaneous industries should be developed. A man with ingenuity and invention sees his way to satisfy, at a profit, some human want. He requires, however, credit or capital to carry it into effect. As things at present are constituted, municipalities, labour agitators, politicians, and charlatans of all kinds lie in wait for that enterprise. Neither the man of ability nor the capitalist is permitted to undertake the risk, and the labourer, to whom alone there was no risk in the matter, is defrauded of a new market for his services. The air is full of theories of rapine and confiscation ; and the uncertainty of all labour contracts adds additional risk to every undertaking. Credit therefore is shaken, and enterprise dare not venture.

It may here be very proper to remind the reader, that the labourer asks not only for higher wages, but for an increased share of leisure. It is a praiseworthy and legitimate ambition. In this connection M. Leroy Beaulieu has finely said, *La civilisation se mesure à l'accroissement simultané et des produits et des loisirs.* By civilisation this distinguished writer means the orderly growth of industrial society based on the principle of free exchange. Already the services which the labourer brings to the associated "effort" of the community have secured to him some "satisfaction" in the way of leisure.

Mr. Giffen has pointed out by means of incontestable statistics that shorter hours are now worked for higher wages than fifty years ago. This boon cannot be purchased by the trade union policy of keeping up prices by a restriction of output. When effort in any given trade is producing more than sufficiency of supply, the remedy is not restriction, but a passing on of some of the effort to new industries.

Let me attempt to indicate the direction in which these new industries are to be found. We see vast combinations of capital and labour devoted to supplying the rich with luxury and leisure ; the ascent of labour permits, and in the future will permit still more, great developments of industry in supplying luxuries to those who are now poor. Fifty years ago, tea, sugar, and wheaten bread were the luxuries of the poor—they are now tending to gratuity. In the future, healthy houses, leisure, books, and a thousand other refinements must be subjected to the same process. There is a disposition to look too exclusively to foreign and colonial markets for the expansion of our trade, and to neglect this prospect of an inexhaustible demand which lies at our very door. To secure the opening up of these new channels of trade, we have no need of costly filibustering expeditions, often of very doubtful morality, but of peace, retrenchment of public burdens, liberty of enterprise, and security of property. Towards this ideal we shall move more rapidly if we will only recognise and forward, rather than ignore and thwart, the true principle of progress. The Duke of Argyle and Mr. Mallock have based their defence of the private ownership of capital on the obvious advantage accruing to society when ability, by means of capital, is able to direct the industrial effort of the community. There is, however, a

ªrther harmony arising out of the private ownership of capital. It is the device by which men
gain leisure for themselves in the evening of life,
and protection for the widow, the orphan, and the
helpless. Men's desire to purchase leisure, in other
words, a right of deferred consumption, arises from
many complex motives. Many desire to purchase
it, not for themselves, but for those dear to them. In
these feverish days the number of those who, being
able so to do, deliberately choose leisure for themselves is, we fear, comparatively few. In many cases
the demand for leisure would be more correctly
described as a demand for a short day, and plenty
of overtime at a higher rate of wages. It is a
perfectly legitimate desire. A man's first economic
duty is to maintain and provide an endowment
for the helpless persons dependent on him. Till
that is done, to a right-minded man, leisure will
be apt to seem idleness.

The philosophy of leisure is not well understood
in any rank of life. There are situations where
leisure is a crime, but there are also others where a
true wisdom will deplore the exaggerated importance imputed, even by the best of men, to political
power, social distinction, and material wealth, as
things for which leisure is to be ruthlessly sacrificed.
Social distinction and material wealth are innocuous
possessions. It is the struggle for power—for power
to be used for the most part in hindering by

legislation the natural progress of civilisation—
which more than anything else is wasting the energy
of the nation. It is a tempting subject for a
digression, but it is necessary to return to the
labourer.

His facilities for purchasing leisure, for whatever
purpose he desires it, are greater than they were;
and if, as a class, he will be guided by the true
principles of freedom, his progress in the near
future is assured. All is in his favour, the fall
in prices, the ascent of labour, the comparative
ease with which a small capital can be accumulated. The danger, the only danger which threatens
his future, is his excessive and superstitious faith in
politics and trade unionism—occupations no more
conducive to profit and content than the labours
of Sisyphus.

In the foregoing pages the freedom permitted to
a friendly critic has not, I trust, been exceeded.
The right of labour to combine has been fully
recognised, remonstrance has been addressed only
against the suicidal policy of restriction which
underlies so much of modern trade unionist effort.
It is admitted freely that there are many useful
purposes to be served by voluntary combined
action. The benefit and investment side of trade
unions is most valuable, and might no doubt
be largely extended; as centres for public discussion and information they might do much to reveal

to the labourer the real beneficence of his dependence on the market. All this would follow as a natural corollary, if the leaders of the labour world could be disabused of their present superstition.

Plain speaking will not, I trust, be imputed to lack of sympathy with working-class ambitions. An impartial observer must mark and regret the disappointment which inevitably results to the labourer from the use of mistaken methods. Most of all he will deplore the misfortune which surrounds the newly enfranchised heirs of political power, with a crowd of sycophants and charlatans. As token of respect and of sympathy, he will pay them the highest compliment in his power to pay, he will tell them plainly and directly what he believes to be the truth, without fear and without favour.

THE END.

PRINTED BY WILLIAM CLOWES AND SONS, LIMITED,
LONDON AND BECCLES.

www.ingramcontent.com/pod-product-compliance
Lightning Source LLC
Chambersburg PA
CBHW030910270326
41929CB00008B/640